‘*Catching up*’ with David Epston:

A collection of

narrative practice-based papers

published between 1991 & 1996

DULWICH CENTRE PUBLICATIONS
ADELAIDE SOUTH AUSTRALIA

ISBN 0 9586678 5 3

published by

Dulwich Centre Publications
Hutt St PO Box 7192
Adelaide, South Australia 5000
phone (61-8) 8223 3966 fax (61-8) 8232 4441

printed & manufactured in Australia by:
Graphic Print Group, Richmond, South Australia

100% recycled paper

cover artwork & design by: Susy Stiles, Torrensville, South Australia
typeset, layout & design by: Jane Hales, Melrose Pk, South Australia

Contents

Contents (cont'd)

Introduction

It is somewhat daunting trying to corral all your published papers from over half a decade between the covers of a single text. And when I did round them up, no matter how hard I tried I could not press them into some 'progress' towards some higher purpose or some form of emergent theory. When I thought about it, how could this be? Most of what I had written came from the concerns for, and reflections on, a day-to-day practice, nothing more and certainly nothing less. After all, it was the very gaps and novelties that are always there in any practice that excited my mind. These were the incentives for me to consume myself with questions rather than rush to some purported answer or other. I have always committed myself to generate practice from the ground-up rather than theory-down, although I have no qualms about raiding theory whenever it suited my purposes. I have never been very faithful to theory but more attracted to metaphors that have you looking where you hadn't looked before.

And I was always eager to 'co-research' the small miracles of everyday resistance. I use 'resistance', not in the psychological sense but rather those ways and means by which the influence of a Problem over lives and relationships is repudiated. That has been my angle of vision, my perspective. There have been obvious sources for it but, most notably, the ironic critical practice of Michel Foucault. Over this past half decade I have felt more and more at home thinking of myself as an 'ethnographer of the particular', drawing as close as I can to the experience of others - often problematic - as they live in their everyday/everynight lives. This drawing closer is best captured by Michael White's revision of Foucault's 'solidarity':

> *And what of solidarity? I am thinking of a solidarity that is constructed by therapists who refuse to draw a sharp distinction between their lives and the lives of others, who refuse to marginalise those persons who seek help; by therapists who are prepared to constantly confront the fact that if faced with circumstances that provide the context of the trouble of others, they just might not be doing nearly as well themselves.* (White, M., 1993: 'Commentary: History of the present.' In Gilligan, S. & Price, R. [eds], *Therapeutic Conversations,* p.132, New York: W.W.Norton.)

Notions such as 'communities of concern' and practices of 'co-research' naturally derive from such a drawing closer. This is in contrast to the 'great divide' that opens up when the subjects of psychological science are appropriated as objects of that knowledge.

I would like to think it is a commitment to such solidarity that might bring together these papers, which, at first reading, may seem so disparate.

1

Benny the Peanut Man[1]

In 1983 I was asked to deliver a plenary address at the Australian Family Therapy Conference in Brisbane. I was given plenty of time to prepare. The topic was: 'What are the influences on your work?' I agreed to it, thinking all I had to do was to systematically review the books I had read, the workshops I had attended, the training video-tapes I had witnessed, and what I had gained from my supervisors, mentors and colleagues. I was ill-prepared for what eventuated. The conventional sources seemed inadequate to the task and then, in a kind of epiphany, I 'remembered' the 'genealogy' of the 'heart' of my practice - Benny the Peanut Man. I came to realise that I had been my father's apprentice on how to treat a visitor and have a respectful conversation. I can hardly ever recall my father or mother speaking about someone they had met without marvelling at some aspect of their lives. I had no formal training, no curriculum, no 'tests'. You just did it, day-in and day-out. Such a personal experience has left me the legacy of a keen interest in the 'genealogies' of such knowledges. Each time I ask others the sources of their knowledges, I distinctly remember my mother and father in me.

I had just presented a two-day workshop organised by Karl Tomm and his colleagues in The Family Therapy Program, Department of Psychiatry, University of Calgary. It was at the end of a severe cold spell that had blown down from Alaska.

Although the residents were somewhat relieved as the temperature had warmed to a twenty-seven degree below zero day, coming from a New Zealand summer hadn't prepared me for such severe temperatures. I was relieved when a number of the workshop-goers joined Karl and Bill Tomm and me in the nearby university bar which had a generous open fire. As the evening wore on, those who remained discovered we were all men. Frank Young, well known for both his wit and his martial arts, proposed that instead of talking as men do, that we talk like women. This suggestion met with strong approval as I imagine we all privately concluded that there was nothing more tedious than men talking around alcohol. Frank proposed that, as my workshop had to do with the 'storying' of experience, we should tell each other stories about turning points in our own lives. He requested I go first. I did so without hesitation and told the story of my father's apparent contrariness, and how he had confounded me with the revelation of his intentions. This led to a series of recollections about our relationships with our fathers.

But first let me tell an expanded version of the story I told that night:

> *I had turned sixteen and had just got my driver's licence. My parents had permitted me to borrow their car that night. And this night just had to be a night to remember. Things were getting pretty serious with Judy. We had had our first kiss on our last date. And now she had accepted my invitation to a dance at the Brock Street Hall. Although we had gone to dances at the YMCA, the Brock Street Hall was something altogether different. On Wednesdays, they had Pro-wrestling with the likes of Bobo Brazil, The Masked Marvel, Gorgeous George, and Tiger Tasker; the rest of the week service clubs ran Bingo evenings to raise funds for charity. On Saturday nights they had Rock and Roll dances and many of those attending weren't high school students. They worked at the Canadian General Electric and for me that was a vast mythical place of transformers and switch-gear. Everything in Peterborough depended on the CGE. Over 4,000 employees meant prosperity and anything less meant a downturn.*

Looking back, I don't remember much about the dance. What I do recall was what happened afterwards. Judy and I got into my parents' Pontiac and set off down Brock Street. We were being followed closely but I didn't make anything of it. The traffic lights turned amber as I approached the intersection but, as the streets were icy, I speeded up at the same time thinking what a well considered decision I had made on the spur of the moment. I felt so manly that I was encouraged to put my arm around Judy. I didn't have much time to consider my luck before the car that was following us pulled alongside so that I could read 'Provincial Police' emblazoned on its side. I pulled over to the kerb. Two sinister figures approached us, one from either side. I rolled down my window, trying to keep my composure. 'Whatja go thru the red light for, kid?' I summoned up all my courage and started to give my reasons for running the amber light. 'Shuddup kid ... gotta driver's licence?' I handed over my licence which was examined by torchlight. He then looked curiously at me. All his Mickey Spillane toughness vanished as he politely enquired 'Are you Benny the Peanut Man's boy?' I admitted I was although I probably would have confessed to almost any allegation. 'Look kid ... you went through a green light and don't let anyone tell you different. Say 'hello' to Benny for us. I'm Jack. Come around here Jerry, and meet the Peanut Man's boy.' We exchanged greetings and they drove off.

This was my first clue to the mystery of my father, a man so self-effacing that I barely knew him; a man who spoke endlessly to and of others. But let me get back to 'Benny the Peanut Man'. His name was Benjamin, but everyone in Peterborough, both young and old, called him Benny. 'The Peanut Man' was new to me and quite embarrassing. To some extent my father was always an embarrassment to me. He and my mother ran a lunch bar with twelve round stools that rotated on stainless steel pedestals on one side, with peanuts and nuts for sale that he roasted himself on the other side. Their store was called 'The Nuttery' and was on the main street right across from the Paramount, one of the three movie houses. My father worked, on the average, 70/80 hours every week, Monday through Saturday night, so we didn't get to see him that much. But that just built up our anticipation for Sunday, a day he devoted to my sister and me. We started the day by joining our parents in their bed for an hour or two of 'Rifkay and Barrell' stories, of which my father seemed to have an inexhaustible supply. He would then take us on secret adventures, often accompanied by the other neighbourhood kids. Our destination was not revealed till the last possible moment. Sometimes we went skating on the Trent Canal, visited a friend's farm to see a newborn colt, fished for sunfish off the floating causeway, went to the zoo, or explored native Indian caves for hieroglyphs. He always insisted that it was to give our mother 'some peace and quiet', but I distinctly had the impression that he enjoyed our adventures as much as we did.

Although my mother tried to convince me of my father's virtues - that he was a journeyman electrician by trade; that there was nothing he couldn't fix; that he was kind to old people - my father, by contrast, did everything in his power to have me follow in someone else's footsteps. He forbade me from using his tools and instead encouraged me to read 'The Book of Knowledge'. We had the complete twenty volume set. He urged me to be 'aggressive' and study law. He kept everything about himself from me so I wouldn't admire him. Or perhaps he didn't admire himself? The only matter he took pride in was his capacity to amuse people, to make them laugh and it was all the better if it was at his expense. It didn't seem to matter. What was most important was making people laugh. He was always making ridiculous bets with people that they always won and he had to pay up with hamburgers and boxes of nuts.

Still, as I grew older, I became more and more impatient with him without knowing why. He just didn't seem like other people's fathers. He didn't have real friends - just all those people who used to hang around 'The Nuttery'. And the men who came and spend hours over a cup of coffee were always strange, like Fat Bill who worked at Canada Packers as a slaughterman, and Bruce who had been given a sinecure at CGE after an overhead crane dropped something on his head and he was, as my father put it, 'never quite the same again'. And George the Dane. My father taught him English by speaking Yiddish to his German and in return George provided us with Danish pastries.

My parents lived frugally so my sister and I could live beyond their means. And I think I took this to suggest that I deserved more than my parents. And I had further evidence of my entitlement. I could read library books and they couldn't. I became convinced that the Peterborough Library on George Street was the repository of the wisdom of all ages. It was all there under one roof. All I had to do was work my way through it and wisdom would certainly be mine. I was so earnest that I was allowed into the Adult Section at a precocious age and had ambitions to be an archaeologist. Most of my 'digs' were in the neighbour's rubbish tins where I sought artefacts to put on display in my private museum down behind the furnace in the basement. With age, I advanced from ghosted autobiographies of baseball players to more erudite tomes. My ambition in life was to get twenty out of twenty in the Reader's Digest 'Improve Your Word Power' section. My father stood aside while I became a juvenile pedant until a concerned teacher approached my parents, worried that my bookishness was putting me at odds with my classmates. However, I only found this out sometime later. What I did know was that my father started flooding the snow on our lawn late at night after work and miraculously it turned into a skating rink. He then would invite me to play hockey with him, one against one and, despite some hotly contested games, the score always ended up in my favour. I found it hard to respect a man my father's age who could be so consistently beaten by his son. The rink attracted other kids who turned up with their skates and hockey sticks. More and more, when I would urge my father to play, he said he couldn't because of one injury or another and he would have to remain on the sidelines for that day. He retired altogether when I got up the nerve to approach Mr Olmstead whose brother, Bert, actually played for the Chicago Black Hawks, for a trial with his PeeWee Black Hawks in the City Hockey League. My father then accompanied me to the games until I asked him if he wouldn't come anymore as I felt I could tie my own skate laces.

In my last year at high school, my distaste for my father increased. He was pretty much a non-drinker, but when I told my parents that I had started drinking with my friends, he arrived home with four or five bottles of spirits - gin, vodka, whisky and bourbon. When I asked why, he said that he had started wondering if hard liquor was as strong as it used to be when he was my age. He concluded the only way to find out was to try some out. He asked if I would like to come along for the ride. I couldn't wait to tell my friends. He was giving me liquor whereas they had to water their father's scotch to acquire their supply. I drank with my father as he mused about how strong whisky was compared to how it used to be. We then started comparing how strong bourbon was to gin, and vodka was compared to whisky. I began to feel smug outwitting my father yet again.

Then matters got worse. He suddenly developed what I took to be an extremely irritating habit. By then, I had become a member of a secret intellectual elite at Peterborough Collegiate and Vocational School. We called ourselves 'The Group of Seven' after an early 20th century avant-garde group of impressionist painters. It was de rigeur in this group to compare IQ scores which we had learned by infiltrating the school files. As the youngest of this group, I had a hard time keeping up so I had to redouble my efforts at the Peterborough Library. I realise now that this marked the onset of my father's very irritating habit. He would often come home midday for a nap as he worked until 10pm every night. It must have been then that he would enter the privacy of my bedroom and read the dust jackets of my library books. And then every opportunity he had, he would dispute the premise of the book in question. It seemed as if he was being disagreeable on purpose and, as I had never known him to be anything but agreeable, this turn in his character infuriated me. In fact, I became so vengeful that I took to researching our points of disagreement further and then would submit full essays, with lengthy bibliographies, proving my point. He would, after some consideration, remove his objections. However, he was unrelenting in his research of my researches, even though I assumed all this was quite beyond him. I became enraged with him at times, as he seemed so insensitive to me and my newfound knowledge. This disrespect was bad enough but what galled me most was his contrariness. He seemed out to vex me for no apparent reason. Once I got so angry that I kicked him from behind when he left my bedroom. Luckily I missed him and he never knew I had made an attempt. What was so perplexing was that he continued to be so kind, unassuming and generous to all his friends at 'The Nuttery'. Why was he picking on me all of a sudden?

I wasn't to find out for another ten years when I had returned from New Zealand to visit Canada. My father seemed to have returned to his old self in relation to me. I reminded him how oppositional he had been, almost to the point of what I took to be irrationality. I was shocked into incoherence when my father apologised, but said 'Son, I did it on purpose'! This renewed my old outrage and I asked why he possibly could and would have caused me such distress. Benny the Peanut Man replied, 'I was so worried about you. You seemed to be so willing to accept other people's ideas. I really wanted you to be able to think for yourself. So that's why I did it. I'm really sorry if it upset you.' He seemed so regretful that I was speechless. My mind went blank. It took me another ten years to figure out the significance of his comments and by then he had died.

Back in the Calgary University bar, in many of the men's stories the son-father relationship changed through an incident whereby the physical strength or capability of the son was tested by the father, and the son prevailed. The relationship was reshaped through power in an atmosphere of imminent or actual violence. I understood at long last what a singular man my father had been, and why it was no wonder he had so few male friends. I thought back to his death when I was approached by some elderly people who referred to him as 'an angel' and some young men, unknown to me, who referred to me as 'brother'. One even told me that my father had given him his electrician's tools. I realised then that I had been reared by a counter-father, a man not of his time.

Acknowledgements

Both Sarah Sandley and Isobel Rose assisted me to make this more literary.

Note

1. First published in the 1991 No.1 *Dulwich Centre Newsletter*.

2

A Proposal for a Re-Authoring Therapy:[1]

Rose's revisioning of her life and a Commentary

'Marissa' (see Epston 1989, pp.128-136) and 'Rose' were people who convinced me to pursue the 'narrative metaphor'. I remain deeply indebted to them. As is often the case, it has taken me this period of time (1989-1996) to 'unpack' the significance of my meetings with them and what they had to tell me about their 're-authored' lives. An Australian colleague, Kevin Murray, one of the first 'down under' narrative psychologists, consented to provide us with a commentary.

In the social sciences at least, it is now generally recognised that it is not possible for persons to have direct knowledge of the world; that an objective description of the world is not available to us, and that no one has a privileged access to the naming of reality, whatever that reality is.[2] And it is generally accepted that what we know of the world, we know only through our experience of it; our experience of the world is all that we have, and that is all that we can know. We cannot even know another person's experience of the world. The best that we can do is to interpret the experience of others; that is, the expressions of their experience as they go about the business of interpreting it for themselves.[3] *Whatever sense we have of how things stand with someone else's inner life, we gain it through their expressions, not through some magical intrusion into their consciousness. It's all a matter of scratching surfaces* (Geertz 1986, p.373). And to interpret the expressions (and thus the interpretations) of others, we have to rely upon our own lived experience and imagination. The most we can do is to 'identify' our own experience of the experience as expressed by others. Thus 'empathy' is a critical factor in the interpretation or understanding of the experiences of others.

So this is all we have - our lived experience of the world, but this turns out to be a great deal. We are rich in lived experience. To quote Geertz: *We all have very much more of the stuff than we know what to do with, and if we fail to put it into some graspable form, the fault must lie in a lack of means, not of substance* (1986, p.373).

Certain questions are raised by any serious consideration of this proposal about the world of experience:

- *Given that what we know of the world we know through our experience of it, what is the process by which we develop an understanding of our experience and give meaning to it?*
- *How do we make sense of our experience to ourselves, and how do we make sense of our experience to others?*
- *If we are perpetually involved in an attempt to articulate our lived experience to ourselves and to others, what processes are involved in our interpretation of it?*
- *What is it that facilitates the expression of our experience?*

- *And how does the expression of our lived experience affect our lives and relationships?*

These questions focus our attention on an investigation of the ways in which we make sense of our lives to ourselves and to others; they focus our attention on the processes through which we interpret or attribute meaning to our experience.

In order to give meaning to our experience, we must organise it, frame it, or give pattern to it. To understand an aspect of our experience, we must be able to frame it within a pattern of experience that is known to us; we must be able to identify aspects of lived experience within the context of known patterns of experience.

Stories or Narratives

Those social scientists (J. Bruner, Gergen, and Harré in psychology; E. Bruner, Geertz, Clifford, V. Turner, and R. Rosaldo in anthropology; H. White, Mink, Gaillie in history, to name but a few) whose work is oriented by the 'interpretive method' and who embrace the text analogy propose that the 'story' or 'narrative' provides the dominant frame for lived experience and for the organisation and patterning of lived experience. Following this proposal, a story can be defined as a unit of meaning that provides a frame for lived experience. It is through these stories that lived experience is interpreted. We enter into stories; we are entered into stories by others; and we live our lives through these stories.

Stories enable persons to link aspects of their experience through the dimension of time. There does not appear to be any other mechanism for the structuring of experience that so captures the sense of lived time, or that can adequately represent the sense of lived time (Ricoeur 1983). It is through stories that we obtain a sense of our lives changing. It is through stories that we are able to gain a sense of the unfolding of the events of our lives through recent history, and it appears that this sense is vital to the perception of a 'future' that is in any way different from a 'present'. Stories construct beginnings and endings; they impose beginnings and endings on the flow of experience. *We create the units of experience and meaning from a continuity of life. Every telling is an arbitrary imposition of meaning on the flow of memory, in that we highlight some causes and discount others; that is, every telling is interpretive* (E. Bruner 1986a, p.7). In considering the vital role that stories have in relation to the organisation of experience, it can be argued that:

1. It is the stories in which we situate our experience that determine[4] the meaning that we give the experience.
2. It is these stories that determine the selection of those aspects of experience to be expressed.
3. It is these stories that determine the shape of the expression that we give to those aspects of experience.
4. It is these stories that determine real effects and directions in our lives and in our relationships.

Performance as Shaping

In the foregoing discussion, we have argued that experience structures expression. But it can also be argued that expression structures experience. To quote Dilthey: *Our knowledge of what is given in experience is extended through the interpretation of the objectifications of life and their interpretation, in turn, only made possible by plumbing the depths of subjective experience* (1976, p.195). Thus, the stories that we enter into with our experience have real effects on our lives. The expression of our experience through these stories shapes or makes up our lives and our relationships; our lives are shaped or constituted through the very process of the interpretation within the context of the stories that we enter into and that we are entered into by others.

This is not to propose that life is synonymous with text. It is not enough for persons to tell a new story about themselves, or to assert claims about themselves. Instead, the proposition carried by these assertions about the world of experience and narrative is that life is the performance[5] of texts. And it is the performance of these texts that is transformative of persons' lives; however, these performances must be before relevant audiences or made known by some form of publication. [T]*he participants must have confidence in their own authenticity, which is one reason cultures are performed. It is not enough to assert claims; they must be enacted. Stories only become transformative in their performance* (E. Bruner 1986a, p.25). Thus the idea that lives are situated in texts or stories implies a particular notion of authenticity - that a person arrives at a sense of authenticity in life through the performance of texts. This notion of authenticity may be affronting to many a cherished belief that carries propositions about the 'truth' of personhood or of human nature; those beliefs that suggest that, under particular and ideal circumstances of life, persons will be 'released' and thus become truly who they are: authentic.

Indeterminate Nature of Stories

If persons' lives are shaped through the storying of experience and through the performance of these stories, and if there is a limited stock of familial stories about who we might be and of cultural knowledges about personhood, how is it that we are not replicas of one another? Perhaps this question is best approached by considering the interaction of readers and literary texts. To do so would be to extend the text analogy in our attempts to understand more fully the processes involved in the ascription of meaning, and to liken life as lived under the guidance of stories to the reader's experience under the sway of the literary text. And since good stories are more transformative of the reader's experience than poor stories, this consideration could bring us to a review of the structure of texts of literary merit.

In following this premise, we believe that Iser, a literary theorist, assists us to find an answer to the question, 'How is it that we are not replicas of one another?'

> ... *fictional texts constituted their own objects and do not copy something already in existence. For this reason they cannot have the full determinacy of real objects, and indeed, it is the element of indeterminacy that evokes the text to 'communicate' with the reader, in the sense that they induce him to participate both in the production and the comprehension of this work's intention.* (1978, p.21)

It is readily apparent that all stories are indeterminate.[6] There is a degree of ambiguity and uncertainty to all stories, and, as well, there are inconsistencies and contradictions. This fact will be appreciated by those who have read a novel that was particularly engaging and then gone to a movie of the same novel, only to find, to their dismay, that the movie director had got it wrong! In such circumstances, what is clear is that the director arrived at a different interpretation of the story through his or her unique negotiation of its indeterminacy.

So literary texts are full of gaps that readers must fill in order for the story to be performed.[7] And, in likening the interaction of readers and literary texts to the interaction of persons and the stories they live their lives through, we become more aware of our need to fill the gaps in daily interaction. Just as these gaps in literary texts recruit the lived experience and the imagination of the reader, so do the gaps in the stories that are 'lived by' recruit the lived experience and the imagination of people as they engage in performances of meaning under the guidance of the story.

Thus with every performance, persons are re-authoring their lives and relationships. And every telling encapsulates, but is more than the previous telling. The evolution of lives and relationships of persons is akin to the process of re-authoring, the process of persons entering into stories with their experience and their imagination, and the process of taking these stories over and making them their own.

The indeterminacy of texts and the constitutive aspect of the performance of texts provide good cause to celebrate. Clifford Geertz quotes Lionel Trilling's lament, 'How come it that we start out Originals and end up Copies?' Upon situating our work in the world of experience and narrative, and in accepting the idea that we must start with a story in order to attribute meaning and give expression to our experience, we would have to reverse Trilling's question, 'How come it that we start out Copies and end up Originals?' To this question Geertz finds an answer that is 'surprisingly reassuring: it is the copying that originates' (1986, p.380).

We have little choice but to start out with copies. We cannot perform meaning in our lives without situating our experience in stories. Stories are, in the first place, given. However, it is the relative indeterminacy - the ambiguity and uncertainty - of all stories that we can only negotiate through recourse to our lived experience and our imagination. And this requires that we engage in a process of 'origination'.

So what might be the effects on a person's interpretation of events in his or her life, if the story that framed, selected, and determined the meaning given to those events was oppressive and authored by perpetrators of child sexual or physical abuse? Kamsler (1990), referring specifically to child sexual abuse, noted a number of 'story-telling' practices associated with it that deny the abused their own 'story-telling rights':[8]

> *(1) it is usually the case that the perpetrator of the abuse has overtly or covertly conveyed to the victim the message that she was to blame for being abused ...*
>
> *(2) the perpetrator will often actively promote secrecy by enforcing it with the child or young woman so that she is divided from other family members;*
>
> *(3) and the various ways in which perpetrator exerted control over the child ... may promote the development of habitual responses of fear and panic in intimacy relationships when she becomes an adult.* (1990, pp.17-18)

And furthermore, what difference would it make if a person who had been situated in an oppressive 'story' - being told - found herself either to be entitled to her own 'story-telling rights' or to have them restored and be enabled to tell her own life and become her own author?

Rose's Revisioning of her Life[9]

From here on, Rose and I request that you prepare yourself for a different set of 'reader responses' as the genres become blurred. If fact and fiction are read differently, how best might you approach 'faction'? The following is an example of a 're-authoring therapy' but that process will be briefly described elsewhere so as not to intrude. So reader, can you find some way that suits you to divest yourself of those 'reader responses' required by academic texts? Perhaps you might set this book down for a while in order to break your train of thought and return to it later. For Rose and I offer you the opportunity of having an experience of your own as you engage with her experience of entering her life's events in an 'alternative' story, a frame of reference at great variance with the 'dominant' story of her life. Louis Mink argues that *It is clear that we cannot refer to events as such, but only to events* under a description*; so there can be more than one description of the same event, all of them true but referring to different aspects of the event or describing it at different levels of generality. But what can we possibly mean by 'same event'?* (1978, pp.145-6). What we could possibly mean by the same event was more than just a historiographical problem for Rose and me. For how Rose 'reads' her life - under the guidance of either the 'dominant' story or the therapeutically co-created 'alternative' story - will prove to have considerable bearing on whether she lives or takes her life, and how she lives that life she chooses to keep.

The re-authoring will be represented to you, reader, by way of those 'letters' I (David Epston) provided for her summarising our meetings, and excerpts from the transcript of the fourth and final meeting six months later. I have taken some liberties here, deleting many of my questions and linking some of her answers. So, reader, are you ready to proceed with my account of Rose's revisioning of her experience as it is brought to life through language?

Rose's employer rang me. I was informed that, despite her compunctions and regret, she had no other option than to terminate Rose's employment as a receptionist/video-camera operator at a busy advertising agency. She only too willingly acknowledged that Rose possessed obvious capabilities. Still, it seemed that whenever Rose was required to attend to a request in addition to an uncompleted task, she would 'crack up' and dissolve into tears.

Her employer drew my attention to the fact that Rose had a genius for food preparation, something she was required to do during a 'shoot'. She had endeavoured to find Rose alternative employment in catering until it dawned on her how impossible that would be. Catering is a task, she commented, that would subject Rose to both urgent and multiple demands. She also told me that Rose had a long history of losing jobs for the same reason. Rose's employer was ringing because Rose had become inconsolable on being dismissed and she was very concerned for her well-being. I suggested she provide Rose with my phone number and that I would do my best to meet with her immediately.

Rose and I met a day later. There was a sense of quiet desperation about

Rose as she recounted her dismal employment history. She did acknowledge that she had a long-standing ambition to become a chef but discounted that, given the demanding nature of the work. She seemed so forlorn that I asked if there was anything more to her 'problem' than that. She grinned ruefully and nodded. 'There's more to it. I don't have a base inside myself.' I inquired, 'Do you feel like a fake person, hollow on the inside?' She greeted this description enthusiastically as if the linguistic resources I proffered her came as something of a relief. I went on to say, 'There must be a story behind this. Do you feel like telling me about it?' She sighed and grinned at the same time, 'That's what I've come for ... I just can't go on any longer like this.' We embarked upon a story-telling with the role of narrator-reflector shared between us. My reflecting questions and her answering led her story through time in addition to disengaging her from entering into her father's story.

His authorship over her experience of his physical abuse had been compelling, given his hegemonic parenthood in addition to his moral sanction as a parish minister in a fundamentalist Christian church. The latter particularly confounded her as his parishioners would regularly comment after church services on her good fortune to have such 'a good and kind man' for a father. Her mother was a bystander to this violence, who defended her silence as the only way she had available to her to contain her husband's violence towards their children. Still Rose felt very bitter towards her, even though she acknowledged that her mother took the action to divorce him when she was thirteen, insisting that Rose be sent away to a distant boarding school. This action was without precedent among her co-religionists.

An 'alternative' account was written up from my notes, taken during the meeting and forwarded to her by post.

Dear Rose,

It was a very pleasing experience to meet up with you and hear some of your story, a story of both protest and survival against what you understood to be an attempt to destroy your life. And you furthered that protest yesterday by coming and telling me that story. I would imagine that you had not been able to tell anyone for fear of being disbelieved. I feel privileged that you shared it with me and hope that sharing it relieved you of some of its weight. I can see how such a history could have left you the legacy you described - a sense of not seeming 'to have a base'. How could you under the circumstances of your growing up when your home - most people's base - was the site of your father's attempt at disappearing you? No wonder you are currently finding life difficult and have mixed feelings about trusting relationships with men. I consider this inevitable under the circumstances. And no wonder, despite all your abilities, talents, and personal attributes that are so obvious to others with whom you have come into contact in the course of your life, you feel somewhat hollow and 'fake' on the inside. No wonder you feel like caving in when you experience other people's demands on you!

You tell me that you were the third of four children, born to a father who 'didn't want children' and since he had them, insisted on 'obedience' to his rule and the Victorian child-rearing policy that 'children should be seen but not heard'. From the beginning, you had some life force that refused to buckle under and submit to his authority. You paid dearly for your vocal nature and were physically beaten for it. Still you refused to deny yourself, even though you came to feel that he was out to destroy you. From what you tell me, he was mood-controlled, violent, self-important, and holier than Thou. In some ways, it must have been a relief to get sent away to boarding school, even though that resulted from your parents' separation.

It seems to me that you are entitled to your resentments towards your mother for not protecting you more. However, I suspect that you don't know the full extent to which your mother endured violence and intimidation. After a certain degree of abuse, the abused person often starts to believe they deserve it. Also your father had a moral sanction, arising from his work. Some day, I believe your mother will confide in you more suffering than you know. And she may have been right that the only course open to her was to silently sit by because, if she opposed him, he would have redoubled the severity of your beatings. I wonder if she has some story that is too terrible to reveal, perhaps even to herself?

Despite your father's attempts to rub you out, you ruthlessly opposed him. You did this in the face of his public image as 'a good man'. You could easily have taken his opinion of you and dismissed your own. If you had, my guess is that you would not be here today. Some special wisdom must have informed you that he was bad, not you. If not, how were you able to see through his hypocrisy?

At eighteen you returned to your father, thinking perhaps he would now be able to appreciate you, an appreciation you so richly deserved. You were to discover, probably not surprisingly, that 'you can't expect anything approaching a caring father-daughter relationship'. Still, you were able to distinguish between his inadequacies and your self. This was a critical distinction, one that I believe has been life saving for you.

Although it must have been very difficult, you were able to create for yourself a very good personhood. You must have had a lot of courage to travel abroad for 4½ years and 'survive' as you put it. Surviving in such circumstances proved to you once and for all that you had 'grit'. You were able to experience some pride in yourself for having managed so well ... You said that 'when I am up against the wall, something makes me get going ... a survival instinct'. I believe that your 'survival instinct' is your life force, a force that never submitted to your father's disciplines and ruthlessness. That life force added a lot to itself during your travels. I wonder if it was then that you became more substantial as a person and started believing in yourself?

Was it then that you started seeing yourself through others' eyes rather than through your father's eyes? When was it that you no longer accepted your father's definition of yourself as 'garbage'?

It must have happened sometime or other; otherwise, you would have gone around looking for garbage collectors and a dump for them to throw you on! Somehow or other, you were able to keep your own picture of yourself alive.

And you rejected that widely shared myth that women solve their problems by being 'rescued by men'. I guess you must have found that difficult to swallow, given your history with your father. I was also impressed by your unwillingness to seek sympathy or special concessions. You have determined to see your own way through this and to make yourself up into the person you want to be. It was interesting to note that you start appreciating yourself most when you are on your own.

I wonder if seeing your two older siblings make up their own lives, despite the violence they suffered at your father's hands, has inspired you with the hope necessary for you to do the same? Obviously they had some advantages in finding partners at an early age who must have really appreciated them, so they could appreciate themselves.

I suggest that you might like to be curious how your older siblings were able to construct viable, loving relationships, ones in which they were able to realise themselves as 'good' persons. Another question you might like to entertain is this: Why didn't you fall for your father's type?

I look forward to meeting you again to assist you to write a new history of the events in your life, a new history that could predict a very different kind of future than your old history.

Yours sincerely, David.

We met a month later. Nothing could have prepared me for what had transpired in the interval. Two days after receiving the letter, Rose had applied for a job as a sous-chef and was not only successful but so impressed the owner/chef that he had invited her to take over sole responsibility while he took his holidays. On his return, she had been made head chef. She now felt her life was 'on the right track' and that she 'had made a start on it'. She had renewed her relationship with her mother and now felt both a sympathy for her and a new connectedness. She had also rung up all her siblings and met with them, one at a time, over the letter. They all legitimated her experiences of physical abuse, and took her side to the extent that they advised her to break off all contact with their father, as the two eldest siblings had done. She took her own advice here and decided to keep her relationship with her father open. Rose was radiant and witty as she contemplated her future, a future she was now anticipating. This meeting was summarised in the following letter.

Dear Rose,

Reading the letter, which provided you with a different story, seems to have led to 'a sense of relief ... it was normal I had problems ... it wasn't my fault ... I had previously felt weak and vulnerable ... and that I should have got it all together by now.' Instead, you began to appreciate more fully that 'I felt I had made a start ... I was definitely on the right track'. And I suspect now that you are realising that you have been on the 'right track' for some time now; if not, as you put it, you would have become 'disillusioned ... and ended my life.' Well, there is a lot of life in you and it is there for all to see!

In a spectacular advancement several days after we met, you applied for a job as a chef and in no way permitted 'terror to stop me', put yourself on the line, and discovered much to your satisfaction, that you are very competent, so much so that you were requested to take over the restaurant while your employer has been on holiday. You feel you have been able to learn a lot in a short time and that this may be the career you have been looking for. As you put it, 'I'm realising I have all these opportunities ... and I am just beginning.' I can see that you have just opened a door and there is a lot of room to explore there.

Feeling so accomplished, you were then able to appreciate your mother's contribution to your abilities. She too 'had an enquiring mind ... an appreciation of other cultures ... it was something from within her'. Despite this, 'she still didn't have much self-confidence' but then again, what would she have become if your father, as you put it, didn't 'treat her like a door mat?'

You were also able to discuss some personal matters with your brother and sisters and they concurred with the letter. Their advice to you was to reject your father as they have. I believe your approach is more courageous and will have more embracing results. Still, it must have been satisfying for them to side with your story and, perhaps because of this, you have obviously been able to see yourself through others' eyes. The result of that is for you to appreciate yourself more and to develop a more comfortable relationship with yourself.

From here, you proposed that 'I feel I have to take some time out and work on Rose .. I want her to grow .. I want her to be strong and independent.' You proposed a month of consolidation rather than further experiment, especially in relation to your competence in your new career, to develop more self-appreciation, to experience fully your success and that degree of success is 'enough for now', and to resist the temptation of loneliness to drive you into an unsatisfactory relationship. Here you will have to challenge yet again the cultural myth that women complete themselves in relationship to men.

I will be very interested to meet you next time to hear of your further adventures. It was a pleasing experience for me to hear how much you are pleasing yourself and how far you have come in such a short time.
Best wishes, David.

We met another month later and Rose was more full of life than ever. She had taken charge of the restaurant and had expanded her range of catering abilities. She expressed great caution about a relationship with a man she had met, as she reported her determination to fashion a different kind of relationship from her previous ones, in which she had 'felt drained'. 'I understand what mistakes I've made. I have been giving my power away and making myself available for abuse by not taking responsibility for myself.' She said she had decided to evaluate this relationship as it went and to sustain her self-respect by communicating her own needs and desires: 'I am going to decide if this relationship is positive for me as a person ... I no longer will be diminished. I am actively working at not letting it happen. I feel so much better about myself.'

Six months after our first meeting, I invited Rose to join me as 'a consultant to others' and followed the protocol outlined in Epston & White (1992):

> *Therapy is concluded with an invitation to persons to attend a special meeting with the therapist so that the knowledges that have been resurrected and/or generated in therapy can be documented. The knowledges will include those alternative and preferred knowledges about self, others and relationships and those knowledges of problem-solving that have enabled persons to liberate their lives.* (p.17)

'A consultant to others' implicates an audience, and those audiences that are recruited contribute to the authentication of the person's preferred claims derived from rendering his or her life's events meaningful according to the 'alternative' story. And reader, you have become a member of that audience. Rose herself was provided with both audio-taped and transcribed versions of this consultation, from which the following is an edited excerpt.

DE: Can I ask - what difference did it make to you having your story available to you, do you think?

Rose: *It helped me understand what had happened and possibly why it had happened ... my reactions to what had happened and the end result. Looking at it and following it through gave me a sense of relief and understanding ... It was relief that it wasn't my fault ... that there were things that had happened to me as a child and I had been basically reacting ever since ... A lot of the negative feelings I had about myself had been enforced when I was younger by a parent figure (father?). And I took that attitude, consciously or unconsciously, and continued to think that way about myself. Having the story gave me a point of reference to look back at , to read it through, to think about it and form my own opinions from what we had discussed and draw my own conclusions. I remember getting the letter from the letter box, making myself a nice cup of tea, sitting down and reading it. I had feelings of 'Yes ... that's it ... that's the* whole *story!' Thinking about it, re-reading it ... and feeling a lot better about myself, possibly understanding myself and possibly what direction I wanted to go in. Without it, I think I'd still be confused ... I know I'd still be confused and have the same feelings of inadequacy as a person and not knowing why I felt the way I did.*

DE: How did having your own story validate you? If you had felt you were a fake, phoney, hollow, nothing inside of you, not a true person, how did you legitimate yourself so quickly?

Rose: *It was a number of things. I think I had all these suspicions floating around and I wasn't too sure what was real, what was right, what was following through and what wasn't. Possibly having my own story helped me to find out my own attitude and thoughts. And from that so much grew ... I just immediately started feeling so much better about myself. I started feeling I had validity. And that I had so many untapped opportunities that I had been too frightened to look at or thought I didn't have a right to them. Basically feeling so much better about myself allowed me to consider a very different kind of future for myself. If this hadn't happened, I would have remained a very unhappy person. I had got to the stage that I didn't want to go out there again and compete and have another go at finding employment. I'd got to the point where it was make or break about living. Either I did something about it ... or I'd pull the pin and forget about living ... Ultimately, I think because I separated myself, in my case, from my father's opinions of who I was and formed my own opinion of who and what I was. I realised the danger of being made up by others. I had to make myself up although I think other people contributed to it. They weren't the people I expected or counted on and there is a real sense ... a lot of feelings about all that - anger, resentment ... a lot of pain. Somewhere along the line, you've got to accept ... accept? Accept isn't quite the right word ... understand and leave it behind.*

I summarised this 'consultation' once again by letter:

Dear Rose,

I am just writing to thank you for sharing your 'knowledge' with me and for your willingness to make it available to others. It has also added to my stock of 'knowledge' and has certainly encouraged me to pursue further the idea of the significance of people having their own 'story' rather than their abuser's 'story'. I can't tell you how struck I was that once you had a 'story' that was truer to your own experience of the events in your life, you filled in yourself that 'base' that you had described to me earlier as lacking. To some extent, I see you as having made yourself up and having done so, were then able to realise many of those abilities that were there for everyone to see, but invisible and unavailable to you. Once you saw yourself through your own eyes, you started to see yourself as other see you. It was very pleasing for me to have witnessed you taking up a more comfortable relationship with yourself and to see you realising many of your capabilities. As time goes by, I would imagine that there will be more of this. If you have the wish to keep in touch with these developments, I would be glad to hear from you.

Best wishes for a future of your own design.

Yours sincerely, David.

A Re-authoring Therapy: Premises and Practices

This therapy is premised on an idea that lives and relationships of persons are shaped by the very knowledges and stories that persons use to give meaning to their experiences, and certain practices of self or of relationship that are associated with these knowledges and stories. A re-authoring therapy intends to assist persons to resolve problems by: (1) enabling them to separate their lives and relationships from knowledges/stories that are impoverishing; (2) assisting them to challenge practices of self and relationship that are subjugating; and (3) encouraging persons to re-author their lives according to alternative knowledges/ stories and practices of self and relationship that have preferred outcomes.

Externalising the problem[10] as one of living according to her father's story of her, Rose and I soon came to realise that a great deal of her lived experience could not be accommodated by the 'dominant' story. Many events in her life, seen through her eyes or the eyes of others, just wouldn't fit and thus Rose had been unable to acknowledge or register them. The translation of experience into meaning was 'pre-figured'[11] by the extant narrative with certain events ascribed as meaningful and others unregistered as meaningless. The performance of her life according to the 'dominant' story led her to self-reproach and self-blame in relation to herself as a person and to fear and self-doubt in relation to the enactment of her own capabilities. An 'alternative' story became very plausible as 'unique outcomes' were identified and new meanings performed around them and the 'dominant' story began to be revisioned.[12] Rose recruited her own audiences for purposes of authentication, as did the 'consulting to others' meeting.

Commentary

by Kevin Murray

'Take charge of your life'. 'Be the person you've always wanted to be', 'Declare your independence'. The slogans of popular psychology books can be seen to grant the potential to mould oneself into the person one desires to be, in spite of what one imagines others think.[13] Is re-authoring therapy another version of this culture of self-reconstruction? Some consideration of this question is important in placing this clinical practice in a broader social realm.

The first obvious difference between re-authoring therapy and popular psychology concerns their respective media. Though re-authoring therapy draws on the power of textual documents, it is carried out under the gaze of the therapist as a helping *service*, whereas popular psychology appears to be largely a consumer *product* that is taken home and performed in the private act of reading. This is a difference between a *dialogical* process, in which oneself is reflected in the eyes of the other, and a *monological* process, in which the only audience for oneself is oneself.[14] This distinction is a little blurred: the reader of popular psychology texts does have some relationship with the author, albeit an abstracted one. Nonetheless, the author of a self-help manual is unlikely to respond to the ways in which the book's advice is taken up by a particular reader. The presence of a person who witnesses one's own responses is what seems here to distinguish psychotherapy from the self-analysis of reading popular psychology. The significance of this difference rests on the necessity of having one's change recognised by a legitimate audience. In popular psychology, it is enough to introduce the book's themes into one's own private narrative, whereas re-authoring therapy partly involves setting up an audience in which forms of change can be authenticated.

For example, in David Epston's letter to Rose he writes: 'it must have been satisfying for them [Rose's family] to side with your story and perhaps because of this, you have obviously been able to see yourself through others' eyes. The result of that is for you to appreciate yourself more and to develop a more comfortable relationship with yourself.' Here a family is organised as a mirror in which to compel the client to accept a more powerful self-narrative.

This dimension of practice in re-authoring therapy raises particular questions for an understanding of what is involved in practices of self-transformation. To what degree does re-authoring therapy diverge from recent developments in psychoanalysis which place emphasis on the reconstruction of self-narratives?

Over the past two decades, American psychoanalysts have been introducing the phenomenon of narrative into their understanding of the therapeutic process. Roy Schafer and Donald Spence are two psychoanalysts in the forefront of this development. Schafer (1978) has examined how psychoanalysis is constituted in narrative form - as comedy, romance, tragedy, and irony. According to Schafer, narrative form provides a vehicle for fundamental dimensions of human nature, such as the malleability of character, the compatibility of individual and society, and potential for happiness in life. What the introduction of narrative does for psychoanalysis in Schafer's theory is to make those assumptions appear as matters of choice rather than essential components of theory. Differently narrativised versions of psychoanalysis may suit different contexts: for example, comic psychoanalysis suits a social work situation, whereas ironic psychoanalysis is more appropriate for long-term analysis. For Schafer, anyone who employs psychoanalysis chooses more than a picture of reality - they also implicate themselves in an ethical vision.

As a theorist Spence (1982) is less concerned than Schafer with the formal narrative structures involved in the therapeutic process. His emphasis is on the skills of the analyst in finding the appropriate structures in language for expressing the unconscious anxieties of the analysand. Spence names this quality 'narrative truth'. Narrative truth is not a literal representation of the past, but rather it is a picture that by virtue of its 'aesthetic finality' gathers unrecognised experiences into a manageable whole. Spence presents a truth that is measured by its therapeutic effect, rather than its accuracy. This introduction of narrative brings to the fore the creative skills of the analyst in making up a good story.

The narrative psychoanalysis represented in the world of Schafer and Spence concerns itself with a refusal of the classical paradigm of historical truth within psychoanalysis. Rather than a specific set of truths revealed in analysis, it is the particular 'form' in which that truth emerges which is seen to contain the healing potential. It is this form which most sharply distinguishes narrative psychoanalysis from 're-authoring therapy'. The factors at play in the psychoanalytic setting are limited to the clinic. This limitation is at one with the general framework of psychological healing which is to see the problem mainly 'in the head' of the client: if you look at the problem differently, it will be alleviated. Though this interpretation does not do justice to the sophistication of the narrative psychoanalytic approach, it does form a major difference between it and 're-authoring therapy'. The emphasis in Spence on the use of psychoanalysis in finding a 'home' for experience in language looks at language outside of its everyday dialogical setting - it doesn't seem to matter if no one else but the analysand and the analyst understand the problem.

One can argue that the approaches of both narrative psychoanalysis and popular psychology are fundamentally limited to this narrow context. If one looks at agency as a resource that is distributed by others - being granted the right to speak - then what others think of oneself must be taken into account; it is not sufficient simply to change one's own picture of oneself privately; one must in addition have a convincing picture to show others.[15]

It is this dialogical principle which also conditions the nature of re-authoring therapy. To a certain degree, the ideology of such a therapy stresses the *freedom* of the individual to construct his or her own life. Such therapy states as one of its ideological principles that it is giving *freedom* to the individual to construct his or her own life story.[16] With all freedoms there is necessarily some exclusion that makes them possible: a negative makes a positive. This limitation can be found in the dialogical context. One can ask: why is it that their new story is credited by their conversational group? What do others have to gain from this accreditation? These are questions which seem to rest an inch from the nose of most accounts of therapy yet, because of that, pass largely unnoticed. The criteria by which an audience will accept a client's claim to have changed through therapy is a form of what Gergen (1989) calls 'the conditions of warrant'. Change in this sense is a licence that must be purchased form an audience in forms of currency that are seen as legitimate. Personal change is a restricted economy. It is one of the sparks of genius particular to re-authoring therapy that it recognises the power of the text to authenticate forms of personal change.[17]

This development creates a space in which other forms of family therapy might follow. What is primary is a sensitivity to what it means for a person to 'change' in the group context. In certain Australian families, for instance, the experience of being overseas is seen to provide a legitimate demonstration of the capacities of its members (White & Epston 1990). Travel here operates as a rite of passage that is customised by families according to their social location. At its extreme, a child is not acknowledged to be capable of an independent life until he or she has been able to return home with stories of trials in foreign settings. Such stories usually make a point that relates to the conversation between members of that family about human nature. For instance, one conversation might concern the question of whether deep down people are the same or different. A child who returns home with evidence about this in his or her experience of exotic peoples can be seen to contribute to the conversation that maintains the family.[18] The child participates in what Bruner (1987) describes as the 'meshing' that incorporates different points of view within the kind of conversation that brings families to the same table.[19] Here it is possible to examine change within the dialogical context provided by the family: change is acknowledged when it contributes to the moral picture of the family. The implication of this for family therapy is to extend the kind of sensitivity to the dialogical setting evident in re-authoring therapy to the importance of understanding the narrative ecology that already exists within the family - it is to sue the family not only as audience, but also as editors and script-writers.

Re-authoring therapy exists as a licence to move outside the abstract relations which typify established therapeutic interventions. To this extent, it is not just telling a story, it is also listening to the audience.

Notes

The introductory discussion and Rose's narrative are by David Epston and Michael White; the commentary by Kevin Murray.

1. First published 1992 in McNamee, S. & Gergen, K.J. (eds), *Therapy as a Social Construction*. London: Sage Publications. Republished here with permission.
2. This is excerpted from M. White (1989/90).
3. Victor Turner wrote that these expressions are 'the crystallised secretions of once living experience' (1982, p.17).
4. By arguing for the proposal about the extent to which stories determine the meaning attributed to experience, we are not suggesting that the context of our lives is single-storied. Rather, we believe that the context of our lives is multi-storied. There is a range of alternative stories for the interpretation of experience in which we and others may situate our lives. Also, despite this assertion about the story-determined nature of meaning, it turns out (as discussed later) that all such stories are, in fact, indeterminate.
5. When discussing the performance aspects of ritual process, Turner states: 'The term 'performance' is, or course derived form Old English parfournu, literally, 'to furnish completely or thoroughly'. To perform is thus to bring something about, to consummate something, or to 'carry out' a play, order, or project. But in the carrying out, I hold, something new may be generated. The performance transforms itself' (1980, p.160).
6. Turner (1980), when discussing the ritual process, relates indeterminacy to the subjunctive mood of verb: 'Indeterminacy is, so to speak, in the subjunctive mood, since it is that which is not yet settled, concluded, or known. It is all that may be, might be, could be, perhaps even should be ... Sally Falk Moore goes so far as to suggest that 'the underlying quality of social life should be considered to be one of theoretical absolute indeterminacy'. The relation of indeterminacy to the subjunctive mood is also discussed by J Bruner (1986).
7. For further discussion of those aspects of the structure of stories that encourage the reader to enter the story, to take it over and make it their own, see J Bruner (1986).
8. This phrase is taken from Shuman, 1986.
9. For another story that has parallels to the following, see Epston (1989b) with a 4½-year follow-up 'consultation' (Epston 1989a).

10. 'Externalising is an approach to therapy that encourages persons to objectify and, at times, to personify the problems that they experience as oppressive. In this process, the problem becomes a separate entity and thus external to the person or relationship that was ascribed as the problem. Those problems that are considered to be inherent, as well as those relatively fixed qualities that are attributed to persons and to relationships, are rendered less fixed and less restricting ... The externalising of the problem enables persons to separate from the dominant stories that have been shaping their lives and relationships. In so doing, persons are able to identify previously neglected but vital aspects of lived experiences - aspects that could not have been predicted from a reading of the dominant story. Thus, following Goffman (1961), I have referred to these aspects of experience as 'unique outcomes' (White 1989a,b) ... As unique outcomes are identified, persons can be encouraged to engage in performances of meaning in relation to these. Success with this requires that the unique outcome be plotted into an alternative story about the person's life.' (White & Epston 1990, pp.38-41)
11. Hayden White (1973) makes a historiographical case that histories are 'prefigured' by their narratives. E Bruner makes a similar point on doing ethnography: 'In my view, we began with a narrative that already contains a beginning and an ending, which frame and hence enable us to interpret the present. It is not that we initially have a body of data, the facts, and we then must construct a story or theory to account for them. Instead ... the narrative structures we construct are not secondary narratives about data but primary narratives that establish what is to count as data. New narratives yield new vocabulary, syntax, and meaning in our ethnographic accounts; they define what constitute the data of those accounts' (1986b, p.143).
12. Patraka defines revisioning from a feminist perspective: 'Rich defines "Re-Vision" as 'the act of looking back, of seeing with fresh eyes, entering an old text from a new critical direction' until women can 'understand the assumptions in which we are drenched' in order to know ourselves (1979, p.35). To give speech to what has been requires describing, naming and reinterpreting past reality. To change what is calls for an analysis of the sources of that reality and the reasons for its persistence' (1983, p.1).
13. For a more detailed discussion of the values of popular psychology texts, see Murray (1986).
14. This difference is articulated at length in the discourse of the Russian theorist Mikhail Bakhtin (1981).
15. The work of Erving Goffman (1968) in mental institutions can be used as a demonstration of the role of the audience in controlling the kind of agency one has in a situation.
16. The most significant principle that seems to inform the practice of 're-authoring therapy' is self-fashioning. This is a concept initially popular in the dramaturgists of the Renaissance and now re-discovered by readers of Foucault's histories of sexuality. Its most extreme form is found in the performances of artists, who shape their lives into a work of art. Rather than see a life, as under Freud, as being a quest

for a certain knowledge about oneself, which when found transforms one's existence, a life is looked at as a material to be fashioned according to whatever aesthetic or ethical principles seem fit. One of the criticisms of this principle is that it assumes that our condition of being is one of complete freedom. As such it ignores our debt to structures of meaning such as myths and language.

17. White and Epston (1990) contains reports of the seriousness with which clients took the therapist's letters - carrying them around and showing them off to others.
18. This claim is based on thus far unpublished research on travel talk (K Murray, 'Life as fiction: the making sense of personal change'. PhD thesis, University of Melbourne).
19. Jerome Bruner's (1987) account of the conversational dynamics of the 'Goodhertz' family provides a subtle example of how a family might develop a discursive ecology which both individuates and binds family members.

References

Bakhtin, M.M. 1981: *The Dialogical Imagination: Four essays,* tr. M Holquist and C Emerson. Austin, TX: University of Texas Press.

Bruner, E.,1986a: 'Experience and its expressions.' In Turner, V. & Bruner, E. (eds), *The Anthropology of Experience*. Chicago, IL: University of Illinois Press.

Bruner, E. 1986b: 'Ethnography as narrative.' In Turner, V. & Bruner, E. (eds), *The Anthropology of Experience*. Chicago, IL: University of Illinois Press.

Bruner, J. 1986: *Actual Minds: Possible Worlds*. Cambridge, MA: Harvard University Press.

Bruner, J. 1987: 'Life as narrative'. *Social Research*, 54:11-32.

Dilthey, W. 1976: *Dilthey: Selected writings*, Rickman, H. (ed). Cambridge: Cambridge University Press.

Epston, D. 1989a: 'Marisa revisits.' *Collected Papers,* pp.128-136. Adelaide: Dulwich Centre Publications.

Epston, D. 1989b: 'Writing Your History.' *Collected Papers*, Adelaide: Dulwich Centre Publications.

Epston, D. & White, M. 1992: 'Consulting your consultants: The documentation of alternative knowledges.' In Epston, D. & White, M., *Experience, Contradiction, Narrative & Imagination: Selected papers of David Epston and Michael White, 1989-1991*. Adelaide: Dulwich Centre Publications. (Previously published in the 1990 No.2 *Dulwich Centre Newsletter*.)

Geertz, C. 1986: 'Making experiences, authoring selves.' In Turner, V. & Bruner, E. (eds), *The Anthropology of Experience*. Chicago, IL: University of Illinois Press.

Gergen, K. J. 1989: 'Warranting voice and the elaboration.' In Shotter, J. & Gergen, K.J. (eds), *Texts of Identity*. London: Sage.

Goffman, E. 1961: *Asylums: Essays in the social situation of mental patients and other inmates*. New York: Doubleday.

Goffman, E. 1968: *Asylums*. Harmondsworth: Penguin

Harré, R. 1983: *Personal Being: A theory for individual psychology*. Oxford: Blackwell.

Iser, W. 1978: *The Act of Reading*. Baltimore, M D: Johns Hopkins University Press.

Kamsler, A. 1990: 'Her-story in the making: Therapy with women who were sexually abused in childhood.' In Durrant, M. & White, C. (eds), *Ideas for Therapy with Sexual Abuse*. Adelaide: Dulwich Centre Publications.

Mink, L. 1978: 'Narrative form as a cognitive instrument.' In Canary, R.H. & Kozicki, H. (eds), *The Writing of History: Literary form and historical understanding*. Madison, WI: University of Wisconsin Press.

Murray, K. 1986: 'Finding literary paths: the work of popular life constructors.' In Sarbin, T.R. (ed), *Narrative Psychology: The storied nature of human conduct*. New York: Praeger.

Patraka, V. 1983: 'Introduction.' In Patraka, V. & Tilly, L.A. (eds*), Feminist Re-visions: What has been and might be*. Ann Arbour, MI: University of Michigan Press.

Rich, A. 1979: *On Lies, Secrets, and Silence: Selected prose (1966-1979)*. New York: Norton.

Ricoeur, P. 1983: *Time and Narrative*. Chicago, IL: University of Illinois Press.

Schafer, R. 1978: *Language and Insight*. New Haven, CT: Yale University Press

Shuman, A. 1986: *Story-telling Rights*. Cambridge: Cambridge University Press.

Spence, D.P. 1982: *Narrative Truth and Historical Truth: Meaning and interpretation in psychoanalysis*. New York: Norton.

Turner, V. 1980: 'Social dramas and stories about them.' *Critical Inquiry,* Autumn:141-68.

Turner, V., 1982: *From Ritual to Theatre*. New York: Performing Arts Press.

White, H. 1973: *Metahistory: The Historical Imagination in Nineteenth-Century Europe*. Baltimore, MD: Johns Hopkins University Press.

White, M. 1989a: 'Family therapy and schizophrenia: Addressing the "in-the-corner lifestyle".' In White, M., *Selected Papers*. Adelaide: Dulwich Centre Publications.

White, M. 1989b: 'The process of questioning: A therapy of literary merit?' In White, M., *Selected Papers*. Adelaide. Dulwich Centre Publications.

White, M. 1989/90; 'Family therapy training and supervision in a world of experience and narrative.' *Dulwich Centre Newsletter*, Summer.

White, M. 1990: 'The externalisation of the problem.' In White, M. & Epston, D., *Narrative Means to Therapeutic Ends*. New York: Norton.

White, M. & Epston, D. 1990: *Narrative Means to Therapeutic Ends*. New York: Norton. (Also published 1989 as *Literate Means to Therapeutic Ends*, Adelaide: Dulwich Centre Publications.)

3

Voices[1]

'Voices' certainly demands some explanation. It all began when Gunthard Weber and Fritz Simon (Heidelberg, Germany) sent a letter to Michael White who then sent it on to me. The letter was a formal request for Michael to contribute to a festschrift, *a book to be published in honour of one Carl Auer. There was what I took to be a rather impertinent suggestion that Michael would wish 'to take this opportunity to acknowledge Carl Auer's obvious influence' over his work. I thought I knew Michael pretty well; so who was this Carl Auer? He certainly had never mentioned him to me. What was even more bewildering was Michael's note to me: 'Did you save our correspondence that we had about Carl?' The grounds of 'reality' suddenly became very slippery beneath my feet! I can't remember for how long; nor can I recall how I learned that* kalauer *translates from German into English as 'pun, wit, or play on words'.*

What a fitting way for a social constructionist publishing house - Carl-Auer-Systeme-Verlag to make itself up as a 'language game'. If you had any confusion over the post-structuralist assumption that language is an intervention in the 'world' rather than a representation of it, this makes the point. If a 'life' is constituted of the stories told about it, could Carl Auer be 'constructed' after the fact by the reminiscences of a community of family therapists from around the world? You will have to read Carl Auer: Geist oder Ghost? *(1990) /* Strange Encounters with Carl Auer *(1991) to settle this for yourself.*

Relieved of the usual conventions surrounding the preparing of a 'paper', I entered a 'space' where fact and fiction merged into each other; where one story seemed to tell another. I sat down at my typewriter as in a fever and arose some hours later with 'Voices' more or less intact.

4/8/89

Dear Michael,[2]

I received your letter today with a copy of Gunthard Weber's request for our reminiscences of Carl Auer. I guess it's not really a surprise as Auer is a hard person to forget. Like so many people say about their encounters with Milton Erickson, his thoughts 'go with you', seemingly poised to burst to life by the appropriate circumstances. Don't worry; such was the strange spell he cast over me that I did save our correspondence from 1985 and I didn't have to dig down too deep in my filing cabinet before I dug them up.

And what do you think of this? Coincidence? Or paranormal? Today, I met for the second time a thirty-five-year-old man, oppressed by an obligation life-style. He told me he had been a 'little less under the obligation of his obligation life-style' since we last met. He hears 'voices' which persuade him that he has an unpaid debt to a friend or has left the door of a friend's refrigerator ajar. At times, the 'voices' add insults such as 'dummy', 'cheat', 'rip-off artist', 'irresponsible', 'careless'. As he put it, 'they have ways to bring me around to their way of thinking'. I 'collapsed time' with him and he said that if he was convinced by his 'voices' more, his own sphere of influence would contract so that in the end he wouldn't be able to escape from his bed and his 'voices' would totally prevail over him. But, in reflecting on this dismal prospect, he recalled a 'unique outcome'. And was it unique! Keep reading!

He recalled travelling in Europe last year: 'When I was troubled by my voices nagging me about things, I reached the conclusion that I should start challenging the reality of the voices - their allegations against me. When I started putting up a counter-case, I could sometimes break away from their grip.' I asked my usual questions: 'How did you discover this? How did you make this discovery?'

He told me he had been hiking near Heidelberg and was resting at a gasthaus, perched overlooking the Neckar river. As usual, when he had paid for his schnapps, his 'voices' started harassing him about whether he had paid up or not and he persisted in asking the waiter if he had done so. He could not be reassured. He had been travelling for so long now that he had got into the habit of talking aloud without being aware of it. An elderly man in lederhosen leaning on a stout walking stick was sitting nearby and finally turned to him and - in a reasonable version of New Zealand English - said 'Gidday, mate! Your 'voices' are not a matter for psychiatry. They are a matter for rhetoric - the art of persuasion.' My client was taken aback on a number of counts, least of all this man's appearance. The description should have given him away but it didn't.

I was dumbstruck myself as his story unfolded. After a brief discussion (or was it a consultation), he suggested my client do the following: that he should invite them (the 'voices') to attend a recording session, pointing to my client's tape recorder. When my client queried their willingness to accept his invitation, the man advised him to incite them by acting like a 'bad boy'. He said that my client might consider that the 'voices' had something of importance to tell him. He proposed my client then record them into what he called 'your little machine' and then submit them to close scrutiny, especially their rhetorical aspects. My client had little knowledge of rhetoric so the old man, thanks to a classical education, assisted him at some length. He then advised him to tape his own 'voice', a voice that presents 'your counter-case', as he called it. These are my words but the old man said something to the effect that he imagined his 'voice' would argue again his further submitting to obligation and its side-effects. He said: 'Give voice to your advocate's voice and tape it likewise'. He then proposed that he study his 'case' for a free life, free from the impoverishment of obligation and always measuring up to others' expectations.

I don't know why I am going into such detail because the important thing was that this was so close to the conversation I had with Auer on my way from Christchurch to Auckland in 1985. Remember, you flew directly to

Adelaide and we parted company in the airport. It just had to be old Auer and when I checked some details, sure enough it was. What do you think of all this? What do you think of Auer's 'therapy'? You know what they say about Auer that 'once met, never forgotten'. Auer's life is like a Dickens novel in its dependence upon coincidence. Flabbergasting, is it not?

Yours Auer-ly, David Epston.

PS: Find enclosed my letter from Oct. 9, 1985.

9/10/85

Dear Michael,

A remarkable thing that happened on my flight to Auckland. I was pretty weary after the workshop as I imagine you were.

As is my custom, I had planned to bury myself inside some headphones and rock-and-roll myself home. I had an aisle seat. An elderly, 'foreign' man excused himself and pressed past me. I had no interest in making contact with anyone after the workshop but there was something about him that attracted me. He looked old but acted young. His eyes were vivacious and when I couldn't suppress my curiosity, I guessed by his leather satchel full of weighty books that he was an Oxford don here on sabbatical. I started sneaking glances at him which wasn't hard to do as he seemed quite in a world of his own. A DC-10 was just another university carrel to him. He vigorously slashed his way through a manuscript with a fountain pen. I remember thinking that I hadn't seen such an antiquated pen in use before.

He seemed to satisfy himself in regard to his editing, sat back and pulled out, of all things, Bateson's *Mind and Nature*. I couldn't contain myself any longer and thought I might start up a conversation with him. I did the usual opening airplane gambit. 'Have you enjoyed your stay in New Zealand?' His reply baffled me on two counts: first, he spoke with quite a reasonable New Zealand accent and second, he said: 'As an anti-positivist, is has had a special significance to me. But it was nothing like arriving here in 1942 with my late friend, Karl Popper. We both had secured Junior Lectureships at Canterbury University where we weathered the storms of the war years.' He then enquired if I knew who Karl Popper was. I indicated I did and that was all it took for him to commence lecturing, much like I am told Wittgenstein used to at Cambridge. More or less, I became a witness to him having out-loud a conversation with himself. Aphorisms were followed by oracular riddles, several of which he attempted to solve, much to his own amusement. I didn't quite know what to make of all this, so I remained attentive. I thought to myself that this wasn't rock-and-roll but my mind felt like it was getting a dry-cleaning. Abruptly, he discontinued his discourse and said: 'Tell me the story of your life, young man - or would it be better put, "story" your life's story.' Without any opportunity to try a reply, he broadened his question by further musing, chaining together a number of unanswered questions:

'How does one render events or episodes out of the flow of lived experience? How are those events construed as a story? How is storied experience warranted? Does one tell one's story or is it told? What would become of a person whose story was "untellable"? What if people's lives were considered to be "texts" and how would it be different to be a "reader" or an "author"?' One question seemed to breed another. It didn't seem important to him to stop and try to find an answer. I am not at all sure I understood a word of this, although it was pleasing to consider how this man's mind was working. All of a sudden he snapped out of his intellectual reverie, fixed me with intense interest and asked me what I did for a living. I was caught napping and said: 'Family therapy'. Assuming this would make no sense to him, coming from Europe, I qualified my remarks with ... 'something like psychiatry'. He laughed: 'Voices', he said, 'they worry when people hear voices. Their question is badly put - "Do you hear voices?" A preferable question would be: "Which of many voices is most attractive to you?" Psychiatry is like my long-lost friend, Karl Popper. Don't you think psychiatry would be better served by scrutinising its rhetoric? Psychiatry has selected base rhetoric. Why not noble rhetoric?'

With a flourish, he placed *Mind and Nature* in my lap and insisted I should explore its contents. Well, for the first time I felt I could contribute. 'Professor', I said, 'I want you to know that I am a student of the self-same book and that Bateson has had a particular influence on my colleague and friend, Michael White, who lives in Adelaide, Australia.' He looked rather surprised and said that he had been under the impression that Karl Popper had 'popper-ised' us. He said this was certainly the case in the universities he had visited. 'Not in my family therapy', I replied. He said: 'Yes, family therapy ... I have met some family therapists here and there'. He jokingly referred to his plan to climb Ayers Rock the week after. I told him of your attempts to derive a therapy from the ideas of Bateson. He expressed keen interest. By the way, his name is Carl Auer. Be prepared: he's like no-one I have ever met before. I hope you will offer him some of your generous hospitality. Your life may never be the same again.

Fond regards, David Epston.

PS: Write back as soon as you can. Isn't it curious that Auer and Popper were at Canterbury University at the same time and I had never heard of him before. This cannot last forever, I assure you. One day, there will be a *festschrift* for Auer, and New Zealand will be honoured to realise it provided refuge for this man. He has had an influence on me that will only unfold over time. I hope you don't think I have gone crazy.

Notes

1. First published 1990 as 'Voices/Stimmen' (pp.24-135) in *Carl Auer: Geist oder Ghost,* edited by Weber, G. & Simon, F.B. (publisher Carl-Auer-Systeme Verlag: Heidelberg). Republished 1991 in *Strange Encounters with Carl Auer* (publisher WWNorton: New York). Republished here with permission.
2. Both are letters to Michael White, the answer to which has unfortunately been lost.

4

Internalising Discourses versus Externalising Discourses[1]

This was my early attempt to account for the variant effects of internalising as compared to externalising discourses. Here too I was striving to have 'externalising the problem' conceptualised at the very level of 'discourse' rather than as a somewhat unconventional 'technique' from the therapy 'tool kit'. Michael White, reading Foucault, had been rethinking 'externalising the problem' as a discursive practice since around 1985. He commonly would use the Foucauldian term 'counter-discourse'. I was referencing the socio-linguist Halliday's concept of 'anti-language'. More recently, others have been referring to similar linguistic practices as 'transgressing discourses' (see Huspek & Radford 1997). No matter how demanding, I think it is highly relevant to consider such a practice in reference to Foucault's 'antiscience' project. What might happen if therapeutic conversations were no longer conducted for *science and were structured very differently? In this chapter I hoped to explore such a prospect.*

Several weeks ago, I was visiting with my good friend, Michael White, in Adelaide. During our work together, he was interviewed by a psychologist for a study of therapists working in the area of male violence. The interviewer's questioning assisted Michael in reviewing his career and those ideas that were influential in the development of his unique practice. I was invited to join them as a spectator. Near the end of the interview, the psychologist turned to me and offered an invitation I couldn't refuse: 'David, if you were to ask Michael one question and one question only, what would it be?' I was quite flummoxed, as this question intruded into my reflections. Still, I decided to reduce my million and one questions of Michael to the following: 'Michael, if you hadn't invented that "talk" we refer to as externalising discourse, where do you think your work would be today?' Michael's reply was immediate and conclusive. 'Nowhere!'

That one question had been on my mind even prior to receiving the invitation to address this conference. My answer, had I been asked, would also have been 'Nowhere!' I had written something to this effect in 1989:

> *If I were to restrict myself to only one aspect of White's work that I have taken over, it would be that of 'externalising the problem'. This is summarised by his maxim: 'The person isn't the problem; the problem is the problem'. This provided a rationale and a practice to position myself in therapy, that is, to be on everyone's side at the same time and to act with commitment and compassion against the 'problem', whatever the problem might be. It freed me from the constraints of some of the prevailing practices that I found distanced me from the family and reduced my fervour.* (p.26)

I had always been interested in the problematising of the notion of the 'problem'. I credit the Mental Research Institute for pioneering this undertaking and it seems very appropriate that John Weakland is here to represent it. According to one of Karl Tomm's (1989) many aphoristic summaries: For MRI, 'the problem is the attempted solution'; for the Milan associates, 'The problem is the solution'. The Milan associates have ironicised the idea of problem, with an unsurpassed mastery. In my reading of the literature, both MRI's and the Milan associates' revisionings of the idea of the 'problem' were radical departures from the taken-for-granted and by now sedimented and buried-over practices relating to the construction of the 'problem'.

Such practices were the methodologies of what Foucault (1980) refers to as 'regimes of truth', so-called regimes in which power and knowledge were inextricably linked. Those practices had come to be warranted as special forms of procedure leading to a 'truth' and accordingly were considered inviolate. Those professions whose prestige and privileges were founded on those 'regimes of truth' had arrogated to themselves the warrant of establishing the 'lawful' and 'universal' *truth*.

My preference is to conceive of 'truth' as a fiction that has been constructed in line with truth-making procedures into a 'fact'. Latour and Woolgar (1979), in their ethnography of the construction of a scientific 'fact' in a prestigious research laboratory, conclude:

> *Scientific activity is not 'about nature'. It is a fierce fight to construct reality. The laboratory is the workplace and the set of productive forces, which makes construction possible. Every time a statement stabilises, it is reintroduced into the laboratory and it is used to increase the difference between statements. The cost of challenging the reified statement is impossibly high. Reality is secreted.* (p.240)

The professional histories of how they gained access to these truth-making methodologies, of how they superseded the 'untrue', and how they won hegemonic or partial authority over rival claimants to truthfulness, were written as if they were history-taking rather than history-making. No matter what reading you wish to give Foucault (1979) and his critiques of the extant histories of professional practices and his rival historical method (the 'genealogical'), we can no longer be so innocent.

But let me go back to my story. In the late 1970s, freshly qualified, I returned to New Zealand from studying in England and at The Family Institute in Wales. I started working in psychiatry and soon found myself responsible for the supervision of a young social work graduate working in a psychiatric hospital ward. His idealism was as yet undimmed and he found himself distressed, without quite knowing why, when he witnessed those practices referred to as 'grand rounds'. He was currently researching his masters thesis, so we decided upon our own informal research project. We constructed notions of kinds of 'talk': solution talk and problem talk. We hoped these terms would have the capacity to distinguish one kind of talk from the other. Any conversation inquiring of the 'problem' was deemed problem talk and any conversation concerned with a solution was regarded as solution talk.

You might have thought such a distinction would not have been fine-grained enough to separate one kind of talk form another. In fact, the forms of talk were determined by the arrival of the tea trolley punctually at 10am, exactly one hour after the grand round had been called to order. You may wonder how a tea trolley could punctuate a grand round, which must be considered as an exemplar of positivist practices. You guessed it; from 9am to 10am there was nothing but talk relating to the 'problem'. The tea trolley's arrival precipitated an embarrassed, 'Well, what do we do now?' The next two minutes or so were a frenzy of banalities, which seemed to be recycled from one week to the next, a bit like an old threadbare shirt that had fit someone or other sometime or other. Each of the more senior people made the selfsame suggestions. The discussion was concluded when the most senior person settled the matter with, 'Well, why don't we just keep a watchful eye on it?' This was immediately met with agreement and relief. However, this pensive moment dissolved spontaneously in a flurry of activity, with everyone forsaking the grand round for the allure of the tea trolley. All this problem talk can sure make a professional person thirsty!

It is interesting to note that Ben Furman and Tapani Ahola, free-wheeling brief therapy practitioners in Helsinki, Finland, appropriated solution talk for the title of their recently published book: *Solution Talk: Hosting therapeutic conversations* (1992). They define the conduct of such a talk:

> *In our search for alternative ways of talking about problems we have been drawn to the traditions of family and brief therapy. Over the years we have gradually found a number of useful ideas for conducting therapeutic conversations and consultations which we will refer to in this book as 'solution talk'. This way of working is characterised both by an atmosphere of openness and by what could be characterised as a constructive way of talking. This conversational style is achieved by thinking positively and by focusing on subjects that foster hope, such as resources, progress, and the future.* (p.xxiv)

Allow me to review a recent article by Howard Waitzkin entitled 'A Critical Theory of Medical Discourse: Ideology, Social Control, and the Processing of Social Context in Medical Encounter'. I don't think anyone would be surprised by the conclusions of discourse-analytic studies. And Waitzkin, at the same time, punctures any non-medical practitioner's pretensions or smugness by adding: *Similar patterns may appear in encounters with clients and members of other 'helping' professions* (p.223). I feel certain that they do.

What does Waitzkin find when what professionals really 'say' is scrutinised, rather than what they say about what they say? According to him, the 'talk' is disengaged and uncritical of social context. In fact, unwittingly, *medical encounters tend to convey ideological messages supportive of the current social order and these encounters have repercussions for social control* ... (p.223). He goes on to say: *The technical structure of the medical encounter ... masks a deeper structure that may have little to do with the conscious thoughts of professionals about what they are saying and doing* (p.227). He also argues on the basis of his earlier research that the 'traditional format of problem-diagnosis-plan' is used 'as an organising framework' of medical encounters.

What is a medically proper diagnosis and what effect does that have on what is said, recorded, and thought? Mischler (1984) reveals that medical language encourages the saying of some things and the leaving unsaid of others.

If thought is enacted through talk, what would happen if a person were to live their life medically? To research such a question by, say, rearing a person in such a way as to exclude him/her from all other discourses would be an ethical outrage. I wouldn't have even been able to formulate such a prospect if I hadn't met the Medical Model Man on the 27th day of February, 1990, in my office in a very modest suburb of Auckland, New Zealand. As I was to learn as we got talking, his life so far had been a kind of 'natural' experiment. But I don't want to get ahead of myself.

It was early in my work year. I was just back from my summer holidays. At such times, my preference is to meet with calm, considered people. I don't have anything in particular in mind, just so long as people aren't too alarming. That was the frame of mind I was in when Rob and Sandy entered my office. Both were in their mid-to-late thirties. Rob extended his hand to me. I responded in kind and nominated myself: 'Hi! I'm David'. His reply disconcerted me, to say the least: 'Hi! I'm the Medical Model Man'. Before I could say anything, Sandy fiercely announced her presence with a tirade: 'There he goes again. I have had enough of this. This has been going on now for six months. The moment this interview is finished, I'm leaving and I won't be back for a week. He's already spent $20,000 on psychiatrists. And what did he end up with but ECT. The rest of the time I had to nurse him, with him crying four, five hours a day.' She then looked at me with a cool intensity and warned, 'You had better watch out or he'll try to out-doctor you!' I thought this might be an out and said, 'He can't. I'm a social worker. Do you think you've gone to the wrong professional?' Rob was quick to reassure me that he had been referred to me by two psychiatrists in another country and that settled the matter for him.

Rob seemed as eager to get on with the consultation as Sandy was to have a holiday from Rob. They had just repatriated themselves after being overseas for less than a year. Six months of this period Rob had spend in bed with depression, alternating between crying and reading psychiatric texts in preparation for his next psychiatric consultation. Talking to him was like talking to a history of psychiatric nosology; melancholia, neurasthenia, and more current terms like anhedonia. It seemed that Rob had become depressed during what he described as 'a brutal time'. The job that had been promised him turned out to be in a company on the brink of financial collapse, and their first pregnancy was stillborn.

The following was a letter I sent to them summarising our meeting together:

Dear Rob and Sandy,

I enjoyed meeting you both very much. Rob, for a depressed person, you make very good company. In the company of Sandy and myself, you were far more a 'person' than a 'patient'. Sandy, I certainly experienced Rob as you did during the seven years of your anti-depressive relationship. You said that you had regraded him, refusing to see him as fragile, requiring medical intervention, but instead saw him 'as a strong human being', as you put it. You both agreed that your relationship was 95% anti-depressing then. And Rob, you were able to appreciate Sandy's appreciation of you. You said, 'Sandy was proud of me'. Sandy, you also enjoyed Rob's lively sense of humour, his creativity, and his decency. Here, I gather you were alluding to his sense of justice and fairness and in your words: 'his goodness'. You also considered that Rob has 'perspective ... he can tell chalk from cheese'.

However, your trip to America was a 'brutal time'. The business enterprise you joined was on the brink of financial collapse. And the birth of your first born was stilled. Sandy, you responded to this unexpected tragedy with all your feelings. When it was your turn, Rob, you 'medical modelised' your feelings and turned yourself into a case study.

From what you told me, Rob, you had been trained in the family you came from that any distress should be put to bed with a few Valium for good measure. I wish I had asked you the following questions:

- 'Do you think your father was providing the best for you when he prescribed Valium instead of sympathy?'

- 'Do you think your father wanted you to grow up to be a Medical Model Man?'

- 'Did your father treat himself to the same treatment?'

- 'Did your father treat your mother to the same treatment?'

- 'What do you think he would have thought if he knew you arranged some ECT for yourself after he had died?'

- 'Did you think that your father, by treating you rather than talking to you, was preparing you for a medical career?'

- 'Do you think he was disappointed when you only got a MBA?'

- 'Did you feel a failure, even though you topped your class?'

- 'Did you think that if you couldn't be a good doctor, at least you could have a great patienthood, one in which you could out-doctor doctors?'

- 'What sense do you make of your patronage of psychiatry?'

- 'Do you feel indebted to psychiatrists?'

- 'How did you convince them to ECT you?'

- 'What do you think they thought about a person who supported questionable psychiatric practices more than they did?'

- 'Do you think they realise that you were a living Medical Model Man?'

Ever since you 'medical modelised' yourself and your feelings, you have been bed-ridden and a 'good patient': passive and devoted to psychiatric nosology, which must have given you some satisfaction. Still your medical modelising is starting to hurt. It seemed that you were getting 'sick' of your depression, even though it has become your preoccupation and, as you put it, 'my hobby'. Depression, according to you, is 'my raison d'etre ... my reason for living' but it seemed to me that you were beginning to question whether you wanted to be an 'object' of your medicalisation anymore. You have found that depression now has taken priority over all other pursuits, including your relationship. Your medical modelisation has tried to recruit Sandy into nursing you, but Sandy, you gave me the undeniable impression that you had had your fill of that.

Rob, you said that depression had taken over 100% of your life. Sandy, you said that depression had taken over 100% of your relationship.

Sandy, I wish I had had the.wit to have asked you a few questions:
- 'Do you think that Rob's depression is good for your relationship?'
- 'Why have you decided not to go along with the medical modelisation of Rob's life and the life of your relationship?'
- 'Do you get the impression that Rob is more attracted to the medical model than to you?'
- 'How far has depression come between you?'
- 'How far do you think it will go, if the weight of your relationship is not pitted against it?'
- 'What is Rob's depression doing to your love and respect for him?'
- 'Is Rob's depression reducing your intimacy with him and do you feel constrained to act towards him more like a nurse than an intimate partner?'
- 'Is nursing Rob's depression an attractive undertaking for you?'
- 'Rob, do you have any wish to take your life back from depression or is being a doctor to yourself more appealing?'

Last week I met a woman whose life had been 'medicalised' recently. Following that experience, she had a dream which might interest you. She dreamt that she was paralysed on an operating table, helpless and speechless. She looked up to see what she described as 'technical looks' on her doctors' faces. Then, and only then, did she discover to her horror what they were doing. They were taking her heart out. And that reminds me of a quote from Michel Foucault, the French philosopher and historian of medical, psychiatric and penal ideas. In 'The Birth of the Clinic' (1973) he writes: In relation to that which he is suffering from, the patient is only an external fact; the medical reading must take him into account only to place him in parentheses.

Rob, it struck me that you have put your 'heart' in parentheses and medical modelised it. It may be preferable, if you are to pursue a medical modelising course in life, that you consult cardiologists rather than psychiatrists. You could conceivably have your heart removed and replaced with some technology that won't respond to grief and disappointment. All that will be required is another micro-processor.
- 'Rob, is it time to critically scrutinise whether you wish to continue medical modelising your life?'
- 'Do you think it would interest you to set aside depression for a while and undertake an archaeology of the seven years of anti-depression in your

relationship?'

- *'Don't you think that would be worth digging up?'*

The questions you might ask yourself are:

- *'How do we keep depression at bay?'*
- *'How did Rob specialise in being a person rather than a patient?'*
- *'Sandy, how did Rob make you respect and love him before depression first turned you into his nurse and then estranged you from him?'*
- *'Rob, do you think you might bring your studiousness to bear on the mess depression is making of your life and relationship?'*
- *'How did the tragedy of a stillbirth separate you rather than bring you together?'*

Yours in anti-depression, David.

Just before the end of our meeting, I informed Rob and Sandy that Margaret Newmark and Chris Beels would be joining me the week of their next appointment. I added that Chris had formerly been a professor of psychiatry at Columbia University in New York. Sandy vehemently opposed my proposal that they join us, alleging that Rob would out-professor the professor. Rob grinned and looked rueful. He said, 'I'd love to meet him but I don't feel depressed now'. I tried to save the day by saying, 'Don't worry about it ... fake it and they won't know the difference'.

Rob rang me soon after he received the letter. He informed me that Sandy had retired to a beach cottage for a rest from depression. However, he avowed his desire to become a 'person'. In the meantime, he had found a job three days after our meeting and had brought a new car. Sandy had arrived home the night before our next meeting and telephoned me in a state of alarm. She warned me that Rob was going to kill himself. 'How can you tell?' I inquired. She said that he was yelling and shouting. 'At whom?' I asked. 'His father and mother!' she replied. 'Has he ever done this before?' She said, 'Never!' 'Sandy, I think he's becoming a "person". What do you think?' The tone of her voice dropped in hushed reflection. 'You're right ... sorry about disturbing you ... I'm looking forward to seeing you tomorrow.' 'Can't wait to catch up with you both.'

At the beginning of our second meeting, Rob presented me with a thirteen-page document, which began:

So how do I begin to record my feelings about my life and my seemingly uninterrupted battle with what's been variously labelled as 'depression', 'affective disorder', 'arrhythmic cyclothymia', 'melancholia', etc. These terms trip off my tongue/pen with such ease and perverse pride - it's as if they represent some kind of accreditation. Certainly they take precedent over my ability or desire to define myself in human qualities. Frankly, I feel devoid of any human qualities. I'm a medical case, not a human being, I no longer relate to the world as a person or character.

We were to meet five more times, during which Rob constituted himself as a 'person' and his depression subsided. Probably the most important event was when Rob met with his male friends and told them that he had lied to them about his physician father. His father had not been a great man but rather a 'drunk'.

I rang Rob to ask his permission to tell you (at this conference) about our meetings. He asked if he could address you:

Dear David and Colleagues:

I address this letter to you, primarily, David. But I also invite you to verbally share it with your professional colleagues. Why? Because I think it motivating for you all to realise the importance and usefulness of your collective work. Specifically, as a result of six or seven one-hour sessions over the last fifteen months (with a seven-month hiatus over the spring-summer of 1990-91), I have been freed from the doubts and limitations imposed by the well-intentioned 'medical model'. Such bondage existed for at least twenty years on and off ... thankfully much more of the latter than the former.

As I once said to you David, the medical school of mental diagnosis and treatment has several shortcomings. It turns acute conditions into chronic problems. It is problem-orientated, not solution-driven. It therefore uses drug therapy to treat weakness, not human insight to lever a person's strengths. You introduced me to the latter approach. Thanks! Its pharmacological prescriptions become junk-mail subscriptions. Getting away from 'them' is like trying to convince American Express you don't want your card renewed ... and so on.

I'd appreciate you keeping my name anonymous but I find it appropriate that I acknowledge your help in this slightly formal way.
Yours sincerely, Rob.

This leads me to review what Michael White (1990a) has referred to in his earlier publications as 'the externalisation of the problem', which some would relegate to the realm of technique, tactic, or strategy. As Karl Tomm (1989) has said, 'To do so would certainly be both naive and limiting'. It is my purpose, in what is to follow, to locate externalising in the realm of discourse. White (1990b) has proposed the notion of 'counter-discourse'. Elsewhere I have argued for externalising in relation to a problem as 'counter-cultural'. I am now wondering if externalising problem discourse (Madigan 1992) qualifies as what Halliday (1978), the noted sociolinguist, has described as an 'anti-language'.

I should first like to acquaint you with the notion of *discourse* and those discourses, in particular, that frame problems. Secondly, I would argue that discourse is always situated in a cultural and historical context. Thirdly, discursive practices relating to problems have very real effects on how the problem is experienced by the parties to it - whether the problem is experienced as a state of being or as an influence on one's life and relationships. It is also critical whether the 'problem' speaks to and of the person and his/her identity or whether the person speaks of and to the 'problem'. The latter refers to the matter of 'position' in discourse and I would like to refer to that as the 'grammar of experience'.

Lowe (1991) makes the point that:

> *... one way of characterising postmodern experience would be to describe it as being* 'discourse-sensitive'. *Discourse has become a central concept, not only in postmodern thought, but in the general sphere of contemporary social and cultural theory. The term can be confusing because of its varying usages, in different fields, but there appear to be two related usages ... In the first, discourse refers to the process of conversation ... The postmodern repudiation of a representational view of language suggests that meanings are not given or 'found' through conversation, but are progressively made or fashioned through conversation itself ... The second use of discourse relates to a broader and more overtly political form of analysis which began in the 1970's, generated by reaction against aspects of the prevailing intellectual movement of structuralism ... Poststructural theory tended to displace attention from language to discourse. Discourse* 'historicises' *and* 'politicises' *the study of language use through emphasising the historical specificity of what is said and what remains unsaid. It is this sense of discourse which is most typically*

associated with postmodernism and particularly the work of Foucault. (pp.44-45)

For Foucault, the familiar objects of the social world, whether they be disease, death, madness, sexuality, etc., are not 'things' set apart from and independent of the discourse. They are realised only in and through discursive practices which surround the objects in question. He argues that discourse is not a narrow set of linguistic practices but is composed of a whole assemblage of activities, events, objects, settings, and epistemological precepts. Discourse and practice walk hand in hand and my inquiry concerns itself with those practices linked to a distinction I want to draw between externalising and internalising discourses.

Foucault, along with others, traced the rise of Western medicine. I would add an internalising problem discourse, emphasising the power and influence of clinical and experimental pathology in its development. He cites Morgagni's (1761) treatise *De sedibus et causis in morborum* as transitional to the notion that one can pinpoint the site of death and mortality within human anatomy, writing, *From the point of view of death, disease has a land, a mappable territory* (1973, p.17). In other words, disease was internalised within the living bodies of individuals. Anatomy superseded pathology in the late eighteenth century and came to monopolise clinical medicine in the nineteenth century. Here anatomical space became causal space, the home of both death and disease. This was followed by the body being regarded as the repository of human qualities. Mind, intelligence, madness, and a myriad of human qualities were regarded as located in living bodies. This is a superficial version of a history of the siting of human problems. Karl Tomm (1990) brings us up-to-date in regard to the DSM-III-R, probably the most significant contemporary text:

> *The authors seemed oblivious to the theoretical significance of their individualistic presuppositions. There was no mention of another point of view. They simply ignored the body of knowledge based on an alternative assumption, namely that human behaviour, the mind, and its disorder, may be more fundamentally grounded in social phenomena than individual phenomena.* (p.6)

I believe that the same historical developments relating to the siting of problems could be traced for other disciplines, e.g., psychology, but I do not have the space to survey them here.

So what are the effects of positioning oneself differently in relation to a 'problem' and construing it as *external* rather than *internal*? I propose the following effects: Persons/couples/families are more likely to become agents rather than patients. They do not appear dulled and stupefied as patients often do; rather, they are creative, enlivened, enthusiastic, and can call upon problem-solving capabilities that are surprising even to them. However, their surprise, in my experience, is quickly overtaken by delight. They are more likely to enter into various development/identity projects as 'persons' in relationship to themselves and others. They seem to take more pride in themselves and their relationships and never degrade themselves to that condition, described by Goffman (1961), of 'utter shamelessness' (p.121). These were 'patients' who had been entered into and entered themselves into what he referred to as 'psychiatric stories' or 'sad tales'. An externalising discourse seems to position people so that they have access to other culturally available storylines. Here the characters they play are often heroic ones or what Goffman (1961) refers to as 'success stories'. Foucault (1979) commented on the significance of the 'case' and the 'case history' in general:

> *The turning of real lives into writing is no longer a procedure of heroisation. It functions as a procedure of objectification and subjection. The carefully collated life of mental patients or delinquents belongs ... to a certain politics of the function of writing.* (p.192)

If persons fade away or are absorbed into descriptions of their problems that are foundational to an internalising discourse, in an externalising discourse they seem to emerge and come to life as protagonists in their life stories, which can now admit of a life lived forwards rather than one transfixed in various versions of chronicity. People speak of and to their problems, thereby becoming speaking subjects. When people are rendered into problematic descriptions of themselves, they seek authorities vested with 'disciplinary' power/knowledge to speak of them and for them. Problems then can speak of a person's identity - but who speaks the 'truth' of the problem? No wonder so many patients have to 'lie' to tell their 'truth'.

I connect the distinction between externalising and internalising discourses with Goffman's (1974) 'primary frameworks'. The first he calls natural, in which events are seen as the result of unguided, unmotivated, and purely physical processes. The second he calls social, in which human agency, will, motivation, and purpose are embedded. The same sets of events can be interpreted, he contends, in either framework. Both may incorporate concepts of causation, though with an entirely different meaning.

Wolfgang speaks

Wolfgang was a man in his mid-thirties. He confessed to me that he was killing himself slowly, such was his despair. He had been advised to manage his kidney disease through careful attention to diet, no smoking, and drinking in moderation, all of which he was doing to excess. I learned that, at fifteen, Wolfgang had had a mild stroke which resolved itself, leaving him with virtually unnoticeable traces around his mouth and eyes. After the stroke and rehabilitation, he had never discussed his concerns with anyone, even his wife, from whom he had recently separated after seven years of marriage. In fact, he had married her because of her physical attractiveness. He thought that when he was in her company all eyes would be on her. He described himself as 'paranoid' and found himself unable to go out in public, except after dark or under certain circumstances. Making arrangements to meet together was very difficult, as he insisted on entering my premises unseen. At the end of the second session we externalised 'self-depreciation', and within the next two months he stopped smoking and drinking and maintained a sensible diet. He had also become actively involved in training for public speaking, engaged in a number of social activities (including lunch dates with his former enemies), and confided in a friend about his stroke. During the fourth session, Wolfgang commented:

> *I can recognise self-depreciation now. Before it was my way of life. I am catching myself doing self-depreciation - the chatterbox. I now see it from a distance. It's not so close to me. I used to accept whatever I heard most of the time and I even agreed with it. The sentences are now the same but they are from a distance. I've known it for most of my life - this chatterbox. It can be so powerful. I have to be careful. But now I have weapons. My most important weapon is I know that it's not true. My growing self-esteem is also a weapon. I can be aware that it can take me over ... the way I look at myself. It's not vanished ... it's not gone away. Before I took it to be like an illness in my body. Now it's out there and it wants to come back. It wants to return to the position of dominance it once had over me.*

Natalie speaks

I met Natalie, who was almost ten at the time, along with her parents, Sally and Mike, and her older sister, Jane, aged eleven. She had what they described as an intractable soiling problem that had defeated eight interventions - four medical, three psychiatric attempts, including a hospitalisation, and family therapy. They informed me that it had now been declared a lifelong problem for young Natalie. However, Natalie would retire to her room every night, crying both in pain and despair. Her mother could bear this no longer and had tried to kill herself. She survived and starting working night shifts as a nurse to save her sanity. However, Natalie would leave notes on her pillow which she would discover on her return home. 'Mum, what's wrong with me? My tummy feels all squishy and watery. My knee feels like it has been cut in half. I can't work properly and I just feel sick all over. PLEASE HELP ME.' So, despite all the help they had received, they felt obliged to attempt yet another therapy, even though they felt hopeless about it.

The following is the summary of our first meeting (the approach I detailed was akin to that described by White [1989], but employing the metaphor of 'detective work/clues', etc.):

Dear Sally, Mike, Jane and Natalie:

It didn't take me long to understand what a mess Sneaky Poo was making of Natalie's life in particular, but you all in general. Sneaky Poo has kept Natalie at a five-year-old level, made her have to hang around toilets instead of friends, and, in fact, stopped her from visiting friends. It has even stopped her from swimming in pools. Sneaky Poo has started to stink her life up so that no one will have anything to do with her because of the smell. But what was most tragic was that it has caused her to switch off her mother and father 50% of the time. This means that Sneaky Poo has deprived her of 50% of the learning she might have learned from the two people who care about her most. Sally, no wonder that you feel that 'I can't get through to her'. It must be very depressing to lose 50% of your daughter. Jane, Sneaky Poo has been getting through to you, too, by embarrassing you and making you reluctant to have friends round to stay.

I got pretty depressed myself, thinking what a mess Sneaky Poo was making of Natalie's life; what a mess Sneaky Poo was making of her mother's and father's lives and their relationship; what a mess Sneaky Poo was making of Jane and Natalie's sisterhood; what a mess Sneaky Poo was making of this family in general. However, my depression lifted when I realised, at long last, that Natalie was starting to clean up her life. Natalie, you mustn't have allowed Sneaky Poo to grow you down anymore. Look what you went and did.

Last year, Sneaky Poo made your poo sneak out three times a week. This year, you have started out-sneaking your poo more and more and it only snuck out on you once a week. More importantly, Natalie, you have stopped Sneaky Poo from messing up your school, even though there probably still is the smell of it around. When I asked you, Natalie, what your tactics were, you had this to say. 'I work out when I usually go to the toilet and round that time, I usually put my mind on my stomach feelings. I start feeling a soreness in my stomach.' Natalie, you are getting a few clues. The more clues you get, the less sneaky poo will be. For some time, Sneaky Poo must have thought you were clueless. When I asked you how you were able to do this, you told me you were more mature. I wish I had asked you how you were able to mature yourself when Sneaky Poo was trying to keep you a five-year-old. By the way, I thought that Sneaky Poo was pretty mean to keep you young and undergrown. You said that on the inside you were smiling and that you didn't feel sorry for Sneaky Poo, as you no longer wanted to be its playmate. I wish I had asked if there were any other ways you were growing up.

When I asked you, Natalie, whether you wanted to out-sneak Sneaky Poo, that seemed a good idea to you. I guess you must be sick and tired of a messed up life and want to clean it up. So we came up with a lot of ideas to get back at Sneaky Poo and the mess it has made of your life, your mum's life, your dad's life, your sister's life, your mum and dad's relationship with each other.

We met a month later and Natalie announced that she had not done any 'detective work'; she had just stopped soiling once and for all. Three months later, we met for a review. The following is extracted from that interview.

DE: Before, were you scared of Sneaky Poo?

N: *Sort of ... because it was ruining my life. And I didn't have much control, I didn't think I could do it.*

DE: What made you, on that particular day - the 12th day of February - what made you understand or realise you had heaps of control? Is there anything, in particular, that happened on that day... or is there anything anyone said? Did you have a dream or a vision or anything?

N: *I was reading these books. There's a series of Value Books. There's one about Helen Keller ... about determination. And she was blind and she learned. At first, she was determined to be a nasty, horrible person. And then Ann Sullivan started writing words on her hand and it made her understand her thoughts.*

DE: When did you read that book?

N: *I got them about two years ago. I got a whole series.*

DE: So why now - on the 12th day of February - did it have an effect?

N: *When I came to you, I realised what was in the book, what it meant.*

DE: What the book meant? How's that?

N: *Most of the other people just thought I was another patient ...*

DE: What did I think of you?

N: *You were more interested in my problem ... you were like Anne Sullivan. You kept asking me questions.*

DE: Did those other people who thought you were a patient, didn't they ask you questions about yourself?

N: *They just asked how it had been. I went to them every six months.*

DE: Did you think I treated you more like a person than a patient?

N: *Yah...*

DE: How do you see it as different? Say I wanted to teach a person not to talk to a young person as a patient but as a person, how would you do that?

N: *You'd just understand and have faith.*

DE: Did you think I had faith in you?

N: *Yah ...*

DE: How could you tell? I know I did, but I didn't say, 'I've got faith in you'. Or at least I didn't say it out loud. How did you know I believed in you? How could you tell?

N: *The sort of questions you were asking ...*

DE: Do you have any regrets about out-witting Sneaky Poo?

N: *Not that I can think of.*

DE: No way would you want to go back and have a friendship with Sneaky Poo? Do you think there are any tricks you used or any talking to yourself you did that you could tell the other kids? Any pearls of wisdom?

N: *I just understood things more.*

DE: What did you understand?

N: *Before I didn't know Sneaky Poo was bad or anything.*

DE: You didn't! You thought it was a friend? That must be a big difference. So did Sneaky Poo talk you into thinking that it was your friend rather than your enemy?

N: *Yes.*

DE: Well, it's pretty hard to go against your friend. So that is what maybe is at the heart of your success. How do you figure Sneaky Poo was able to trick you into thinking it should be your playmate?

N: *It was sort of telling my mind, because sometimes my mum and dad smacked me for soiling and things. It sort of said in its own special way that they were blaming me. And it was good to have a problem like that.*

DE: Do you feel sort of angry that Sneaky Poo lied to you like that?

N: *Yah.*

DE: Was there something I said or asked you that helped you undo this ... and helped you figure out the trick?

N: *You kept calling him Sneaky Poo instead of the other name and that helped me to understand that he was in the wrong.*

DE: Did you think that you were in the wrong?

N: *Yes.*

DE: Oh, I see. That's sad because if you thought you were to blame that might have weakened your determination. Did you think that when you got free of the idea that it was your fault and it was really Sneaky Poo's fault, you could determine your determination against it?

N: *Yes ... I could have done it all without anybody else. I just had to have faith in myself and believe that I could do things.*

I would like to end my address by paying my respects to Sergej P., who was known almost to the very end of his life as the 'Wolf Man', the psychoanalytic name granted him by Sigmund Freud. His given name became anonymous, as the interpretation of one of his dreams became foundational to psychoanalytic theory and practice. Still, after 60+ years of analysis he refused to accept a psychoanalytic ban to talk only to duly appointed interviewers. Karin Oberholzer (1982) persisted.

> *'It seems that I want you to write something after all', the Wolf-man said once. 'But it must not be published until after my death. You must understand, I cannot do otherwise.'* (p.7)

Sergei P. is remarkable on two accounts: surely, he is the longest follow-up study in the history of psychotherapy (sixty-plus years) and secondly, his interviews with Oberholzer stand as the first time the 'other' speaks back as a person rather than as a case study. And just listen to some of what the 'other' says when he is asked:

Oberholzer: When you read the 'History of an Infantile Neurosis' for the first time, what did you think?

Sergei P.: *I didn't think much about it.*

O: Did you believe at the time that everything Freud had written in the text was correct?

SP: *I didn't think about it. That was because of the transference.*

O: And today?

SP: *There is that dream business. I never thought much of dream interpretation, you know.*

O: Why not?

SP: *In my story, what was explained by the dreams? Nothing, as far as I can see. Freud traces everything back to the primal scene which he derives from the dream. But that scene does not occur in the dream. When he interprets the white wolves as nightshirts or something like that, for example, linen sheets or clothes, that's somehow far-fetched, I think. That scene in the dream where the windows open and so on and the wolves are sitting there, and his interpretation. I don't know, those things are miles apart. It's terribly far-fetched.* (p.35)

By Sergei rehabilitating himself in his dying days, perhaps, he ends what his therapy began: the professional monologue of internalising discourse.

Commentary

by William Hudson O'Hanlon

How about internalising *and* externalising discourses? David implies that internalising discourses are, of necessity, oppressive and always lead to some power-mongering therapy 'expert' foisting his/her TRUTH upon people with whom s/he works. I stand opposed to blaming, invalidation, discouraging, oppressive, and physically harmful interventions, talk, and other activities, whether they emanate from clients or therapists (or from anyone else, for that matter). I do not always externalise, however.

Externalising, the way David and his colleagues practise it, avoids the unhelpful practices of blaming the person (ie., implying or asserting that s/he has bad or pathological intentions or traits) and of confusing the person's identity with some of her or his actions or experiences ('obsessive-compulsive' or 'schizophrenic'), but there are other ways of avoiding these practices. To assert, as David does in his paper, that his and Michael White's work would be 'nowhere' without having developed externalising is a bit of an exaggeration. Both of them are bright, creative, caring and articulate fellows. Without externalising they would be somewhere helpful, I trust, just not where they are today.

I consider externalising interventions (discourses) to be, in part, an invitation from the therapist to clients to develop a different relationship to their concerns or their troubles. The invitation goes something like this:

> *I invite you to consider that you are not your problem(s).* [Or alternately, I invite you to consider that your son, daughter, wife, husband, father, mother, etc., is not the problem.] *You* [or you and they] *have successfully done something other than the problem or not identified yourself with the problem at times in the past. I invite you to notice and tell me about those times when you have opposed or resisted being identified with the problem or letting 'it' control your actions, experience or relationships. From there, I invite you to reconsider your previous conclusions about who you* [they] *are, who you* [they] *can be and what you* [they] *can do.*

Externalising was a means for David, Michael White, and others to find an alternative to (or, in their usual prison/oppression metaphorical frame, to escape from) the traditions of blame and discouragement so rampant in traditional psychiatric and psychotherapeutic practices and discourses, but it is not the only route. To identify the means as the end is a mistake akin to what my dog used to do sometimes when I would point things out to him - he would look at my finger rather than whatever I was pointing to.

In sum, internalising discourses are not equivalent to oppressive, discouraging, pathologising discourses, as David would have us believe. There are internalising discourses which empower, are collaborative, and lead away from an identification with the problem. I would retitle David's paper 'Oppressive Discourses Versus Empowering Discourses'. I think that is what his finger is pointing to.

Note

1. First published 1993 in Gilligan, S. & Price, R. (eds), *Therapeutic Conversations*. New York: W.W.Norton. Republished here with permission.

References

Epston, D. 1989: 'A reflexion.' In Epston, D., *Collected Papers*. Adelaide: Dulwich Centre Publications.

Foucault, M. 1973: *The Birth of the Clinic: An archaeology of medical perception*. London: Tavistock.

Foucault, M. 1979: *Discipline and Punish: The birth of the prison*. Middlesex, England: Peregrine Books.

Foucault, M. 1980: *Power/knowledge: Selected interviews and other writings*. New York: Pantheon Books.

Furman, B. & Ahola, T. 1992: *Solution Talk: Hosting therapeutic conversations*. New York: Norton.

Goffman, E. 1961: *Asylums: Essays in the social situation of mental patients and other inmates*. New York: Doubleday.

Goffman, E. 1974: *Frame Analysis*. Harmondsworth, Middlesex: Penguin.

Halliday, M.A.K. 1978: 'Antilanguages.' In Halliday, M.A.K., *Language as Social Semiotic: The social interpretation of language and meaning*. London: Arnold.

Latour, B. & Woolgar, S. 1979: *Laboratory Life: The social construction of scientific facts*. Beverley Hills, CA: Sage.

Lowe, R. 1991: 'Postmodern themes and therapeutic practices: Notes towards the definition of "Family therapy: Part 2".' *Dulwich Centre Newsletter,* 3:41-52.

Madigan, S. 1992: 'The application of Michel Foucault's philosophy in the problem externalizing discourse of Michael White.' *Journal of Family Therapy,* 14(3):265-279.

Mischler, E.G. 1984: *The Discourse of Medicine: Dialectics of medical interviews.* Norwood, NJ : Ablex.

Oberholzer, K. 1982: *The Wolf-man: Sixty years later (Conversations with Freud's patient).* London: Routledge & Kegan Paul.

Tomm K. 1989: 'Workshop notes.' University of Calgary, Alberta.

Tomm K. 1990: 'A critique of the DSM.' *Dulwich Centre Newsletter*, 3:5-8.

Waitzkin, H. 1989: 'A critical theory of medial discourse: Ideology, social control, and the processing of social context in medical encounters.' *Journal of Health and Social Behaviour*, 30:220-239.

White, M. 1989: 'Pseudo-encopresis: From avalanche to victory, from vicious to virtuous cycles.' In White, M., *Selected Papers*. Adelaide: Dulwich Centre Publications. (First published 1984 in *Family Systems Medicine,* 2(2):150-160.)

White, M. 1990a: 'Externalizing the problem.' In White, M. & Epston, D., *Narrative Means to Therapeutic Ends*. New York: W.W.Norton.

White, M. 1990b: Personal conversation, Adelaide.

5

Internalised Other Questioning with Couples:

The New Zealand version[1]

Internalised Other Questioning with Couples - and anyone else for that matter - remains a vital form of my everyday practice. Like most of the chapters in this book, such a practice emerged, in the first instance, to solve a 'problem' around meeting with couples divided by extreme conflict. When repeated trials led to more positive outcomes than errors, I endeavoured to 'explain' this to myself and others, having discussed the beneficial experience of such questioning with many couples. It was at this point that Karl Tomm took over and did 'internalised other questioning' a great service. I only wish Karl would publish his 'theorised' versions of internalised other questioning which he has presented at various workshops. Internalised other questioning has also assisted me in calling forth 'audiences' and providing some of the membership for 'communities of concern'.

I devised a practice around 1985 which I then referred to as cross-referential questioning. This practice of questioning owes a great deal to Michael White's (1989) innovations relating to both the purposes and methods of questioning in therapy. In particular, I am indebted to his 'hypotheses regarding the couple's prescription for the therapist and the outcome if the therapist inadvertently conforms to the couple's prescription' (White 1984). From discussions with Karl Tomm from between 1989-91, I have taken his designations of 'internalised other questioning' to describe this practice, although he has certainly elaborated what I refer to as cross-referential questioning to many other therapeutic contexts.

This format of questioning was invented to disrupt those warring couples who construed couple counselling as a venue to contest their differences. These couples seemed to lack any conception of themselves as bound together, for better or for worse, in a relationship. It seems that without a 'relationship', they can only act out of individual interest and contest their differences within one or more domains, each of which allocates certain practices and specified roles for the participants. In addition, each domain assigns the therapist/counsellor both a role and specified functions. These domains of practice are (1) the juridical, (2) the ecclesiastical/moral, and (3) the politics of reality. These prototypes are derived from cultural institutions and have rather obvious analogues in the courtroom, ecclesiastical courts of the Inquisition, and the psychiatric/neurological interview.

Those practices and stances modelled on the courtroom are usually pale reflections of tactics of attack/defend, counter-attack/counter-defence, and discredit/discredit. In this domain, the therapist is required to adjudicate the competing claims submitted to him or her and find parties innocent or guilty or to establish that neither has a case to hear or establish that no ruling can be made. Should either party to a relationship have recourse to this model, he or she will work hard preparing a 'case' and gathering supporting evidence to undermine the anticipated counter-claims. A partnership soon dissolves into prosecuting and defence attorneys.

Those practices modelled on the ecclesiastical court of Inquisition also position the partners in opposition to each other. The only difference between the court of law and the ecclesiastical court is that the 'case' is argued not on the issue of lawfulness, but rather on the morality of innocence versus sinfulness. Here the therapist is positioned to adjudicate the competing claims in order to find between innocence and sinfulness. The sinful party in the dispute is assigned penance and the innocent party is morally elevated.

Those couples who have been organising their differences according to the psychiatric/neurological interview assume not only a 'world' that is objectively present but also one to which one can have direct and persistent access. Furthermore, it is taken for granted that others experience the 'world' in an identical fashion. So what happens when persons responding to the same 'world' experience and/or describe it in disparate or contradictory ways? The solution is to question the adequacy of the methods through which the 'world' is being experienced and/or reported on by the other. One then calls into question the mental capabilities of the other either by critiquing his or her method of observation or by attributing pathology. The partner in the couple who assumes the role of the psychiatrist/neurologist claims a privileged and uncontestable view of the world. Accordingly, any counter-claims or counter-experiences must be due to specious or inadequate perception or an underlying pathology. In such a situation, you have either a reluctant or recalcitrant 'patient' who won't comply with prescriptions or two pseudo-scientific opinions at odds with each other. Here the therapist is positioned as the consulting expert in the field in order to add greater weight to their junior colleague's prescriptions for his/her 'patient' partner.

I have found that if I don't do something to the contrary very quickly, many of my meetings with couples rapidly assume the shape of the courtroom, ecclesiastical court, or psychiatric/neurological interview, with me being recruited very unwillingly into one of the abovementioned roles. Such couples often become both perplexed and vexed if I decline to participate accordingly. With an interest both in avoiding these recruitments and in disrupting the couple's familiar relationship tactics, I have devised a format of questioning that allows me to decline these roles and permits each partner to experience something of the other's experience.

I have found it necessary to add both a *prologue* and *apology* prior to embarking on what was then referred to as 'cross-referential' questioning. The prologue goes something like this:

> *If you aren't a 'one in a million' couple with a problem, I believe I can safely predict that you both have been asking each other a lot of questions and that those questions have not relieved the situation in any appreciable way or brought you closer to a mutually satisfying solution. My guess is that, if anything,*

you have found the situation deteriorating right before your eyes. I can safely predict, too, that you have been asking yourselves a lot of questions and those questions have not brought relief or a mutually satisfactory answer. I base these conclusions on the fact that you are here. Am I right in thinking that all your questions have not so far provided an agreeable answer?

In that case, this leads me to a conviction that it would be folly for me to ask you the questions that you have asked either of the other or of yourselves. So I propose that I ask you questions that it is very unlikely you have asked each other or yourself. If you had, I would guess that you wouldn't be here today. And if by any chance I slip up and ask you a question already asked, please draw my attention to this so I won't waste your time by asking a question that has already been tried and found fruitless. I give you full credit for having tried your questions and , given the state your relationship is in, it would be unwise for us to employ the selfsame questions that have not stopped your relationship from being brought to its knees. Do I have your agreement to depart from the divorcing direction these questions are leading you to and to experiment with some questions that conceivably could lead to a reunion in your relationship?

The apology is very necessary to prepare the respondents for the difficulty in first construing the questions and then answering them. For that reason, they are forewarned as to how they might experience these questions.

As these questions are very likely questions that you have never thought of before or never asked yourselves before, I need to warn you of their difficulties and to seek your permission to pursue a course that may cause you discomfort. You might not have quick or ready answers. If you had either a quick or ready answer, I would distrust your seriousness, as these questions will require you to think what you never or rarely have thought before. You can expect to take a while to get the gist of these questions, but you will if you persist. And I think I can guarantee you that it will take a minute or two or even more to think up the answers. In fact, the longer the better. So I apologise to you now for their difficulty. You may be stretched in ways you have never been stretched before. Do I have your permission to go ahead with this questioning process?

After having received the couple's permission to proceed, I ask: 'Who would like to go first?' I request that the person who goes second listen to his or her partner's answers. I make it clear that they both will be subjected to the same line of questioning, after which both will be provided with equal opportunity to inform the other to what degree (or how close) their partner came to understanding their experiences.

Assume that I am interviewing a hypothetical couple, Jack and Jill, whose relationship has been deteriorating over the last 10 years. Jill has offered to go first, so I direct my questions to Jill:

> *Jill, what do you think Jack would say if I asked him the following question: 'Jack, how do you account for the deterioration in your relationship over the past 10 years?'*

In very adversarial and other-blaming couples, the form of this question seems to have the effect of taking the vindictiveness out of the answer. Essentially, Jill is invited by the questions to render Jack's complaints about her, even though the question is directed at their 'relationship'. In this instance, it is very likely that Jack will be restrained from reacting by jumping to his defence. Instead he may seem spellbound and curious as to how Jill will represent his complaints (or, in fact, blame herself). Even if Jill's answer is self-condemning (e.g., 'Jill isn't giving me enough love.'), I then ask a further question of Jill: 'Jack, what effect has this 'lovelessness' had on your relationship?' If Jill should find this question hard to answer, I would assist her with some questions to introduce some ways of assessing the impact on their relationship of this externalised version of the complaint, condemnation, or accusation: 'Do you think a loveless direction is good or bad (healthy or unhealthy, adds to or takes away from, increases or decreases) the share value of your relationship?'

With some practice (and it is surprising how rapidly people can respond to these questions if the interviewer is comfortable with them), the interviewer can delete the preamble and merely direct his or her gaze at Jill and enquire: 'Jack, you have come up with three theories for the shape your relationship is in. There must be more than that! Are there any little reasons you think are too small to mention out of embarrassment or any big reasons you think are so big you are reluctant to mention them out of fear?'

As the nature of the questions leads respondents (especially men) to reflect in unusual ways, the answers come slowly, cautiously, and are carefully couched. The listener is extremely attentive. Since their complaints are being heard, the partners seem willing and curious to hear each other out without interruption. There is little need to defend against one's own allegations. Even if the mood at the beginning of the session is extremely combative, this is soon replaced by a contemplative ambience, with each person digging deep into his or her experience of the other.

On the single occasion that neither party could answer the questions (a couple who had been married 27 years), the interview was called to a halt and questions were asked of the unknown wife. 'Judy, were you aware that, even though you have been married for 27 years, Dick doesn't know anything about you? Is this a surprise to you?' She replied that it wasn't at all. 'Judy, what effect does this knowledge that Dick doesn't know anything about you have on your relationship to your "relationship"?' Judy then went on to say that she had known this all along but she needed to hear it and that she was ending the relationship right there and then. I then asked Dick: 'If it is now Judy's intention to end this relationship, when did you think it would end?' Dick thoughtfully said that he thought it would have lasted for another 20 years.

The answers are then cross-referenced. 'Jack, Jill thought that you would explain the downfall of your relationship by way of an "I'm all right and you're all wrong" patterning. How close is her representation of your experience to your actual experience of how your relationship is declining?' An ambience of thoughtfulness, curiosity, and a degree of generosity is usually sustained throughout the interview.

I respond by 'marrying up' the different versions of the story of their relationship at the end of our first meeting. This brings the story of their relationship up-to-date, customarily concluding in some sort of dilemma for the future of their relationship.

An example of a letter to a middle-aged couple summarising the information derived from this format of questioning follows:

Dear Terry and Gloria:

From what you told me yesterday, your relationship has come to something of a cross-roads. Gloria, from your point of view, you were 'blackmailed' into the marriage in the first place; Terry, you must have wondered what hit you when Gloria, soon after you married, became dismayed and was called 'depressed'. My guess is that at that time you both would have found it very difficult to understand what was happening to you, especially as it was quite contrary to the images you had of what your married lives would be like. Gloria, without wishing to discount your suffering, those events in your life could now be considered 'teachings'. Your tuition was a long and gruelling ordeal, but look what you have made of yourself. When I asked you to tell me about yesterday's person, you described that person as lacking in assertion, 'not knowing what I wanted and how to get it', 'totally revolving around the needs of others', so much so that you became an other-sensitive person at the same time as being insensitive to yourself. This led you into what they called 'depression' and you thought the way out was a chemical life-style. So weaning yourself off that was just one more struggle that had to be overcome. One of your most important learnings was that you had 'grit' and that was there for me to see.

At the same time, Terry, you became Gloria's nurse and looked after and cared for her the more she became dismayed. There was a price you paid for this and that is the neglect of your own pursuits. You cared for, supported, and promoted Gloria into self-discovery, so much so, in fact, that yesterday's person has almost been eclipsed by today's person. I wouldn't be surprised, Terry, if you were wondering if you didn't do too good a job. You have been so successful at promoting Gloria that you may have fallen behind her. As you put it, 'She's hard to keep up to ... I'm being left behind ... I'm still back doing the same old job ... I feel stuck.'

Terry, I wonder if you aren't feeling dismayed in the sense that things haven't worked out at all in the way you might have thought they would. In addition to all this, it would have been inevitable that you both would have been required by the departure of your children to turn and face each other again without them in the way. All couples need to, if they are going to last the distance, go through a period of review and re-evaluation. I got the impression that that was exactly where your relationship is, with each of you wondering whether you want to do the next half of the marathon together or on your own or with someone else? I can see, too, that you, Terry, have also started to feel the pinch and have started taking some initiatives on your own, firstly joining a men's group and coming here to couple counselling. Both of these ventures are quite new for you.

You tell me that your relationship is imperilled and that if left to its own devices, according to you, Gloria, will go on to the rocks in six months or so and, according to you, Terry, could survive for a few more years. You could let your relationship drift and find out whose estimate is closer to the mark. On the other had, you could, if you desired it, take your relationship out of the water and survey it. It may require a refit if you wish to sail in deep waters. If you do so, will you restore it to the fashion of the '60s or bring it up-to-date by the appropriate modifications.

I await your decisions on behalf of your relationship and I cannot conceal my curiosity as to what you will make of it or by continuing on a divorcing course, break up on the rocks. However, despite my appreciation of the dangers to your relationship, I found it very easy to like and respect both of you as persons.

Yours sincerely, David.

Such an account entails a 'double externalisation', as it externalises both the problem(s) the partners are experiencing *and* the relationship itself. This paves the way for a trialogue between, say Gloria, Terry, and their relationship, replacing Gloria versus Terry. The latter only allows for the establishment of guilt, sinfulness, or pathology. The process of therapy from here on can now become a meta-commentary on the direction of their relationship as it heads for the metaphorical rocks or, by their determining a new direction for it, gets out of danger or departs from the problem(s). This is achieved by the deployment of some newfound or recovered relationship tactics or the reorganisation of their relationship according to some other 'recipe', 'design', or 'plan'.

Such paradigmatic questions can inquire about anything but always invite the respondent to answer from his or her experience of the other's experience. This has the effect of undermining those cultural practices that affirm an objective reality. It seems to me that when a problem is understood in terms of an objective reality, most couples immediately seek recourse in practices that are detrimental to their relationship. The problem-solving practices derived from the analogues of the courtroom, ecclesiastical court, and psychiatric/neurological examination tend to divide partners rather than reunite them. It is hoped that the practices described in these pages can serve to offer a remedy to this less than useful way to conduct a relationship and the prescriptions for the therapist that follow from it.

Note

1. First published 1993 in Gilligan, S. & Price, R. (eds), *Therapeutic Conversations*. New York: W.W.Norton. Republished here with permission.

References

White, M. 1984: 'Marital therapy: Practical approaches to long-standing problems.' *Australian & New Zealand Journal of Family Therapy*, 5:27-43.

White, M. 1989: 'The process of questioning: A therapy of literary merit?' In White, M., *Selected Papers*. Adelaide. Dulwich Centre Publications.

6

Imaginary Friends:
Who are they? Who needs them?[1]

co-authored by
Emily Betterton & David Epston

'Imaginary Friends: Who are they? Who needs them?' and 'The problem of originality' are a series of considerations about the suppressions of 'specialness' and what I have come to refer to as the 'weirdly abled'. These papers are some of the first steps in what I came to write about at some length in several more recent publications (see 'Weird and special abilities' in Freeman, Epston & Lobovits 1997).

Emily, aged ten, came to catch me up with exciting developments about the actions she had taken to resist her thumb-sucking habit at night. We had met several times when she was eight. At that time, her habit was ruling her both by day and by night, and no-one could recall ever having seen her without her thumb in her mouth. She acknowledged this was very distressing for her, and she worried that she would have a misshapen jaw and teeth. And there certainly was visible evidence of that at the time. Soon after our second meeting, she was able to intervene in the 'life' of her thumb, and went on to have a life of her own by day. Everyone was so pleased about this that thumb-sucking by night was set to one side. So it was now two and half years later and Emily was clearly excited about something or other. And it didn't take me long to find out. Emily reported that she had now gone five nights in a row not sucking her thumb.

Naturally enough, I was extremely curious about this, and asked her to let me in on her secrets. She informed me that it all had to do with her imaginary friends: Jim Harritt, Jim's mother and father (I will have more to say about him), and John and Lisa, aged fifteen and sixteen. I was not surprised Emily had been granted older imaginary friends, as she seemed somewhat beyond her years to me. It turns out that Jim Harritt's father is in charge of assigning imaginary friends to weirdly abled kids. Now what or who are the weirdly abled ? Well, they are kids who are so abled that less able kids and adults think that their abilities are weirdnesses. This can mean, as Emily told me, that you can 'get teased and pushed around', and greatly misunderstood by kids and adults less abled than you are. The weirdly abled have special abilities that mean that 'they can see things that aren't there' or 'see things in a different way from others'. 'At times they can think that the real world doesn't matter too much.'

I decided to take this opportunity to learn more about imaginary friends for the weirdly abled and what part they might play in their lives. I asked Emily lots of questions and she was very generous and kind in telling me who they are and who needs them. In return for her favour, I said I would tell any weirdly abled kids I meet in the future about Mr Harritt and how they might apply to him. He is the New Zealand agent for imaginary friends.

'How do you apply to Mr Harritt for an imaginary friend?' I asked. Emily told me that, in your imagination or in secret writing, you let him know, firstly, your age according to your birthday, but, more importantly, the age of the person you feel at home with. You also tell him what kind of person you are. For example, Emily said in her application that she was 'a kind person, a helping and strong person'. You then tell Mr Harritt what your interests are and what special abilities you have that you have found it best to keep from most people your own age and certainly from adults. You also tell him your favourite things, such as music, books, food, clothes, etc., and any spare time activities you particularly like doing. It is also a very good idea to get a photograph of yourself so that Mr Harritt can get a good idea of your outside appearance. Emily thought you may be surprised to learn that Mr Harritt's head office is under the sea somewhere between Tasmania and the Cook Strait. I asked

Emily: 'If there were only so many imaginary friends to go around, and if there were too many applications to be filled right away, who would go first?' She answered me immediately: 'The most lonely weirdly abled kids'.

I started wondering, to myself first and then out loud so Emily could hear me: 'How have your imaginary friends helped you in your life so far?' I was very surprised how large a part they had played and continued to play in Emily's life. First of all, Emily said: 'They help me when I'm feeling lonely or when I'm in trouble at home or at school'. I could have guessed that, I suppose, if I had really tried. But there was more. And most of what Emily then told me I could never have guessed, no matter how hard I tried. Emily's imaginary friends 'help me with homework that I can't work out. They give you helpful hints but never do it for you! They also give you personal strength to overcome habits which you don't want or like, for example, thumb-sucking or crying all the time.' I hadn't been aware that Emily had been crying all the time as she was always so bright and happy when we talked together. Maybe that was because she knew I knew she was weirdly abled. I asked: 'What would make you cry?' 'A little hit or word would set me off crying, but now I am turning crying into laughter!' 'Have your imaginary friends helped you with teasing?' I asked. 'As for teasing, you can almost automatically see the funny side and show it. The teasers can no longer get you worked up!'

'Quite apart from what has been bothering you, have your imaginary friends done anything to make your life a better life than it was before you knew them?' Sure enough, they had. 'They have helped me be more adventurous. I am no longer scared of heights. I used to be scared of thunder but now I look forward to a storm, hoping there will be some thunder. I am not scared of spiders anymore.' I marvelled, and said: 'Hold on now, spider fears are hard ones to overcome! How did they encourage your bravery there?' Emily told me of an imaginary friend approach that I had never heard of before. I think it was imaginary friend John who came up with this anti-fear approach. This is what Emily told me about how it works: 'John told me that this anti-fear approach had worked for him within a day. He told me and asked me if I wanted to try it. Even thought it was weird, I liked the sound of it. What he did was have a spider in one cupped hand and some lollies in another cupped hand, and refused to tell me which was which. Then he told me to hold my hand out. Well, I did, and it only took five times before I wasn't scared of spiders any more. I did have to throw a few spiders away, but they really didn't hurt when I think about it.' I asked if there were any more weirdly abled ideas like this. Sure enough, there were. It seems that once Emily was afraid of crabs in rockpools. John showed her how to first have a long stick and then keep getting shorter sticks until she could pick a crab up with her hands without getting nipped by its claws! This meant that Emily could enjoy herself a lot more walking from Palm Beach when the tide was out over the rocks to Boatshed Bay (in New Zealand).

I suppose I could have expected this from Emily, but she saved the best for last. 'What's really good about imaginary friends is that they are good practice until true friends come along, as they will.' And 'imaginary friends treat you the way you would like to be treated'.

Here is my last question of Emily: 'If you could thank your imaginary friends for one thing, and one thing alone, what would you thank them for?' Emily replied: 'I've come to understand the ways of myself, my real abilities (even though they are sometimes thought weird by my classmates and adults), and my shortcomings like spelling and in Physical Education when balls come at me. But I am even starting to overcome that!'

Well, I guess you can see that Emily recommends imaginary friends to lonely people who have to wait a while to find true friends and, unfortunately, can be thought to be weird, despite the fact that really they are weirdly abled. They are so able that often people their own age, and some adults, think they are weird.

After talking to Emily, I wondered if imaginary friends always know that you are really wonderful and weirdly abled. If you have imaginary 'friends' who try to convince you that you are bad, fire them and get in touch with Mr Harritt for imaginary friends like Emily's imaginary friends!

Note

1. First published in the 1993 No.2 *Dulwich Centre Newsletter*. Republished here with permission.

References

Freeman, J., Epston, D. & Lobovits, D. 1997: *Playful Approaches to Serious Problems: Narrative Therapy with Children and their Families.* New York: W.W.Norton.

7

The Problem of Originality[1]

Roslyn[2] was referred by her school counsellor - who knew her very well, for her refusal to attend school, her 'depression', and the fact that she had, in a manner of speaking, retired from life. Roslyn passed almost all her day in bed watching television. The school counsellor informed me that Roslyn was one of a kind, and suggested that I would certainly savour our meeting.

Even with such a forewarning, I was quite unprepared for our meeting - and I doubt if there was anything I could have done to adequately ready myself. For, when I went to the waiting room and invited Roslyn and her mother to join me (her parents had separated when she was very young), they both stood and followed me down the corridor but, just before my door, Roslyn turned on her mother and forbade her entry in no uncertain terms. Her mother, who seemed familiar with such treatment, deferred to her and turned back towards the waiting room.

Quite unperturbed by these events, Roslyn resolutely entered my room, extracting ear plugs from her ears at the same time. She must have observed my puzzlement, for she was quick to explain that she could not bear the sound of her mother's voice and suspected that I might find that somewhat unusual. I was quite immobilised by her extreme self-possession. She obviously observed this, because she suggested I take my seat.

Even before I was settled into my chair, she informed me: 'David, I've got so much misery. Let me tell you all about it!' I was scrambling to take the initiative in the session when she once again confounded me. She did so by holding out her right hand, crossing her thumb underneath her outstretched four fingers - her gesture was so portentous. She looked over at me, waiting for me to discern the significance of this sign. All I could guess was that she was indicating four somethings or other, but she withheld any further explanation. I joked, 'What! You are four years old?' She was now quick to make her reply: 'Four suicide attempts, and they weren't cries for help. I was serious!' It was in this context that she told me of her all-abiding interest in Marilyn Monroe. To check on this, I enquired: 'What was written on the doorway of the home in which she died?' Without any hesitation she replied: 'Cursuum Perficio'.[3] This confirmed to me the extent of her Marilyn Monroe knowledge.

Something told me that it would be prudent to steer away from Roslyn's invitation to keep her misery company, despite her obvious enthusiasm for me to do so. Instead, we got talking about the problem of originality. I asked her if she knew much about Sinead O'Connor. Her information about O'Connor was cursory, so I provided her with an audio-tape that I happened to have at hand, so she could familiarise herself with the lyrical sentiments and politics of her music. I thought it might be helpful for her to add Sinead O'Connor as another potential alter ego. Our conversation was intense and ranged widely between the problem of originality and some of the lifestyles she felt were currently available to her, and the misery that, according to her, had driven her backwards in her life, to what she described as a 'six year old level'.

The following correspondence represents summaries of our meetings, along with questions for Roslyn to entertain, and her thoughtful replies.

Dear Roslyn,

You are a unique 16 year old! So, is it any wonder that you are finding it hard to fit in with the lifestyles that are currently available to you. And the price you have paid so far for your decision not to go along with the familiar 'courses' in life have been 'self-doubt', some 'self-hatred', and even 'despair'. You have even come to feel that others are 'hating' you. When we listed the lifestyles you had available to you, you came up with the following:

1) a Barbie doll lifestyle, following 'all the trends';
2) pregnant and married at 19, living a life full of regrets;
3) a Marilyn Monroe lifestyle, living your life through men's eyes and, when they look the other way, you wonder if you are anything or were anything; and,
4) a yuppie lifestyle complete with BMW, personal computer, designer partner, and designed children.

Roslyn, it would have been much easier for you if you had decided to conform to any or all of the above lifestyles. If you had, then it would have been very easy for you to follow in others' footsteps. By choosing to be original, the hard thing about that choice is that you have to both make and find your own way. And to do that, you have to believe in yourself until you are believable to others. And to prove your originality takes more than just saying you are original. I am afraid you have to prove it, some way or other. I cannot say exactly how you will do this, and if I could, you would be far less original than I think you are.

So I can understand to some extent how you find yourself wanting others to appreciate you at the same time as wishing they didn't. No wonder life is confusing for you: for example, if you became the most popular young woman at your school, what would that prove except how conforming you had become! Still, it must be hard to envision a future, a unique future. It is easy, especially as you are a sensitive and capable young person, to prefer giving it all away and giving up on yourself. I can understand that growing down to the level of a 6 year old could seem like a viable solution to you. When you were 6, all you had to do was follow your parents' instructions and not think much for yourself. However, this has the effect of you trying to go forwards, looking backwards. No wonder you are surprised and befuddled that you are tripping over everything and convincing yourself that you are a failure. And when you are most successful at doubting yourself, you end up 'in a whirling tunnel' of despair and misery. It is like being on a misery-go-round.

Still, it was interesting to note that you can get off when you want to and have the odd good day. It seems that you are fated to live your life and 'sometimes I can like myself'. It was impressed upon me by your account of being yourself all by yourself. This occurs when you are making yourself up in the mirror. And at such times you can appreciate the person you see and like that self-same person. And you can find good reasons to appreciate that person, the Roslyn you are designing; you thought she was 'confident, attractive' and original, but not understood by others. Right now, not many know your originality; all they can see is that you refuse to go along with their trends, trends they would give their lives for. No wonder, they must think you are a 'snob', but it seemed to us that it was more a matter of choosing your own course in life, rather than following in others' footsteps.

Roslyn, I think it is very hard, indeed, to face up to your originality even though it will pay off in the long run. Still, right now it must be hard to face up to. There will be 'some pain and hurt' to face, but do you think it is worth it to live a life of your own design?

You admitted that 'I am out of my shell a bit' and having a good look round. You thought you 'need to show the world what Roslyn can do'. Sure, but there is no rush! You have a lot of life ahead of you, and you seem to think that travelling is the adventure you are seeking. I can understand how you came to such a conclusion.

This was just a thought: it sounds as if your mum has lived a life that hasn't fulfilled her. My guess is that, as she sees you falling prey to misery, she feels like a failure as a mother and as a woman, which leads her to get more busy in your life. Do you think you could start seeing if you could convince her she's been as good a mother as was possible under her circumstances?

I thought I would leave you with a few questions to stretch both your mind and imagination a bit:

Marilyn, I feel like I am an original, and I believe you were an original but got taken over by Hollywood and they made you up, and maybe you even started believing in their made-up you. But, in the end, you found you were just tinsel ... lonely tinsel. And even everyone you met believed you were the person they had made you up to be.

- *Marilyn, if you could speak to me from beyond your grave, how would you think I should lead my life?*
- *How can I survive at school without conforming?*
- *How can I make myself up into the person I want to be?*
- *How can I realise myself rather than others' designs on me?*

- *If you were 16 and were me, what would you face up to and what would you ignore?*
- *Is there any hope for me if I grew backwards and stayed a forever 6 year old?*
- *If you were looking into my 17, 18, 19 and 20 year old futures, what can you see in my futures that I cannot see?*
- *If you were to ask Sinead O'Connor these questions, what do you think she would say?*

Sinead, sometimes I think I am a 16 year old woman like you were a 16 year old woman, although I was not abused and beaten by my mother. I feel like I am an original like you are. I know from what I have read about you that you have refused to conform and, even now that you are famous, you continue to be who and what you are.

- *Sinead, how did you deal with all the pressures on young women to conform and go along with the way things were?*
- *How did you face up to other people thinking you were a 'bitch' for pursuing your own course in life?*
- *Were there times you felt lonely in your originality?*
- *Were there times you felt despair and depression?*
- *Did you ever feel like giving up on yourself and your life?*
- *Did you keep going because you had some vision of a good future for yourself ... when your originality would sooner or later be recognised?*
- *Do you shave your head bald to prove your originality and refusal to go along with women's fashions, etc?*
- *Did you ever lose your nerve?*

I look forward to reviewing these questions with you.

Yours sincerely, David.

21st March

Dear David,

*I thank you for your wonderful letter and the tape which I have dubbed. I went to see my school counsellor today. I had a great talk with her. I was feeling absolutely miserable. I was away Tuesday and Wednesday - I couldn't face being in school. I just can't seem to grow up! In many ways, I want to grow up **so** much yet I keep looking back into the past - being little.*

Half the time I am in 'fairy land' and when I plonk myself down into 'reality' I run away from things because I get scared and I can't handle it. I don't want to live my life like this!! It's awful and so frustrating!! I do not know what I want for my future and I look at it and I think: 'Can I get there?' Living in the present, I shrivel up at times and look back to when I was younger. For security, I suppose. I'm so sick of life (or maybe, ME), bored. I just sit there and my life is passing by. My life is like a film. I'm standing there watching it flicker away!

I want people to like me and to love me, yet I'm in this cycle of continually pushing and pulling people both away and towards me. I feel so lonely at school, but when people try to get close to me, I shove them back! I'm punishing myself! Not only with people and friends, but grades at school. I've missed assignments and tests - I'm ruining 'Roslyn'. Sometimes I feel nuts. I wish it would all vanish, but I know it won't be easy - but is it going to get any harder? I'm sick of waiting!! I know I do wallow in my misery but it's so damn hard. I feel like I am being sold at an auction - yet the people buying are my inner selves.

Another thing I'm finding hard is looking at my family through rose-tinted glasses. I still get upset at not having the 'happy family' like in TV ads. I just get so sad it's like an aching hollow feeling that I really want to disappear.

I have carefully considered your letter and I will discuss that with you then. I hope this letter hasn't depressed you! It wasn't meant to.
Yours sincerely, Roslyn.
PS: What I most of all want, David, is to love myself for the person I am!

28th March

Dear Roslyn

Your school counsellor agreed with the letter that you are an 'original' and one original thing about you is your preference, at the moment, for keeping misery company. However, we observed that poetry-writing was one way you had stumbled over to separate yourself from misery for a moment or two. It sees that, by expressing it, you put it outside yourself. It seems too that in the past you have used your mother as 'an emotional punching-bag'.

You also started to inform yourself about Sinead who you agreed was 'one of a kind' too. You thought that you two 'wouldn't get along' but that a friendship would emerge out of respect for one another's originality. You guessed she has a 'heart of gold' along with a 'sharp tongue'.

I thought it was interesting when you put your life in Marilyn Monroe's hands. Her advice to you was as follows:[4]

Stay put and put up with what's going on. Finish school. I didn't finish school. You need an education if you are to realise your ambitions. At the moment you are not showing your originality ... you don't need to show it right now. You are not ready to unveil yourself. You are only ¼-baked. You can survive at school by keeping to yourself and being a loner. This is the price you have to pay. Otherwise you will have to surrender your originality. Making yourself up into your own person will take time. It just has to take its course. So beware of impatience. Do not allow your life to be impatience-driven. Remember, it is quicker for someone else to make you up than for you to do it. It used to only take my make-up artists five hours to make me up into their image of me. Roslyn, you have to find yourself. And don't expect to find all of you in one place or at one time. And don't be impatient. Go to life rather than expecting life to come to you. You cannot find your life in TV-land. Don't get suckered into a TV version of your future, your present, or your past. So don't be too patient either waiting for life; otherwise, I fear you will be frustrated by cobwebs. Face up to your requirement for an original life and all that will mean for you. And an original life cannot be found by escaping into TV-land, fantasy-land or Walt Disney. Don't fall for the fantasies propagated by TV on young minds. Be true to yourself even if it hurts. Growing backwards will do you no good whatsoever. That's where you are heading now, and look where it's leading you - into misery. I can see the future you desire, and it isn't a miserable one. Your future will be a creative one.

Roslyn, I hope I was able to convince you I appreciate your misery. I think I can dimly understand that any original who was living their life through TV, growing backwards, waiting for life to come to them rather than going to life, would be desperately unhappy, dissatisfied, and sickened by the thought of life passing you by. The worst torture I could think of would be to force, say da Vinci, to watch TV from morning till night. I doubt if he could bear it. I believe he would have gone mad. Roslyn, misery seems to know how to trick you into it, and unwittingly you go along with its deceitfulness and walk into its trap. Do you think misery will make you happy? Do you think being the most miserable person in the world will be your originality? So, Roslyn, please forgive me if I refuse to go along with you as you go along with misery.

If I did, I think I would be very unhelpful to you. Very unhelpful indeed! So that is why I will not join you in the misery of your misery. To jump in the pit with you would mean that both of us would drown in misery.

I wonder if you would mind jotting down your thoughts as to what Sinead might advise you as to how you might go about your life so as to express your originality in some other way than in being the most miserable person in the world. And I am not suggesting that there is not some misery to endure.

Also, what about asking Marilyn Monroe the following questions:

- *Marilyn, if I become the 'original' miserable person, will that make me happy?*
- *Marilyn, do you think I should have a 'Disneyland' life?*
- *Marilyn, if I talked David into joining me in the trap misery has laid for me, where do you think our therapy will go and end up?*
- *Marilyn, if I started reading some autobiographies of people (their stories of how they got made up or made up their own lives), what could I learn?*
- *Would their stories give me more ideas to make up my own life or should I stick with 'Neighbours', 'Young and Restless', or 'Days of Our Lives'?*

Roslyn, although misery loves company, and that is well known, this therapy will keep you company as you start exploring your life, by making this present into some future that will permit you to express your originality. If you, in any way, feel I don't have a deep enough understanding of your misery, either send me some poems or we could set aside 5 minutes at the beginning of each session for you to express your misery, a misery I won't keep company. This therapy will not be a miserable therapy - rather it will be a liberating therapy, liberating you from the hold misery has and could have over your present and future.

Yours anti-miserably, David.

A week later, Roslyn's mother rang in great distress fearing for her wellbeing. I agreed to write her and brought her next appointment forward. The details of that conversation are in the following letters.

4th April

Dear Roslyn,

Your mum rang me and I told her I would write you and let you know she did.

In addition, I couldn't help but think of you over Easter. I couldn't help but think you were walking into a trap. I think you dimly perceive this but I don't think you know how dangerous it is. And I wondered if you had been tricked into thinking misery would lead to happiness, and that an escape from life would ensure a good life for you. I know misery has its temptations, but it is a trap that has taken many people's lives before today, and spoiled their futures.

Roslyn, do you or don't you know the trap that you are innocently entering? Please let me know the next time we meet.

I hope you haven't found this letter intrusive. It's just that I had second thoughts after our last meeting.

Yours sincerely, David.

8th April

Dear David,

Thank you for both *your letters. Replying to your second letter, I think you are quite right. I don't think I really know the trap that I am entering, that an escape from life would make a good life for me. I really do think it might be true.*

Going to Australia was one escape that I believed would make me happy. I rang my aunt this weekend and had a really good talk with her. At that time, I felt crushed because my way of escape - going and living with her - was finished, gone. I had nothing to hang on to.

I have *realised now that I was running away from my present life. I know it* did *take a lot of time to realise. But I have and I know that I have to live in 'reality' no matter how hard it gets. I try to find escapes because I know I cannot kill myself or die.*

Your letter was a real eye-opener. I rang up Lifeline after my aunt said I couldn't live with her. It was good talking on the phone. I was thinking about a lot of things and deciding too.

Remind me, please, to tell you about what happened in the weekend with these new friends I have befriended. It seems I always wish what I haven't got, and when I have it I'm not satisfied or I don't want it anymore.

I agree with you in your first letter that I have *used my mother as an 'emotional punching bag'.*

Answering your questions: 'No, I do not think going to misery will make me happy'. 'No, I don't think being the most miserable person in the world will be my originality.' 'And I certainly wouldn't expect you to go along with my misery. I understand that' and 'Yes, you would be very unhelpful to me.' 'I would also think you would be nuts to do so.'

I am really trying not to fall into the 'misery cycle'. I am seeing the school counsellor about a job working after school. And I haven't been shutting my friends out and I've rejoined the hockey team.

I know I do have to stay here and battle it out. I have jotted down some thoughts on Marilyn Monroe's advice which I will discuss with you next time.

Yours sincerely, Roslyn.

PS: I thought your 'Yours anti-miserably' was hilarious!! Very funny ... thanks.

11th April

Dear Roslyn,

I read your letter of the 8th of April with great interest. And you know, I didn't have to fight back against the slightest temptation on my part to join you in misery. For it seems you saw the trap you were innocently walking into without really knowing the kind of future being trapped might predict for you. At the same time, I gather from your letter that you had to contend with your Australian aunt refusing to go along with your escape plans, and contend with it you did. You say you are reconciling yourself to live in 'reality' no matter how hard it gets.

Roslyn, do you think 'reality' will get harder or easier if you go to it rather than waiting miserably in your bedroom living through soap operas?

Say you were to experience happiness, fun or delight in some small measure, do you think you would be prepared for this after having been in training for so long in misery?

You informed me my letter was a 'real eye-opener'. What did it permit you to see that your misery had blinded you to? What did it illuminate that previously was in the shadows? Was there anything in particular that led you to be more devoted to your own cause?

You really piqued my curiosity with your note: 'Remind me please to mention about what happened in the weekend with these new friends I have befriended'. Matter of fact, I find myself beside myself with curiosity, so I thought I would just guess *instead. Let me know when we meet next time how close or far away I was from the mark.*

Here's my guess *about what happened.*

After you rang your aunty and things sunk in, you said to yourself: 'It's about time I started having some influence over my reality'. And, with that, you decided to show Roslyn off to other people. Well, it was no surprise to you really that when you did so, people were attracted to your originality. It started to dawn on you that originality could pay off, even in the short term. Still, you wondered to yourself: 'Will these new friends stifle my originality? Are they original enough for me?' From hereon, I find it impossible to guess what happened.

What do you think made your mother vulnerable to being used by you as an 'emotional punching bag'? Can you imagine what effects it has had on your mother to be used by her one and only daughter in this fashion? Do you think you adopted your father's practices in relating to your mother? Do you think now, knowing what you know, there is any hope for a women's reunion? Is there any hope for you to both understand and appreciate your mother's experience of her life?

Roslyn, I am pleased that you have let me off the hook in terms of joining you in misery. Misery has never been a particularly good friend of mine.

I will be very interested indeed to review all this with you and what's happened in the meantime. It seems that there is a lot more to talk about ever since you started wrenching yourself free from misery. I can't help myself thinking what Sinead O'Connor would be thinking about what you have gone and done.

Yours anti-miserably, David.

28th April

Dear Roslyn,

What a surprise it was for me to be informed that you sat your exams and, according to you, 'they went alright'. And you did this, despite almost throwing the towel in even before you got there. You played your first hockey game of the year and won 2-0. And you yourself said this about that: 'I really enjoyed it ... it was better than misery'. In fact, you went on. You informed me that my guess was 'bad'. Things turned out quite differently. Here is your version: 'I started meeting new people and hanging out with them. I didn't have that good a time. I went over to Nicky's place on Saturday but felt uncomfortable. I thought to myself - I want to get out of this place. Mum came over and picked me up. I rang my aunty again to escape. Then I rang Lifeline and just thought about a lot of things. I said to myself: Roslyn, you've got to do something about your life or you will go downhill and be miserable for the rest of your life and kill yourself. Instead, I decided to pick myself up and went back to school. I got back into life even though I am in neutral. I had some pep-talks from my mum. By the way, I have decided to live with my mother's voice.'

You also concluded that your Mum 'doesn't have to put up with my crap'. And, as you said: 'It finally occurred to me that we both are a product of my father. He abused my mother emotionally by not talking to her and the whole lot. When Dad left two years ago her voice started to annoy me.' This was interesting, given that you had acted as her advocate before then. What exactly did you mean when you said: 'I think too much of her and I demand too much of her'?

By the same token, you seemed to be in support of her new relationship with Bob because 'he isn't like my dad ... he treats women badly. Bob is in touch with himself and knows how to treat a woman.'

You informed me that your mother 'has always been there for me. She'll do anything she can to help me and make me happy. My father is totally the opposite. If he wanted to help me, he'd do the opposite thing.' You were considering some reparations as 'I do feel guilty ... terrible. I have no thoughts quite yet. I am taking it slowly.'

In relation to misery, you have not had a break away yet but you are seeing through its lies and you have cut the misery cycle from 10 days to 2.

And you also assured me that 'misery has no charm for me'. You said that this had something to do with 'an act of will' on your part. You said too that 'I knew I could do it', but, nevertheless, 'I am a little bit proud'. Also, you got a job at the Town Hall and saw Nigel Kennedy and thought he was another original.

The 'eye-opener'! What was it? 'Writing to a person who wasn't going to join me in misery and didn't really care a stuff how miserable I was'. That was positive. And when we were talking, 'I saw a "picture" of me in the darkness and, at the same time, me getting into life. That was when I finally faced it. I realise now other therapists and my mother in particular got sucked into misery. I finally made a stand.'

You have started reading autobiographies of women like Katherine Mansfield, another original, and thought you might start your own journal entitled: 'A New Life for An Old'. Still, you have decided to carry on in neutral instead of 'expecting too much'. You told me that you and your mother 'don't fight any more ... we are trying to understand each other more'.
Regards, David.
PS: You are not a copy. I still think you are an original.

We were to meet several times that year and, for Roslyn, the events referred to in the above were what she referred to as 'embarrassing learning experiences'. Two years later she wrote out of the blue to tell me that she felt she had at last found herself and a way to express her abilities. She was doing tertiary training in child care and thought she might have found a niche for herself. She did add that she didn't think she was such an original. I leave it to you, reader, to form your own opinion here!

Notes

1. First published in the 1994 No.4 *Dulwich Centre Newsletter*. Republished here with permission.
2. 'Roslyn' was chosen as a pseudonym in honour of the last role Marilyn Monroe played in the Arthur Miller screenplay for 'Misfits'.
3. This translates from the Latin to 'My Journey Ends Here'.
4. This was derived from linking Roslyn's answers and deleting the framing questions. For that reason, this text should be considered as co-constructed.

8

Just hold on for a minute so I can read you these letters[1]

This paper was submitted for publication in 1994 and I read it aloud to honour my friend and colleague, Marie Roberts, at her retirement party following her 30 plus years' career in social work. The events described took place in an adult psychiatric ward in a public hospital in 1980 and the consultation was in line with similar strategically-influenced approaches that I was developing at that time to address problems of tantrumming and violence (see Epston & White 1992, pp.37-74).

Ron, aged seventeen, was referred to an adult psychiatric ward in a general hospital following five consecutive admissions to two different accident and emergency departments. He presented with uncontrollable body spasms that appeared to be epileptic fits. He would thrash his arms and legs around with side to side head movements, accompanied by deafening screams. Ron indicated that the 'fit' usually started with a severe headache. When the headache abated, he would get pains in his legs (thigh and calf). He then would lose control of himself and begin jumping around, and thrashing his legs and arms to relieve the sensations. He was finally admitted to a general medical ward for a neurological examination and EEGs. While there, his 'fits' and bizarre behaviour were alarming both to the staff and the patients. Tests showed no abnormality. In spite of this, there was still some question about potential physical origins of his behaviour.

The family general practitioner had seen Ron and his family repeatedly for ten weeks prior to these hospital admissions. During a six week period, Ron had at least two or three episodes per day, each lasting for several hours. Ron could not explain the episode except to say that he found himself suddenly filled with energy and needed to 'jump around'. He would, however, strike furniture, damaging himself at the same time. Afterwards, he seemed quiet and reported feeling fine. His parents observed that he was not his usual self afterwards, but there were no discernible problems.

On admission to the psychiatric ward, Ron's body was severely bruised and battered. His forearms had to be sutured to close the wounds. His feet were swollen and split open, making walking very painful for him. During the episodes, he would kick his feet up and down with such force that it was feared he would permanently damage them, if, in fact, he had not already done so. His parents were understandably overwhelmed by these 'fits' and had discovered they could help him control them by sitting on his legs and forcibly restraining him or by taking him for a ride on an antique motorcycle, the pride of the family, which his father, brother, and Ron had painstakingly restored over several years.

Early Treatment

I (Marie Roberts) was on leave when Ron was first admitted to the ward. Although he had only been in the ward for one week, the atmosphere could almost be 'seen' as well as felt. He had virtually brought the ward to a halt. On first meeting him, I found him to be a cheeky, cheerful young man with a huge, infectious grin. He was unable or unwilling to tell much of his story. My hunch, which was unpopular, was the latter. Any attempt to interview him was met with a perplexed expression, an uncomprehending grin and much shrugging of his shoulders and 'I dunnos'. Within the ward, the 'fits' were becoming increasingly intense and occupying about five hours of Ron's and the staff's day. By the end of my first day back, it became clear to me that most of the 'fits' occurred in two strategic sites: in the doorway of the nursing station or in the corridor leading to the elevators. Because the psychiatric ward was on the tenth floor of a large public hospital, staff and patients had to step over or around Ron to pass by. Most of the episodes occurred around the time his parents were expected to visit. All previous attempts to manage Ron's behaviour had failed, as all contracts between him and the ward staff had been breached. Nothing whatsoever seemed to make any difference, and Ron was making himself exceedingly unwelcome in the ward by regularly exsanguinating walls and ceilings, overturning nursing lockers, and escalating the duration and intensity of his episodes. There was pressure to discharge him as he could not be controlled in a general hospital. We were to meet with his parents to discuss his discharge and the possibility of committing him to a psychiatric hospital if his 'fits' persisted. Also, because of his uncertain condition, Ron had not previously been medicated and sedation was now under consideration.

We had conducted a number of sessions with his parents and as Ron customarily was having a 'fit' at such times, he had been unable to attend. These meetings with Ron's parents proved fruitful. Ron's parents were naturally convinced that Ron was suffering from some epileptic condition. Once we gained their trust, we found out that the couple had a number of difficulties, as did the family. Ron's mother had persistently endeavoured to provide her children with love and affection in order to make up for what she experienced as her loveless childhood. She was saddened by the thought of her children growing up and leaving home. Ron's father valued competence and independence and urged his sons to assume these qualities. The eldest son was already following in his father's footsteps, apprenticing as a tool and dye maker like his father. Ron was the middle of three siblings but was far less able intellectually than the other children. Consequently, he had left school at 16 without graduating.

There had been a great deal of conflict between the parents about how to raise the children. However, since the onset of Ron's episodes, the parents had managed to work together as a team and Ron expressed some pleasure at this change in their relationship. Ron had also previously been upset by arguments between his father and his siblings, but these too had settled down, much to his satisfaction.

Epston Consultation

Prior to the discharge meeting with Ron's parents, I gained support from my colleague, Dan O'Connor, to consult with David Epston. The ward and the family were willing to give Ron the opportunity to undertake what was described as an '*anger control program*'. Ron, himself, expressed enthusiasm with the idea when it was broached with him. Dan agreed to attend a family meeting, using David Epston's approach with letters and with Ron present, before any further treatment decision was made regarding medication, discharge or subsequent committal.

When his parents made their appearance at the appointed time, Ron, as usual, had an episode as violent and distressing as any other. My colleague and I defied family therapy protocol and dragged Ron into the therapy room, each of us taking him by one leg. In the midst of the commotion, I pulled out copies of the letters and said, 'Just hold on a minute so I can read these letters'. Ron stopped immediately, although he remained on the floor on his back. He readied himself to listen to the promised 'anger control program'. I was not surprised that he interrupted his 'fit' since he had previously done so in order to issue commands or shout obscenities.

The following letters were read and a set of copies given to Ron, his mother and his father. They were on official stationery and signed by myself and Dr. O'Connor.

LETTER 1

RON HAS AN ANGER PROBLEM AND HAS AGREED TO EMBARK UPON A PROGRAM OF SELF-CONTROL.

Mother's Instructions

1. In order to help Ron, you are to remain calm and collected. If this is difficult, put on ear muffs or cotton wool pads in your ears, turn on the radio, stereo or television, or go into another room. Say to Ron when you leave, 'Come and see me when you have finished exercising'.
2. If Ron is exercising to the point that he may damage himself, and his father is at home, you are to go away and leave it to his father to carry out his instructions.

3. If Ron is strenuously exercising and you are on your own, you are to hold up warning cards to him. Time on your watch: Warning 1 - 1 minute; Warning 2 - 2 minutes; and Warning 3 - 3 minutes.
4. Tell Ron that these warnings are to be taken seriously. If he does not stop by the third warning, you are to carry out instructions to get in touch with the Merivale Police. A letter to the police is included and will be sent to that station.

LETTER 2

RON HAS AN ANGER PROBLEM AND HAS AGREED TO EMBARK UPON A PROGRAM OF SELF-CONTROL.

Father's Instructions

1. If you are with Ron and he is exercising, keep saying: 'It's okay. You are safe!'
2. Tell him he is not to damage himself because you value him and tell him that he is not to damage any property.
3. Whisper to him that you have to treat him like a child because that is how he is behaving right now.
4. When Ron demands his slippers, or asks that you turn the lights out (or makes other demands), remove yourself to the other side of the room and ask him to get them, for himself, if he needs them.
5. Assure him that you are aware he has very strong feelings although you don't know what they are about. Tell him that you wonder if he knows what they are about.
6. If he damages himself, his mother is to go away and you are to restrain him. Sit on him or do whatever seems appropriate to you. Tell him this is necessary because 'children cannot help themselves when they are out of control'.
7. Sometime during the evening, help him to select either parent to provide him with a quarter hour of worry time. Have such a worry time separate from the family, and devote it completely to worrying about Ron.
8. If Ron damages himself, he is to be instructed that he will have to

pay medical expenses for himself.

9. If he damages property (like getting blood on the carpets or blankets, or breaking furniture), he is to be responsible for the cost of cleaning or replacement.

WHEN RON'S EXERCISING IS OVER, SOME NORMAL PLEASURE IS ALLOWED

I was aware that most of the accident and emergency admissions were provoked by concerned neighbours phoning the police who then had to intervene. Raising the alarm was very justifiable under the circumstances because of screaming and the destruction of property. Ron's parents were advised that Ron, along with them, was to take a copy of LETTER 3 to all the neighbours in earshot and provide them with any explanation they required.

LETTER 3

TO WHOM IT MAY CONCERN

As you know, Ron is having problems expressing his feelings in a way appropriate to a person of his age. We have provided the Jones family with an anger control program. In the past, Ron has made quite a lot of noise, which you no doubt have heard. For a week or two, you can still expect some noise from Ron, but we would like to enlist your support to bear with this. If it gets too loud, could you please turn on your radio, stereo or television in order that the noise not interfere with your daily living.

Many thanks for your assistance in Ron's treatment program.

LETTER 4 was prepared for the Merivale police.

The Senior Sergeant
Merivale Police Station

Dear Sir:

Ron has a problem expressing his feelings in a way appropriate for a young man of his age and we would like to enlist your help.

He thrashes around on the floor, flailing his arms and legs, making loud noises and demanding attention. This is clearly heard by the neighbours and is upsetting to them. When in this state, he inflicts severe bruises and wounds on himself and can damage furniture. His anger is such that his family finds him impossible to deal with, and it is very distressing for them to see him harm himself.

Ron has agreed to enter into a program to help himself gain better control. Enclosed for your information are the details of this program.

Mrs Jones may need to get in touch with you when her husband is at work if Ron's behaviour gets out of control. Should this happen, we would like you to issue Ron with a severe warning. If there is a further call, Ron may need to be charged as any other citizen would, for wilful damage to property.

Either Dr. O'Connor or myself would be willing to discuss the control program with you should you need further information.

Your co-operation would be greatly appreciated. Thank you.

Ron consented to do as instructed but was expressionless and did not comment. His parents were amazed at his co-operation and could only ask if Ron was all right. They also asked what they could do when faced with another 'fit'. They were concerned about whether we were experts in the field and we tried to reassure them on that count. We referred them to the 'letters' and advised them to take instruction from them. Ron, still stunned, wriggled on his back the twenty yards down the corridor and then finally got to his feet to enter the elevator. That is the last I saw of Ron although we met with his parents on two further occasions two weeks and one month later. They admitted that Ron's 'fits' had vanished and that he had returned to his old self.

Follow-up

During the period of the 'fits', Ron lost his job, and six months later was referred to a rehabilitation agency for work skills training. He attended there for a further nine months. When a colleague enquired about his hospital stay, Ron was reticent about that period and only commented that they were not very nice to him there. His parents seemed mystified about the period of hospitalisation and indicated that Ron had not really received any treatment at all, although they were glad they had had the opportunity to discuss their relationship as a couple. They felt that Ron had benefited mostly from visiting a hypnotherapist one month after his discharge and one month after the cessation of his 'fits'.

Intelligence testing at the rehabilitation agency indicated that Ron's Verbal IQ was in the 'borderline' range but that his Performance IQ was 'average'. This difference suggested to his assessors that he had sustained brain damage and further testing substantiated this. Odd movements, for example, falling down and walking with an odd gait were noted. But when ignored, they disappeared, especially as Ron gained confidence and developed work skills. Eventually, Ron found a job that suited his abilities. He appeared to have developed considerably as a person and had a girl friend and a range of activities. His parents were eventually reassured by his successes. It also came to light that Ron, just prior to the onset of his 'fits' had taken out the family's restored antique motorcycle without permission and scratched it.

On a number of occasions, I (David Epston) have presented the above case to psychiatric nurses in the final year of their training. I purposefully describe Ron's behaviour and then ask the nurses the following question: 'What treatment would Ron have received if he had been admitted onto the last acute admitting ward you worked on?' The proposed 'treatment' shows a high concordance from respondent to respondent. A typical reply would be, 'Admitted to locked ward; doctor takes out committal papers and seclusion papers; given sedation probably intravenously; no clothing and blankets; possible strait-jacket; room with mattress on the floor; assessment by nurse and doctor about mental status, pre-morbid personality, precipitating factors'. I marvel sometimes that a scratch on a motorcycle almost led to this.

Note

1. First published 1994 in *Progress: Family Systems Research and Therapy*, Summer, pp.1-18. Co-authored by Marie Roberts & David Epston. Encino, Ca: Phillips Graduate Institute. Republished here with permission.

References

Epston, D. & White, M. 1992: *Experience, Contradiction, Narrative and Imagination: Selected papers of David Epston and Michael White, 1989-1991*. Adelaide: Dulwich Centre Publications.

White, M. & Epston, D. 1990: *Narrative Means to Therapeutic Ends*. New York: Norton. (Also published 1989 as *Literate Means to Therapeutic Ends*, Adelaide: Dulwich Centre Publications.)

9

Expanding the Conversation[1]

This paper about the practice of 'letter writing', long associated with narrative therapy, was written more or less over the phone in a series of question-answer dialogues with Laura Markowitz of the Family Therapy Networker. *She sure taught me a thing or two about interviewing. She elicited knowledges that I didn't know I had. Thanks, Laura. I always considered that it was unfair that you were not cited as co-author.*

Conversation is, by its very nature, ephemeral. After a particularly meaningful session, a client walks out aglow with some provocative new thought, but a few blocks away, the exact words that had struck home as so profound may already be hard to recall. Two of us reconstructing a conversation we had even minutes before may not agree on what was actually said because we each hear selectively. Family members accustomed to their usual fights may listen only for what they expect to hear and simply not register anything unfamiliar.

But the words in a letter don't fade and disappear the way conversation does; they endure through time and space, bearing witness to the work of therapy and immortalising it. A client can hold a letter in hand, reading and re-reading it days, months and years after the session. I have had clients tell me that they regularly re-read letters I sent them years ago to remind themselves what they endured, how far they had advanced their lives, and the extent to which they considered themselves to have changed. I often felt that my job as a therapist is to be a kind of amanuensis, a scribe who faithfully notes down the proceedings for posterity and makes readily available a client's history, capturing on paper the particular thoughts and understandings with which they now make sense of their lives. From the very beginning of my career, this is what I have considered to be one of my principal roles.

In 1977, I secured my first job as a family therapist at a child psychiatric outpatient unit in New Zealand. In that medical environment, case notes, or 'the file letter', as we called it, were sombre documents written to an imagined quorum of colleagues or to oneself, but certainly never meant to be shared with patients. I felt a certain distaste for the customary practice of reducing clients' rich and complex stories to a sterile, medical diagnosis. Although I had never been taught to do this in my training, nor had I ever heard of other therapists doing so, I found myself writing a letter to my very first client family after our initial session. It seemed to me the most natural thing in the world, like an extension of the conversation we had been having. I also put a copy of it in their case file in lieu of the standard clinical assessment. I was sure the typist, a very formal woman near retirement, would disapprove of my unorthodox case notes, but she became my biggest supporter, confiding to me that my letters were so much more enjoyable to type than the usual diagnostic pronouncements.

The family was surprised and gratified to receive my letter, and we read it at the beginning of the next session to give us a jumping-off point. We were all so pleased with having a letter in hand to refer to that I wrote to them again at the conclusion of the second session. Since that first letter, I have written thousands of letters; the great majority of my clients have received one after each session. We begin every therapy hour with a reading of the last letter, which not only reminds us of what had been discussed, but also inevitably connects us to where we were the week before. Even now, if I pick up a file and pull out a letter written to a client years ago, just reading it will carry me back to the session's emotional tone and collapse the time and space that separated us. Clients have described feelings of sorrow, delight, elation (even a compelling urge to dance!) upon reading these accounts of our conversations together.

Because therapeutic letters evolved as a way for me to include - and privilege - the clients' viewpoint in the official record, I tried to stay very true to the exact words they used, quoting them as often as possible. In the beginning, I needed more than an hour to write each letter, because I mentally had to reconstruct the session to compose what I hoped was an accurate accounting of the meeting. Then, I began to ask my clients if they minded if I took notes, explaining that my purpose in doing so was to summarise our discussions and send it to them in a letter. No one minded - in fact, many began to request I do so when they came back the next week. Over time, I began not only to take session notes as if I were a journalist, writing verbatim everyone's comments, but also to read these notes back to the clients during the course of the hour. With a woman who was having a hard time getting out of bed and going to work, I might ask, 'Did I get you right here, Diana? Did you say you are "through with protesting against depression and would like to give in to the impulse to sleep all day"?' Diana would answer, 'Well, not exactly. It's more that I am tired of protesting the depression, but I intend to keep it up.' And then I would write that down and read it back to her, and she would amend it again, or agree that this accurately described how she felt and what she intended.

One serendipitous advantage to scribbling these notes is that it slows the therapy down. It allows me time to think as I write and to reiterate important points by reading them back to the clients. Doing this is helpful for externalising the concerns clients bring to these conversations - in other words, assisting clients to see that their problems are separate from who they are as people. They are not the problem themselves, but are beset by a problem that is external to their personhood. This creates a possibility that they can intervene and make changes, rewrite their stories so that the problem has less influence over them.

As I read my notes back to them during the session, restating their answers to my questions, I am reinforcing this notion that the problem is a separate entity acting on them and their relationships in one way or another. And, on another level, I am also allowing us to externalise the therapy itself, so that even as we are in the session, the conversation taking place between us can be called into question, scrutinised and reflected upon.

However, these letters are more than simply a summary of what takes place in a session. A hypothetical 'neutral' observer sitting in the room and writing down everything that was said would certainly produce a very different document than I would. For example, I am extremely conscious of the metaphors people use to tell their stories and describe their problems, as well as vigilant for 'unique outcomes', or moments when the problem is subverted, critiqued or protested. I might ask ten questions in a session that, to my thinking, didn't develop any useful narrative line and therefore wouldn't be in the letter. In my letters, I am always tuning in to what opens up new possibilities, any glimpse of an alternative to the clients' problem-saturated story.

A few years ago, I saw two brothers, ages ten and thirteen, who had quite violent fights with each other, including hitting, biting, kicking and near strangulation. Their father lived in another country, and their mother was at her wits' end trying to keep the peace between them. Every moment in the day seemed to spur these battles, from deciding who would sit in the front seat of the car on the way to school to who would have a turn selecting the television show that night. If the mother was perceived as taking sides with one boy, the other boy would exact violent vengeance on his brother later in the day. The lingering traces of black eyes bore testimony to the seriousness of the matter.

The first thing I did was help externalise the problem. I had immediately noticed the malevolent looks between the boys, so I inquired, 'Has your brotherhood become hateful and hurtful over the years?' They agreed that it had. 'Are hatefulness and hurtfulness the lowlights of your brotherhood?' Again, they both agreed. 'What came first - hatefulness or hurtfulness, or did they arrive hand in hand?' This string of questions enabled both boys to concur that hatefulness and hurtfulness were the problem in their brotherhood. People's everyday language is littered with metaphors, so finding a metaphor or name for the problem is generally quite easy if you know what to listen for and are willing to submit for consideration some likely candidates. I am like a butterfly catcher, waiting for the metaphor to rise up so I can net it and then display it to the clients, who, if not gratified by the first attempt to have a concrete way to describe the concerns that are plaguing them, usually satisfy themselves with some revisions.

I asked the boys, 'What's wrong with hatred? What purpose might you have in opposing hatred? What are your reasons for going against it? It can be intoxicating - why not get drunk on it? What's wrong with it, anyway?' These questions may seem odd, but they allowed the boys to formulate in their own words their hope for a different kind of brotherhood, and when I read back what they said, they each began to hear, aloud, their own commitment to overcoming hatred. I listened for the moments when their commitment to undoing hatred seemed clearest. And around this time in our conversation, out popped a unique outcome, an instance that could not have been predicted given their story of mutual hatred. Both boys remembered that recently there had been 'less hitting, shouting and abuse. I can play with his computer games. We play together more and more and are starting to respect each other. We share things more. We could be in the same room and not fight or shout.'

I questioned each of them to determine if and why they preferred respectful brothering. I asked them if they were considering taking these newfound practices forward into the new history of their brotherhood and whether they had any interest in either elaborating or refining those practices. 'Hatred is getting in the way of harmony', was one boy's answer, allowing me to pursue why harmony is superior to hatred and then how the boys thought they could combat hatred and make room for harmony.

Of course, both children were quite miserable with the constant fighting, so they had a commitment to changing the situation; the problem seemed to be that neither felt he could stop fighting without losing face. Externalising the problem and naming it 'hatred' gave the boys something to point to so they could say, 'I don't really want to fight with you but hatred is getting in the way. What should we do about it?' It allowed their mother to intervene without taking sides; when she saw a disagreement escalating into a fight, she would call their attention to the way 'hatred' was worming its way back into the brotherhood and invite them to collaborate in opposing 'hatefulness'. Writing the externalisation in a letter and creating a strategy for combating hatred allowed the boys to create an alliance where before there only seemed to have been room for antagonism. Receiving the letter and reading it together at home served to reinforce everyone's commitment to substituting respectfulness for hateful and hurtful brothering.

When I sit down at my typewriter after clients leave, I usually only have to edit my notes a bit and the letter more or less writes itself. The therapy conversation generally has its own coherence or internal logic, which I trace in the letter. These days, it only takes me about thirty minutes to finish the two-page letter I typically send. My advice to therapists starting out using letters is not to think of the letter as an intervention apart from the therapy session; see the two as completely and organically intertwined, the one following from the other like the drawing in and letting out of breath. I ask my clients questions and write down their answers and then read them aloud, which sparks off further inquiry, becoming the stuff of the letter. It is all part of the same therapeutic dialogue; all I am doing differently is using the medium of written language to continue and enrich the conversation.

Some clinicians may be intimidated by the idea of putting their thoughts in writing, putting themselves on the line, and it does take a bit of courage. I certainly have made mistakes and have been corrected by my clients, but I find that the letter allows me to salvage a bad session because I can rethink it and acknowledge my mistakes. In the early days, when I felt the therapy hadn't gone anywhere, I noticed I had to search all over my notes to track what happened in the session, and I would ponder this in the letter. 'Did you feel as confused and lost as I did? Was there some way that you would have wanted me to direct the therapy differently?' Whenever I find myself stuck in writing a letter, I often end up including my concern about this in the letter, 'I am wondering if you got anything out of this therapy. Where did I go wrong? The only glimmer was ... but did it have enough substance for you to merit a therapy session?'

Letters allow my thinking about my clients and about the therapy to be as transparent as possible. For example, some sessions can be confusing when it's unclear who is committed to change and who isn't. In a letter, I can put my confusion out for all of us to see, including my confusion - or clarity - about my own commitment to the therapy agenda the clients have come in with. In this way, I am not in the position of being seen as the main advocate for change. I have found this particularly important with couples who are uncertain about the direction in which they want their relationship to go.

A few years ago, a couple came to see me because they were having severe difficulties, In fact, the wife, Jane, described it as 'the marriage from hell'. I had rarely seen a couple so embittered, so deeply divided and so bankrupt of affection and kindness. The husband, Larry, was a well-known courtroom lawyer and, according to Jane, had been interpreting and cross-examining her about everything she said or did for the seven years of their marriage. She had long ago lost any tolerance of this habit and insulted and berated him viciously. He would 'go silent', sometimes for months. During the session, as an experiment for five minutes, Larry tried not to cross-examine his wife, but he didn't even last twenty seconds before he was challenging the accuracy of something Jane said.

Jane came in ready to have what I termed a 'fake marriage', where they would live together but act as if they were divorced - neither felt they could financially afford to divorce - but she changed her mind during the session and said she was willing to work on the relationship, although she gave it a 'one percent chance of working'. I felt there was so much hatred between them that I wasn't sure if the marriage could be worked out - which I told them quite plainly in the letter. We all agreed that should they have even the smallest respite from their current unsatisfying way of relating, it might allow for the possibility of something new to emerge and take its place. I began the letter by repeating what I heard as their tentative commitment to their relationship:

Dear Larry and Jane,

Well, as you put it, Larry, Jane 'went to the wall' and then turned back toward the relationship. Jane, as you put it, 'I don't want us to separate. We have a history that is worth saving. I don't want us to have an arrangement. I could see how that would work if it comes to that. I want to feel good about living together.' Larry, you concur with the above: 'My wish is that we do have sufficient goodwill.' My question to both of you is: 'Do you have enough goodwill to carry you through the revision stage?' In fact, Larry, you suggested that 'we already put some work in. We have made some important discoveries.'

I wanted to be candid about my own reservations about their ability to work out a more mutually satisfactory agreement, and that I was not the one driving them to stay together. In other words, I would not have more hope for their marriage than they had. I continued by outlining some of the things we had identified as being essential if they marriage were to be salvaged:

Larry and Jane, are you willing to go the next step and act on those discoveries? Larry and Jane, does your relationship have the requisite creativity not only to draft a new plan for your relationship, but to put that plan in place? Larry and Jane, has your relationship got the fortitude to remain in the shadow of the old relationship until it overshadows it? Larry and Jane, are you prepared to go beyond interpretation and act upon your relationship until you both feel at home with it? Larry and Jane, instead of forgetting, is your relationship willing not to forget but to organise itself around a perpetual remembering?

I felt the main challenge to this couple was going to be the long-standing bitterness and fury they felt toward each other. Jane, in particular, had mentioned a few insults so grievous that she required that they never be forgotten. By this point in the letter, I had begun externalising the identified patient as 'the relationship'. I introduced the idea that the relationship was what needed to change, giving them both some distance from their own feelings to reflect on whether the relationship was strong enough. By using their names each time, I made it clear that this was their particular challenge, not some generic formula I used for all my clients. Using their names captured their attention and let them know that this was of vital importance to them personally.

You told me your relationship already has some 'wisdom'. It not only knows what controls it but also has given it a name: line dancing, that is, two people close but so far away. Is that even worse than being so far away from each other?

Their metaphor for their relationship, 'line dancing', had emerged after I asked them to describe their pattern of relating. Jane said it was like a kind of dance. I asked what kind of dance and Larry answered, 'A line dance, because we are both dancing to our own steps and never touching'. He got up from his seat and demonstrated what he meant. In fact, this couple lived very separate lives. For example, they each had their own friends, but had no friends in common. Metaphors are like a shorthand, in this case for their profound unhappiness, a reference that both partners understood and related to instantly. As I used it in the letter, I was able to describe in just a few words the emotional state of their relationship.

Often, as I am writing up my notes, new questions occur to me, and I always add them. In these letters, I become my own reflecting team. 'Could this be?' I wonder as I stare at my typewriter. 'Does this mean ...?' 'I wish I had asked ...'

After externalising the problem, I carefully described each one's understanding of how the problem pattern - line dancing - occurs. By writing it down as if it really were steps to a dance, we could all see how the problem emerged, developed, escalated and was resolved. From this breakdown of the events, I then looked for where to intervene and stop the pattern from recurring. Jane would sense Larry's moodiness and ask, 'What's wrong?' Larry would immediately become defensive at being 'grilled on the stand' and refuse to answer, withdrawing angrily. Jane would then 'manufacture' a problem to explain her husband's mood, but after a short time she would get frustrated at being cut off and would demand that he talk to her. Insisting nothing was wrong, he would feel hounded by her 'nagging' him to talk and withdraw even further until Jane would become enraged with him, feeling such strong hatred that, at times, she would have to control a strong urge to physically lash out at him. They would only emerge from this stalemate when Jane 'pushed the right button', according to Larry, restoring them to speaking terms. After I offered a version of these reciprocal events, I wrote: 'Jane, Larry, wouldn't it be nice to push the right button at the beginning rather than making it the ending?' This offered them a glimpse of something they might do differently, a goal toward which to work if they wanted.

But at this point in the session, Jane made it clear that she wanted her bitterness from past injuries to be respected and remembered. I reminded them both of this in the next part of the letter, following the narrative flow of the original conversation. I have found that writing a letter that follows the same chronology as the session is the easiest way to maintain the inner logic of the client's own stories. If I try to move things around too much, I often lose the thread and confuse matters.

> *Jane, you wanted it on record that: 'Jane wants Larry to suffer and enjoys saying 'I told you so'; Jane wants Larry to suffer for eternity; Jane doesn't want to forgive and forget; part of Jane wants to settle and let go.'*

It seemed evident to me that Jane may not have the requisite goodwill to get through the trial-and-error learning that would be required to end the line dancing, so I didn't want to seem too encouraging, nor did I want to be discouraging. But I did want them to understand that they were not favoured by the odds.

> *I propose the following attempt at (1) disrupting line dancing so that (2) you can experiment with some other, more connecting, ways of relating. Undoubtedly, line dancing will happen, and to think it won't is just Pollyannaish thinking. From what you tell me, line dancing pretty much dominates your relationship especially when the going gets tough.*

Then I outlined the strategic intervention we developed together during the session, a complicated plan to help them interrupt their problem cycle. I used words like 'trial and error' and 'experiment' to remind them that they might not succeed all at once. Among the things they were to do was take turns writing up an 'escape from line dancing diary', of their progress while at home

- my way of reinforcing the need for them to keep track of even the most minute unique outcomes. It was also a way of asking for a certain commitment, which I was not sure either one had. I wanted it to become clear to them pretty quickly whether they did or didn't have this commitment. I ended the letter on a note that honestly reflected my doubts.

> *I urge you to be very vigilant of each other's commitment because this session could have been motivated not by a desire for the new but out of fear of the old. I look forward to reviewing this with you. I need not tell you that I am not overly optimistic, although notwithstanding this, I wish you the best of luck. But on the other hand, what has luck got to do with it?*
> *Yours experimentally, David.*

During subsequent sessions, as they pushed themselves to learn the moves to a different kind of dance that brought them closer together and in step with each other, we worked on eliciting an alternative story. I asked them, 'Did you have a romantic courtship, a halcyon time when things worked well? Was the line dancing so apparent back then? What brought those days to an end? Why do you think the act of marriage provoked line dancing and how did it leave love behind?' I helped them articulate some of the things they continued to do well together, despite the line dancing. For example, they had a surprisingly equitable arrangement when it came to doing housework. I asked them to talk to their friends and see if they could find any other couples who approximated such equity in domestic labour.

This couple very gradually was able to revise their relationship, and, over time, hope for a different future for their relationship increased. Their relationship acquired a kind of practical wisdom, grace and good humour. However, perpetual remembering of how the old way of relating had hurt each one was acknowledged as the only just way to redress the injuries each had suffered, and they decided to accept this in the new way of relating.

In *Narrative Means to Therapeutic Ends* (1990), written with Michael White, we describe several different types of letters. Each contains the same elements - a report of the useful moments of the session plus additional reflection and questions from the therapist - but they can be used in different situations. For example, there are what we call 'Letters of Invitation'. Often, if there is a member of the family who is reluctant to come to therapy, a letter from the therapist can be an irresistible incentive. In my experience, most people are surprised and intrigued to receive a letter from a therapist. It gives them a sense that someone actually cares about them and acknowledges their place in the family.

To a family reluctant to come in and talk about their thirteen-year-old son whose doctors had nearly given up on him because he wasn't co-operating on his treatment for severe asthma, I wrote that I would rather meet them to talk about how to help the young man than meet them at his funeral. After they received my letter, they called immediately to make an appointment. Alternatively, I sometimes help family members compose and send a letter to an absent relative. My assistance takes the form of questions, and their considered replies become the text of the letter. Once again, editing is painstaking, and I constantly read aloud my notes and asked the clients, 'How does this sound to you?'

Another kind of letter is what we call a 'Letter of Redundancy', referring to role redundancy in a family. These are, I suppose, a form of epistolary structural therapy. They formally acknowledge how certain members have assumed certain roles and their decisions to change those roles in directions preferred by them. For example, after a particularly difficult divorce in which the mother, Karen, was working full-time and trying to raise two children on her own, the older girl, aged seven, took responsibility for caring for her younger brother, aged two. The children came to therapy with their mother eight years later because the brother, Jim, now aged eleven, and sister, Ann, now aged fifteen, were feuding constantly after Ann moved back from living with her father for six months.

Dear Ann and Jim,

Jim and Ann, it was lucky I met you both so long ago. I think it allowed me to understand what once was and now is. Ann and Jim, I remember watching you two play as young kids and how much you looked after Jim, Ann. It was almost as if, as your mother put it, 'she was more Jim's mother than I was'. And Jim, no wonder you didn't have to bother to speak for yourself or do a lot of things for yourself because Ann did those things for you. Perhaps you are too involved with bickering to remember those times. However, Ann, 'good mothering' leads to good kids and 'strong mothering' leads to strong kids. Ann, do you think you have done too good a job on Jim, now that he not only wants to but can stand on his own two feet? Ann, would you rather have Jim dependent on you? Would you prefer that you still spoke for him and did everything for him? Or are you somewhat pleased with his growing up? Knowing Jim was growing up, was that one of the reasons why you felt you could try out living with your father? Would you have left Jim behind if you thought he couldn't stand on his own two feet? Ann, on your return from living with your father, were you surprised to find that Jim was not so much in need of a 'mother' but wanted you more as a sister?

I used Jim's description of Ann as 'bossy' and explored whether Ann wanted Jim to be her employee or her brother. Then I offered a script we created together in therapy in which the mother will help the two stop their fighting and assert her executive authority as the parent.

Karen, when you see them bickering, you might say, 'Ann, I thank you so much for being 'mother' to Jim when he was a young boy and I needed your help as I was working full-time and had just separated from your father and looked after you both on my own. Ann, you did a wonderful job as Jim has grown up so well, I am proud of you both: Ann, as my daughter, and Jim, as my son. However, I am worried that you will not learn to be brother and sister and that you will lose your relationship to bickering. I know that neither of you wants this to happen, so, if necessary, I will provide you with a golden opportunity to appreciate each other as brother and sister. I will leave you now. Good luck.

These kinds of letters are very handy for reviewing the interventions we set up during the session, so when the crisis erupts in the house, the mother can quickly refer to it, even read from it, and use the situation to practise a new way of intervening with her children. In this instance, the bickering disappeared after a few experiences of brother-sister appreciation.

Another variation of the 'Letters of Redundancy' is when I help clients write a 'Formal Declaration' or 'Discharge Letter'. In a parallel situation, for example, Ron, aged sixteen, thanked his sister Terri, aged twenty-two, for her help in raising him and acknowledged that he would no longer call her names and hit her but would try to act more kindly toward her:

I, Ron, discharge my sister, Terri, from being like a mother to me. This may have been necessary when I was much younger, but it is no longer the case. I have come to realise how worried you are about my success in life and this has probably been going on inside you for some time now. As a result, you have come to feel responsible for me and guilty when you don't feel like putting yourself out for me. You took on this role when I was young and needed looking after. You have done such a good job on me that you can now step aside and let me try my wings. I do not want to be your puppet, so both of us are going to have to cut some strings.

I have decided against violence by having my mother agree to charge me with assault if I strike you again. Until we get used to being equal as brother and sister, it is very likely we will still have arguments, with each of us trying to have the last word. Instead of that, I suggest we put these matters of disagreement to a coin toss, In this way, we will both get used to winning fifty percent of the time. In this way, we will both be equal. I now will not have to prove to you that you are not my superior and I am not your inferior. We are equal and, by being equal, we have a chance to become brother and sister instead of son and mother.

I thank you for what you have done for me when I was young. I think all the caring you did has given you a lot of practice for becoming a nurse.

Signed by: Date: Witnessed by: (mother)

Formalising these changes in relationship on paper, in a kind of contract format - signed, dated and witnessed by the parent - made the new roles more real and tangible for family members, and involved getting everyone's agreement to make the change. In fact, Terri decided, after receiving this discharge letter, that she should discharge herself from the role of 'mother' to Ron and she also wrote a 'Letter of Retirement' to herself. Other discharge letters have included a client's official 'Discharge from the Influence of Anorexia', as well as discharges from previous diagnoses. Lorna, aged thirty-three, declared herself free of bulimia, something that had taken her prisoner when she was seventeen years old:

I declare my freedom from Bulimia.
You no longer have any influence
On my body or my soul;
I pledge my commitment to opposing
Your existence in the world,
and preventing anyone else from falling under your tyranny.

Some things that I find difficult to say to a client's face I can write in a letter, and some things that are painful for them to hear are more easily absorbed when they read it in private. One case stands out for me as having been so painful that I was grateful to have the letter say things I would have found extremely difficult to say in the session.

A mother and her second husband came in with her son, who had been born when she was a teenager. The boy had been raised by his grandmother, who was renowned by all who knew her for her love and caring for children. The grandmother's health had been failing for several years and she had tried to reunite the mother and son, but without success - the mother was not interested in being a parent to the child she hadn't really wanted, and the child resented the mother who had abandoned him. However, the grandmother died suddenly, and ten-year-old Tommy had moved in with his mother, stepfather and two half-sisters. He was having a difficult time adjusting to the new family, and they were having an equally hard time adjusting to him. He had frequent tantrums and, on a number of occasions, had assaulted his half-sister. Finally, unable to see any alternatives, his mother, Linda, had applied to social services to make him a ward of the state.

When I saw them, the parents were seething with hatred for this boy, and the intensity of their feeling frightened me. I wrote them a letter emphasising the progress they felt they had made in their occasional cease-fires, and wove in Tommy's conviction that his grandmother was still a presence guiding him and watching over the family. This common bond to the grandmother proved an effective metaphor for drawing them together, but I still worried about the thinly veiled hatred Linda felt for Tommy, who knew only too well her intention to send him to the Boys' Home. These were the questions I could not bring myself to ask aloud but that I could write to them in the letter:

Dear Linda, Ralph and Tommy:

I request you consider the questions that follow. I believe them to be the most important and far-reaching questions you will ever have to ask yourselves. The answers to these questions could very well have more bearing on Tommy's future than anything else in his life so far, save his birth.

Linda, you made it crystal clear to me that you have 'lost touch' with Tommy and understandably find it hard to get close to him. Not surprisingly, this separation did not occur overnight. As you put it, 'It's been building up ... it's been at a crisis point for the last year and desperation for the last six months.' You had to admit that 'a number of times, I would have liked to have dumped him.' Tommy too, is aware of this in his own ten-year-old way. He described his mother-son relationship as 'utter war ... just a big battle.' So, to some extent, he experiences the person who is usually most loved more like an enemy and, let's face it, it's hard to get close to, get comfort from, confide in or care about your enemy. Enemies are typically hated rather than loved.

Linda, have there been too many disappointments, hurts, etc, that your love for Tommy has died? Have there been so many experiences of 'war' that a mother's love has turned to hatred, that your 'unbelonged' son has become your hated enemy? Has the 'wall' been constructed so well that it cannot be broken down? Linda, do you feel so unbelonged to Tommy that you no longer have the will or desire to seek a reunion, a mother-son reunion, to 'belong' him again in your very own way? Linda, how will you face your mother in this life or the next if you abandon Tommy to his fate? How will you ever face yourself?

Linda, I know these are tough questions but you led me to believe in no uncertain terms that the crisis has now become desperation. I ask you these questions with the best intentions and with concern for both the presents and futures of you and Tommy, and your relationship with your mother. I dare to ask these questions out of my respect, concern and compassion for each and every one of you. And I wouldn't have dared to do so if I didn't know, only too full well, that there is a way to reunite you, son to mother and mother to son, a way for you to 'belong' Tommy once and for all and for him to be 'belonged' by your mother's love.

Linda, I in no way intend a criticism of anyone, I am driven by compassion and my desire to avoid a grave tragedy.
Yours sincerely, David Epston.

Had I said this face to face, I can imagine Linda's reaction - a verbal defence of herself, how she had tried hard with Tommy but he just won't co-operate, how she was worried about her new family and couldn't be asked to handle all of the boy's problems on top of that. She might have attacked me, told me I wasn't hearing how desperate she was. Or she might have shut down and felt guilty, immobilised, perhaps angrier at Tommy for bringing her to this juncture in her life where no choice seemed like a good one. But reading it in the letter, Linda saw my concerns, fear and apologies and, most of all, my respect for her, and she could take the time she needed to let it soak in.

The result of this letter was that Linda, Ralph and Tommy made a commitment to 're-belonging' him to the family. I am convinced that my letter touched them in some way that my spoken words could not. Letters ought to be moving experiences, doorways through which everyone can enter the family's story and be touched by the bravery, the pain and even the humour of the narrative.

Only last year did I solve the mystery of why writing a letter seemed so natural an extension of the therapy for me from the very beginning. On visiting the town in Canada where I had grown up, I met with my parents' best friend, Dorothy, who had lived a mile away from us. We reminisced about my parents and then out of the blue she told me she still had every letter my mother had ever written her. I was confused by this revelation as, for the life of me, I could not recall my mother ever writing Dorothy a letter. After all they spend hours on the phone every day and were neighbours. 'Didn't you know?' she asked me. 'She wrote me a letter after every phone call! She said she wanted to get it down. She said that talk wasn't enough.'

I was struck, learning this about my own mother, how present she must have been on those phone conversations, how deeply concentrated on her friend and their conversation. This is how it is for me as a therapist, taking my notes, typing up these letters: I have to be completely attentive to the family. My mind never wanders to the list of groceries I need to pick up on the way home or the calls I need to make; there is just too much to concern myself about during the session. I am absorbed in the client's narrative, taking my careful notes and completely focused on the alternative story that is unfolding in my office, and then absorbed in the retelling of it in the letter.

Some therapists have asked me if this isn't exhausting. In fact, at the end of the day I often feel much better than when I began. From time to time, I browse through a client's file and read the collection of letters we created together, and I am always humbled and amazed at how clients have skilfully re-authored their lives, often against odds that would have been too great for me.

Note

1. First published in the Nov/Dec 1994 *Family Therapy Networker*. Republished here with permission.

10

Further Considerations Relating to Michael White's 'Ritual of Inclusion'[1]

co-authored with Annette Henwood

This paper was written in response to the intense interest and legitimate concerns on the part of many people who attended presentations relating to the 'ritual of inclusion' developed by Michael White. The paper was also intended to guard against both the misapplication and abuse of such a physical intervention, after the 'ritual of inclusion' was banned by the Department of Justice here in New Zealand following complaints being laid against its implementation at a residential treatment centre in Auckland. When I enquired into this, it seemed that the 'ritual' had been taken out of its context and reduced to a mere physical device to restrain out-of-control young people.

With this in mind, I took care when presenting this work to do so as often as convenient with the colleagueship of Annette and Alastair Henwood, and insisted that those attending take the time to watch on video the implementation of the 'ritual of inclusion' and follow-up meetings. Such a two-day presentation and the questions that arose from it provided both the stimulus and basis for this paper. I am grateful to Amanda Kamsler and the New South Wales Family Therapy Association in Sydney for 'pushing' me to write up this work.

Following a workshop on the 'ritual of inclusion' sponsored by the New South Wales Family Therapy Association in Sydney, a small interest group formed. With the consent of Alistair, aged ten, his mother who had 'belonged' him, and her mother who had acted as support person, the video they had made of their 'ritual of inclusion' was made available to this study group. I quote from their letter, written by Amanda Kamsler, on behalf of the group:

> *After viewing the tape, we had an energetic discussion which raised a lot of questions for us (and the group even started to come up with some creative ideas about possible rituals!). Here is a summary of the questions, which we'd like to have your thoughts on:*
>
> 1. *How do you decide whether or not a ritual of inclusion might be appropriate for a family?*
> 2. *What are the kinds of cues you would pick up on that a child has not been 'belonged' by a family?*
> 3. *How do you prepare yourself and the family for the ritual?*
> 4. *How much do you go through the possible consequences of the ritual beforehand?*
> 5. *How do you know a family is ready for a ritual?*
> 6. *When there is a couple raising the child, how do you decide who should do the holding? How do you deal with the other person during the ritual? What are the instructions about who talks to whom? Do you decide this and discuss it with the family beforehand? Have you ever had complications in relation to changes in the couple's relationship after the ritual? How have you dealt with this? Have you ever had a couple holding the child and each other during the ritual? Would you consider this?*
> 7. *When would you decide not to try the ritual?*
> 8. *Has the ritual ever not worked? Under what circumstances?*
> 9. *Do parents have to feel they are 'belonged' by someone before they can cope with the ritual?*
> 10. *Have you ever done the ritual with a family where the parents were very angry and have not been belonged themselves?*

First of all, I have no 'rules' about determining the appropriateness of the ritual. Secondly, I propose the idea of 'belonging'/ritual of inclusion far more often than I apply it. What probably is more important is the context of ideas surrounding 'belonging' (for example see Epston & White 1992). Now there are some very obvious clues, especially in relation to those young people, who have had multiple foster placements, unsuccessful adoptions, etc. No one would have any difficulty identifying such young people. They have often been abused, malnourished, and neglected. Michael utilised the ritual for young people with uncontrollable behaviour but when we discussed it together, he recalled that many of these young people had what I have called 'unbelonging' histories. Searching the child psychiatric/psychological literatures, I'm confident you would come up with any number of analogous descriptions that aren't as interactional as I would prefer: rejecting, rejected, unbonded, etc. I prefer to steer clear of these conventional terms as they can be taken by any of the parties to be labelling of personal attributes. Many of these terms have as strong a standing in 'folk' psychology as they do in the 'disciplining' psychologies. Still they may help identify these young people.

Many of the young people I have seen felt their lives to be out of their control, paralleling Michael's experience; however, some seem to respond to that very differently from the 'uncontrollable' behaviour he reported. They are withdrawn, worn-out looking, hapless, and miserable. They feel 'hollow' when you talk to them and seem estranged from themselves.

The stories parents tell will often give things away. Let me provide you with a few vignettes: Rogier, now aged nine, was born prematurely in Europe. His parents were not permitted to touch him until he was four months of age. With the birth of their second child two years later, they realised that their connection with their child was, in their words, 'not normal'. This conclusion is often reached through an invidious comparison with a subsequent child. I first met Rogier when he was placed at a therapeutic residential community in Auckland. His mother was only able to approach him up to a two-foot distance separating them, at which point her toothgrinding became audible. She found herself unable to close this gap. Rogier was very promiscuous in his affection towards others, slobbering kisses over relative strangers like myself. He was unable to sustain any friendships despite his effusive social displays. He 'drives people mad', according to his parents. He regularly stole and hoarded the proceeds of his thefts. He had a seemingly insatiable appetite, regularly stealing his class-mates' school lunches and eating out of rubbish bins.

Jimmy, aged thirteen, was the physical size of an eight-year-old. He was being investigated by the Growth Clinic due to his growth retardation. In fact, his parents were considering 'buying' a shotgun growth hormone treatment in another country, as their medical advisers here could not discern any medical grounds for such an invasive procedure. He, too, was excessively talkative, promiscuous with his affection, but friendless. He was so anxious to please that he usually ended up tripping over himself in his efforts to do so. He lied continually (saying what he thought other people wanted to hear). He had been expelled from every school placement from pre-school to the present. He hoarded his thefts, which in and of themselves made little apparent sense, e.g., collections of pencils, pens, erasers, and left socks. His mother, first in private, told me that when she gave birth, she was immediately informed she had borne twins. She recalls through a drug-induced stupor that then both twins were removed from her. She was then informed that one had perished. She was to learn covertly that the cause of death was likely medical misadventure and that the doctor concerned was, according to her informant, consequently forbidden to have further hospital privileges. Her surviving child was kept from her and when she complained, she was told: 'You're a nurse. You should be happy you have one alive.' When she insisted on having the survivor with her, she was offered someone else's child to suckle. The next day, her father arrived at her bedside from their remote farm to seek her assistance as he had raped the young woman who was to 'look after things' in his wife's absence so she could be present at her daughter's birth. The next day, her husband 'cracked up' and was hospitalised. She recalls thinking to herself: 'I've just got to do it' and forced herself to go through with the day-to-day routines. She too realised with the birth of her second son that her relationship with her first 'wasn't normal'. She was unable to touch, kiss, or hug him.

Now these above-mentioned instances are fairly obvious. I have also included as 'unbelonged' those children who, for whatever circumstances, e.g., chronic illness, frequent hospitalisation and obligatory seclusion, pain and suffering, and 'hyperactivity', have been somewhat excluded from connecting up to others. Now you can go to the other side of the 'belonging' relationship: a candidate for 'belonging' and candidate(s) for 'belonging' - the unbelonged newborn, adoptee, etc. Such circumstances such as post-partum depression (I prefer the description of 'dismay'), unwanted pregnancies, pregnancy resulting from rape and violation, or the relationship breaking up around the time of the pregnancy and/or birth, etc., any of which could have pre-occupied the 'belonger'.

Questions that assist me and others both to describe the experience of 'being belonged/belonging another', and to remove it from the taken-for-granted revolve around 'belonging' and other associated metaphors:

- *Do you feel you are as connected to John as you are to Jill?*
- *Do you feel in touch with John as you do with Jill?*
- *When did you realise you were out of touch with John?*
- *Has there been a time when you felt more in touch with John than you did when you were dismayed and demoralised by depression?*
- *Has he remained a stranger to you, no matter how hard you try to get to know him?*
- *Do you have an impression that you know how he's feeling or what he's thinking or what he'll get up to next?*
- *Can you predict anything about him or is he more a mystery to you, if your truth be known?*

You can then explore the following:

- *What happens when you put your disappointment aside and try yet again to get in touch with him?*
- *Does it usually blow up in your face or his or both?*
- *When you try to make a connection, does it sooner or later short-circuit?*
- *When you try to wire yourself up to him by being particularly loving or showing him affection, what happens next?*
- *Do you find that when you try to belong him, he can only take so much and then he, in a manner of speaking, overdoses on it and does something seemingly to disbelong you? If you hadn't been deprived of him at birth because of his prematurity, how would you imagine your mother-son relationship would be different?*
- *How would it feel different?*
- *When you hug him, is it really fake hugging, if your truth be known?*

- *Have you noticed that when things are going particularly well for him or you both, that that predicts a blow-up?*
- *Or that predicts him doing something that you would think was pretty stupid or incomprehensible?*

Quite often, parents, particularly mothers, weep with relief at this point, now being able to appreciate and make sense of their own experience. This is often something they have not dared to discuss with others and if they have, they have been dismissed, reassured that it (the 'belonging') will come in time, or that this is how everyone feels. I think it is very unhelpful to 'normalise' matters as the persons themselves are only too keenly aware that this is not normal. If they feel free to speak about it, they will usually use descriptions such as 'hatred' or that the child is 'evil'.

You can ask similar questions to the young persons, of course taking account of the age and capacity and fitting the questions to those considerations:

- *Have you noticed that your mum seems more connected up to Jill than to you?*
- *Do you have any ideas why this may be so? (The answer is usually that she is 'good' and I am 'bad')*
- *When you are having a good day with your mum/dad, do you find that something tells you that this isn't right?*
- *At this time, do you feel more comfortable (better) with a telling off or a growling?*
- *Have you got the idea that the proof of your parents loving you is how much they growl you? How much they give you hidings?*
- *Do you think it was fair for the 'hyperactivity' to take all your attention so you couldn't pay any attention to your mum's efforts to 'belong' you?*
- *Why do you think the 'hyperactivity' wanted you all to itself?*
- *Do you think the 'hyperactivity' wants you to go through life alone? To go wild?*
- *Do you think it was just for your mother's depression to depress her capacity to 'belong' you?*
- *Do you find that you feel hollow on the inside?*

- *Do you think there isn't very much of you sometimes? That other people have more of themselves than you have of your self?*
- *Do you find that you are inclined to give people the answers you think they want to hear?*
- *Have you noticed that they often call this 'lying'?*
- *Does this confuse you?*

By externalising the problem ('unbelonged - unbelonging'/'un- or disconnected'; 'short-circuiting'; 'in touch/out of touch'), a reasonable account of the evolution of the relationship in a very unsatisfactory direction can easily be constructed. This account usually provides a great deal of relief for all parties as it explains, both dramatically and forcefully, so many incidents and unfortunate episodes, histories, and feelings, etc. that hitherto have remained outside any form of understanding, save the characterological (e.g., she has bad blood) or implications of malevolent intent (e.g., he is trying to kill us). It also, and this is extremely important, allows the therapist to have compassion and sympathy for parents who seem so 'rejecting', 'intolerant', and ungenerous, especially when the young person is one of those who is superficially sociable (even if there isn't much substance to it). I think too that this is a great relief to a young person who perhaps for the first time can comprehend their experience by way of a new frame of intelligibility: 'belonging/unbelonging'. This can overturn and substitute for previous explanations such as 'my badness/stupidity' or the badness/stupidity of their potential 'belongers'.

Another advantage of the 'belonging' description of events and its associated metaphors is that they are uncontaminated by the pathologising discourses of psychology, child development, and psychiatry. This can prevent what Lukacs refers to as '*phantom objectivity*':

> ... *a relation between people takes on the character of a thing and thus acquires a 'phantom objectivity', an autonomy that seems so strictly rational and all-embracing as to conceal every trace of its fundamental nature: the relation between people.* (1971, p.125)

The 'bonding' discourse has been reified and, as Taussig comments:

> ... *through a series of exceedingly complex operations, reification serves to adhere guilt to disease. The real task of therapy calls for an*

> *archaeology of the implicit in such a way that the processes by which social relations are mapped into diseases are brought to light, dereified, and in doing so liberate the potential for dealing with antagonistic contradictions and breaking the chains of oppression.* (1992, p.93)

By proposing accounts that implicate injuries, unjust circumstances, unforeseen events as disrupting 'belonging', guilt/blame can easily be bypassed. The relief provided can, at times, be profound. For example, one mother's two-year long headache disappeared the night of the 'belonging' discussion.

The next stage is the presentation that there is a way to 'belong' people and that it is unlikely that they would have heard about it as it has only recently been invented and tried out. 'However, there is no point in going into detail about it now as it is too involved. If you were merely to accept that 'belonging' Johnny was now a real possibility, would you go away for as long as you wish? Would you consider whether things have gone too far for you to do it? Have hatred, disappointment, frustration, etc. taken too great a toll? Johnny, if you were merely to accept that you could still be 'belonged' by your mother and father, do you think your unbelonged life is too far down the road to turn back and unite with the family that bore you? Have you had too many growlings and hidings and hurts that the possible would seem impossible to you?' I generally leave plenty of time for thinking about this, 'as this could be the biggest decision in your son's/your life since your physical birth/since giving birth to him'. Often months elapse.

The following is a letter to Jimmy, aged ten, his mother, Sue, and his stepfather, John. They had approached the Child and Young Persons' Service to take Jimmy into care as 'we don't want him around the place anymore'.

> *Dear Sue, John, and Jimmy:*
>
> *I request you consider the questions that follow. I believe them to be the most important and far-reaching questions you will ever have to ask yourselves. The answers to these questions could very well have more bearing on Jimmy's future than anything else in his life so far, save his birth.*
>
> *Sue, you made it crystal clear to me that you have 'lost touch' with Jimmy and understandably find it hard to get close to him. Not surprisingly,*

this separation did not occur overnight. As you put it, 'It's been building up ... it's been at crisis point for the last year and desperation for the last six months'. You had to admit that 'a number of times, I would have liked to have dumped him'. Jimmy, too, is fully aware of this in his own 10-year old way. He described his son-mother relationship as 'utterly war ... just a big battle'. So, to some extent, he experiences the person who is usually most loved as more like an enemy and let's face it, it's hard to get close to, get comfort from, confide in, or care about your enemy. Enemies are typically hated, rather than loved. However, lately, Jimmy had to revise this by saying that he thought you both were now creating a 'more average relationship'. In fact, he thought, 'Mum likes me a bit more' and he was of the opinion that he could tell this 'by the way she is quite proud of me'. When I asked him what he saw on your face in the war days, he thought it was 'a hateful look'. It seems that by taking some guidance from his recently deceased Nana, he can now feel her presence in his everyday life, and that has assisted him to 'improve my homework ... stop getting into fights'.

Still, Sue, none of the above denies the feelings you have been feeling for some time now, and now when you try to repair the relationship by doing something especially nice, or giving, everything sooner or later blows up in your face. It's almost as if the mother-and-son wiring short circuits, every time you try to make a connection.

Sue and John, Jimmy is becoming a lost person, and people his age cannot find themselves by themselves. From what you say, Sue, in the overwhelming love and doting of your mother whom he lived with from his birth to age 7, Jimmy got the idea, according to you, that he is 'larger than life'. So was it any wonder, when you think about it, that when he joined your family, now with two younger sisters, that he was 'too big', in a manner of speaking, to fit in? And now everything he does to 'fit in' threatens his place in your family and his future as a person. From what you tell me, Jimmy is becoming a lost person, a person lost to himself, and I have a professional responsibility to inform you that that predicts a most unfortunate future. To my way of thinking, it is impossible to come home to yourself without a home in which to do that. And that home is where the heart is. Sue, you described a 'brick wall' having developed between you, and how his mischief lays down course after course, until now you can't see, feel, or touch each other. So, Sue, each of you is entering the worst kind of suffering I know of - an unbelonged child going wild and a mother whose love is turning into hatred. I fully appreciate and understand your talk about amputating Jimmy from your life, but I must forewarn you of the unendurable 'phantom limb' pain that goes with it and never, never goes away.

Sue, have there been too many disappointments, hurts, etc. that your love for Jimmy has died? Have there been too many experiences of 'war' so that a mother's love has turned to hatred, that your unbelonged son has become your hated enemy? Has the 'wall' been constructed so well that it cannot be broken down? Did you believe that the Berlin Wall would ever come down? Do you know that it stood for 17 years but was destroyed by the will of the people for freedom and a reunited country in one night?

Sue, do you feel so 'unbelonged' to Jimmy that you no longer have the will or desire to seek a reunion, a mother-son reunion, to 'belong' him again and make him your very own this time?

Sue, how will you face your mother, in this life or the other life, if you abandon Jimmy to his fate? How will you ever face yourself?

Sue, I know these are tough questions, but you led me to believe in no uncertain terms that the crisis has now become desperation. I ask you these questions with the best intentions and with concern for both the presents and futures of you, Jimmy, John, your relationship with Jimmy, and your relationship with your mother. I dare to ask these questions out of my respect, concern and compassion for each and every one of you. And I wouldn't have dared to do so if I didn't know, only too full well, that there is a way to reunite you, son to mother and mother to son, a way for you to 'belong' Jimmy once and for all and for him to be 'belonged' by your mother's love.

We will meet on September 12th to review this. However, Nana could very well be making an appearance in Jimmy's life and provide him with guidance. So please keep an eye out for this. In many ways, by doing so, you too will be keeping her alive in your everyday life, not just Jimmy. Perhaps she will find her own ways from her grave. Or, at least, encourage you with hope and desire. I don't know; who am I to say? I have only 'met' Nana through your loving accounts of her and Jimmy's deeply felt grief. You might acknowledge her by paying heed to any influence she seems to be having over Jimmy's actions. John, may I ask one thing of you? If, between now and then, Jimmy seems to get 'lost' again, say this to him: 'Jimmy, you need to feel your Nana's presence more and take guidance from her. I am taking you when I am feeling in the right mood to her graveside so you can talk with her.'

Sue, I in no way intend a criticism of anyone. I am driven by compassion and my desire to avoid a grave tragedy.

Yours sincerely, David Epston

In the matter of Jimmy, Sue and John, the work never proceeded any further towards the actual ritual of inclusion. It is my practice at sessions to review their thinking. I am looking for 'unique outcomes' on the one hand and reinterpreting further incidents to the 'disconnected/making connections/short-circuiting' metaphor: stealing as a wrongheaded attempt to fill his emptiness up, lying as a concerted effort to please others by saying what he thinks they think he should say or do.

For those who wish to take the matter further, there is more preparation. Families are invited to take away and consider transcripts of six-month follow-ups of other families. I will also go through the transcripts carefully with them. The transcripts are interviewer questions/interviewee responses as to the precise details of the experience of the 'ritual of inclusion' and subsequent circumstances of everyone's lives and relationships. If it is within their means, I provide them with Michael White's 'Ritual of Inclusion' paper to take home and read. Thanks to the magnanimity of the Henwood family (Annette and her son, Alistair, aged eleven at the time), I also provide them with a copy of the video-tape which they requested I make for them and an audio-tape of a six-month follow-up of me interviewing Alistair and Annette. This is much like a reminiscence guided by my questioning. Each stage in this process is, at minimum, a session.

However, I continue my search for 'unique outcomes' and not surprisingly this new context of ideas seems to be a breeding ground for them. When they happen, they would have been insignificant outside of this context of ideas of 'belonging'.

Here are some examples: 'When he went to his mother's for the weekend, just before I put him on the bus, I put my hand on his shoulder and he didn't shrug it off'. 'When he saw me crying about my mother's death, he came over and gave me some comfort.' Sometimes there are very overt gestures, for example, the giving of flowers, etc.:

DE: *Why did you give your step-mum those flowers?*

B: *I thought she might be nicer to me?*

DE: *Did it work?*

B: *Not really!*

DE: *What do you mean it didn't work?*

B: *It didn't last.*

DE: *How long did you think it would last?*

B: *A month or two.*

DE: *Gee, you might have been hoping for too much there! How long does a meal last?*

B: *Till breakfast the next day.*

DE: *J, how long did the flowers last for you?*

J: *Two days.*

DE: *That's pretty good? If B's father only showed you affection once every two months, what state would your marriage be in?*

J: *Not a very good one.*

DE: *B, you did a good job there with the flowers connecting up to your step-mum. But you might have had too high hopes. What do you think? ...*

How do you know a family is ready?

Often, the need for a ritual as detailed by Michael White becomes unnecessary, and often some less demanding variant is arranged. I often allow the urgency of the situation to set the timing, but I wouldn't undertake it if the parents weren't desperate: 'This is the last-ditch stand. Is there anything else you can think of that you would like to try before you undertake it?'

So I would often encourage them to experiment with every other possible alternative before proceeding to the ritual of inclusion. However, if they said, 'If things aren't any better by tomorrow, he's out', then that is readiness enough to start discussion and the preparation stage. I would never proceed directly to the ritual.

When would you decide not to try the ritual?

Several family members have decided they couldn't do it. The idea of feeling such intensity terrified them. Usually the preparation stage and viewing the videos would sort these people out. From the outset, I make it clear that the ritual is extremely emotionally and physically demanding and that no one should embark upon it unless they can go through with it. If there is any risk of this, it would be better to forget about it and see if we could draft some other kind of relationship that doesn't require so much 'belonging' in it, e.g., roommates, boarder, etc. Also, if either parent is too angry, spiteful, vengeful, hurt, or embittered, I would refuse to go ahead. It is vital to have developed some compassion on the part of the parents for the young person and on the part of the young person for him/herself. So I am always very candid without wanting to be seen to be merely providing an apology for their children's misbehaviour.

Has it not worked?

Some of my colleagues have told me that it hasn't worked. Some retrospective speculation for the failures proposed inadequate preparation, were not in attendance at the first ritual, and weren't in touch enough around subsequent rituals. As far as I know, there have always been improvements in relationships, although in every case they were so deteriorated that they could only get better. In earlier years, I didn't follow up these families enough, and I think things could lapse over time. But now I caution people repeatedly that this just makes people feel 'normal' rather than ensuring unrelenting good behaviour on the part of their children. In fact, I might add that the behaviour could be much the same, but they might feel differently about it and that it now can be discussed, and those discussions might be 'felt' by the young person.

Do parents have to feel they are 'belonged' by someone before they can cope with the ritual?

This is a very good question and something I wish I had asked a father who refused to consider the ritual. Matter of fact, when I told him about it, he started screaming with discomfort. I don't know what I would do here, but I certainly would think about the idea of 'self-adoption', 'self-belonging', or parallel rituals of inclusion ('This ritual is about being belonged by your Dad, Billy; John, this ritual is about belonging Billy as his father and belonging yourself at the same time into the family you made rather than the family you came from but who weren't there for you').

How do you decide who should do the holding?

The question of who 'holds' can be answered by who doesn't feel 'belonged' or 'belonging'. When it involves both parents, we might all agree that they can take turns. How and when this happens could be left up to them. I have found the young people to be remarkably co-operative at changing the 'belonging' person. Michael White details the requirements of the 'holding' adult and the 'supportive' adult. All the details are discussed at length beforehand. As little should be left to chance as possible, as no matter how much preparation everyone has had, I doubt if anyone could really be prepared for the experience of the ritual. It is beyond words. The idea of one adult 'holding' another is a good one, and some couples certainly have arrived at variations on that. The other possibility is that both persons may be required to ensure the 'hold'. Parents just naturally take turns, probably when distress or fatigue shows on their partner's face.

Everyone in the family is involved in a discussion about how they might feel should, say, Johnny take up a place in the family. This is particularly important with 'good' and 'bad' siblings, and you can predict extreme reactions by the 'belonged' siblings to the new 'belonging' of their sibling. Couples should also be forewarned that this experience could have profound effects on their relationship. 'Do you think your relationship with Jack/Jill could stand up to a fair increase in its belonging? Would either of you feel uncomfortable with a fair bit more intimacy between you? Going through this could very well get you two really in touch with each other on an emotional level. Could that be intolerable? Could you find out something you would rather not know in a way that could not be denied?' At least one couple separated almost immediately after the ritual. However, it was 'just the final straw'. The husband was unable to 'support' his partner nor 'belong' his son.

The following are Annette Henwood's replies to the same questions:

Here are my thoughts on the questions:

How do you pick up cues that the child has not been 'belonged' by a family?

Alistair was always treated differently by his paternal grandparents who told me outright that we were stupid to have more than two children. There is an intense sibling rivalry between him and his older sister (+1) and jealousy over such things as playing with the baby next door. Alistair invariably feels excluded: either his sister has a girlfriend to play and doesn't want him around or his older brother (+3) has mates to play with and doesn't want a kid brother as a hanger-on. Alistair doesn't really have any friends either to phone, visit, or invite to play. His father has never really had time for him and seems to spend quite a lot of time criticising his bad behaviour instead of doing anything positive to help improve things.

Although you explained to me about the ritual, I really wasn't emotionally prepared for the overwhelming feelings of love which came to the surface during the ritual. This I think can only be described by someone who has actually experienced these feelings.

I know you explained the possible consequences, but I don't remember them.

When you first suggested the ritual, you remarked that I wasn't ready because I was too emotionally bruised to cope adequately. I myself know when I felt strong enough to cope.

This possibility didn't arise because I am a single parent and my mother was my support person. You explained everything very clearly beforehand, and apart from a quiet mouthing of reassurance from Mum, I don't think there was any exchange of words at all. You were the one talking directly to Alistair. The closeness all three of us had afterwards was very special, as it really was a form of rebirthing. As Mum had been in Australia at the time when all the children were born, this was as close as she could get to that experience.

Note

1. First published 1994 in the *Journal of Child and Youth Care.*

References

Epston, D. 1992: 'A problem of belonging.' In Epston, D. & White, M., *Experience, Contradiction, Narrative & Imagination*, pp.97-104. Adelaide, South Australia: Dulwich Centre Publications.

Lukacs, G. 1971: *History & Class Consciousness.* London: Merlin Press.

Taussig, M. 1992: *The Nervous System*. New York: Routledge.

White, M. 1989: 'Ritual of inclusion: An approach to extreme uncontrolled behaviour in children and young adolescents.' In *Selected Papers*, pp.77-84. Adelaide, South Australia: Dulwich Centre Publications.

11

From 'Spy-chiatric Gaze' to Communities of Concern[1]

The following two papers describe what I refer to as a 'narrative approach to so-called anorexia/bulimia'.[2] Over the last five years this work has consumed a great deal of my concern and energy. Problems referred to as 'eating disorders' have doubled in incidence since the 1970s and have reached epidemic proportions. They oblige women (and some men) to live their lives out in virtual prisons. The success rates of conventional psychiatric 'treatments' are extremely unpromising; in addition these very 'treatments' often lead to actions being taken against those struggling with the effects of so-called anorexia/bulimia.

A narrative approach allows for working with people against the problem, rather than seemingly working against the person and/or their family. A concern for 'deconstructing' the practice of anorexia (also known as bulimia) brings forth for discussion and contestation the gender, cultural and social contexts of such problems. What is required too is a radical externalising conversation to act linguistically against those discursive practices that have a young woman believing that she is anorexia. Anti-anorexia is a good example of an 'anti-language/counter-discourse/ transgressive discourse'.

> *Neutral dictionary definitions of the words of a language ensure their common features and guarantee that all speakers of a given language will understand one another, but the use of words in live speech communications is always individual and contextual.*
>
> Bakhtin (1986, p.88)

Therapy, like politics, has always rested on the construction and maintenance of social reality. Until recently, therapists practised in accordance with a set of enduring or given 'truths'. Unfortunately, these 'truths' acted to conceal and support our monopolistic ambitions to control information on what constitutes right and wrong, normal and abnormal. The purpose of this chapter is to argue for 'alternative knowledges' (Foucault 1980) that derive from those populations most excluded from power (e.g., clients, inmates, and residents). Our intent is to widen the frame of certain therapeutic traditions regarding the utilisation of client knowledges and to increase the possibilities of utilising these knowledges.

Our chapter proposes 'communities of concern' as a means of revisioning our relationships with people who seek our help. We substitute such communities for the exclusionary professional - other and the degrading practices that seem associated. From our point of view, reflecting team practice (Andersen 1987; Lax 1991; Madigan 1992a; White 1995) exemplifies such communities of concern. Our hope in this chapter is to extend the reflecting team idea into areas of (co)research and political action.

Specifically, the chapter illustrates the practice of circulating clients' local knowledges through the establishment of leagues, letter-writing campaigns, and co-researching practices.

A Looking-Glass History

Since the early 1700s, the deep problems of human concern have been assumed to be the monopoly of a range of health professionals. Therapeutic practice was managed through agreed-on structural, temporal, and ideological tenets. Therapeutic tenets dictated how therapy would be carried out, who would be involved, what information was relevant, how long therapy would take, what constituted a 'cure', and so forth. Tenets of therapy were secured through hard-fought struggles at academic, professional, and governmental levels. Tenets were mediated through policy guidelines that dictated appropriate practice procedure. Since the 1700s, not much has changed. What gets to be said, and with what authority, is not viewed within the landscape of the excluded others' story-telling rights (Law & Madigan 1994). How the problem is defined, who will be involved in the solution of the problem, and how much time is necessary to create change are considered the prerogative of the professional person.

Traditionally, the ideology of professional practice viewed clients/ patients as not having expertise in their own lives (Foucault 1982). Often the existence of a problem is used as prime facie evidence to support such a claim. Health professionals viewed themselves as having 'expert knowledge' and spoke openly of this knowledge with colleagues but not with clients. This expert knowledge marked the health professional off as the 'observer' and distinguished him/her from the 'other'. In fact, the positivist methodologies that undergirded expert knowledge required separation of the observer from the 'observed other', in what Joan Campbell refers to as 'the watchers and the watched' (personal communication, Auckland, July 1994).

Client observation has long been a practice of psychiatry, psychology, and family therapy. From behind one-way mirrors, the family therapy 'eye' expanded to a four-by-six-foot gaze. This provided family therapists with a new eminence which they hoped would make them pre-eminent among their mental health colleagues as looking-glass heroes/heroines. Concealed and quite often anonymous, the behind-the-scenes team offered up ingenious hypotheses and interventions by telephone or in written summaries. Their comments were usually interpretive and strategic in origin as demonstrated by the work of the Mental Research Institute (MRI) and Milan-style 'teams'.

The negative reactions of many families to these 'gazing' practices often went unheeded because negative reactions were often interpreted as signs of perturbation, something that was unequivocally viewed as heralding change. However, both preceding and in the wake of reflecting team practices, questions were being asked as to whose benefit the therapeutic gazing ritual was structured for (Madigan 1991b, in press) and concern was expressed for *some of the clinical, political, and ethical dilemmas of different ways of reviewing and using one-way screens* (Young 1989, p.5).

Postmodernism, feminism, and social constructionism called for reconsideration of our structuralist and functionalist traditions, as was the case in the social sciences at large. Alongside this discussion, the 'other' began to talk back. Anna Yeatman (1994) suggests:

> *Many and maybe most commentators agree that [postmodernism] represents a crisis of authority for the western knowing subject, posed by the refusal to stay silenced on the part of those whom this subject had cast as other: natives, colonials, women and all who are placed in a client relationship to expert, professional authority. By insisting on their own voice and status as subjects, these erstwhile objects of modern western knowledge, have disrupted the epistemological order of domination inscribed within modern, western knowledge.* (p.27)

The professional field of family therapy has begun to review the tenets that long dictated the course of what we understood to be family therapy. Therapeutic ideas and therapy practice have begun the painful shift from being viewed as entitled truths to social constructions (Shotter & Gergen 1989). Who constitutes the self, the status of therapeutic objectivity, structures, and discourse came under revision and have been replaced by co-authoring (Epston & White 1992), the decentring of the subject (Elliot 1994; Madigan 1991a; Sampson 1989), the cultural effects on problem maintenance (White 1995; Waldegrave 1990), and therapist transparency (Epston & White 1992).

It was through the introduction of reflecting teams that therapists began to oblige themselves to make their opinions visible and audible and by the same token, accountable and contestable. Liberated from the distant security of the one-way screen, reflecting team members joined with families they observed and sat in observation of their own comments. Having forsaken any allegiance to grand traditions of 'truth' they felt entitled to offer up a 'smorgasbord' of ideas and not correct interpretations.

They suggested points of view, 'not as rigid explanations but as tentative thoughts' (Lax 1991, p.133). Clients were offered a chance to talk back, interrogate, question, and reflect back to therapists their thoughts about the therapist's thoughts. Within this recursive conversation, clients were intended a different status: one of inclusion and equity.

It is here that the professional monologue that Foucault has referred to, is substituted for communities of dialogue - a process of talking with, rather than talking to. Foucault (1984) writes:

> *In the serene world of mental illness, modern man* [sic] *no longer communicates with the madman* [sic]*; on the one hand, the man* [sic] *of*

> *reason delegates the physician to madness, thereby authorizing a relation through the abstract universality of disease; on the other hand, a man* [sic] *of madness communicates with society only by intermediary of an equally abstract reason which is order, physical or moral restraint, the anonymous pressure of the group, the requirements of conformity. As for a common language, there is no such thing any longer: the constitution of madness as mental illness, at the end of the eighteenth century, affords the evidence of a broken dialogue, posits the separation of the already effected and thrusts into the oblivion all those stammered, imperfected words without fixed syntax in which the exchange between madness and reason was made. The language of psychiatry, which is monologue of reason about madness, has been established on the basis of such silence.* (pp.xii-xiii)

Through reflecting teams, clients participated as partners to the dialogue, co-constructing the very terms and language of the therapy, thereby receiving a chance to be directly involved in co-constructing the language of their own change. Epston & White (1992) found Myerhoff's (1982) 'definitional ceremonies' as apt descriptions of these communities of concern in the manner in which they performed their knowledges and their redescriptions of themselves as persons and families and therapists. They view the performance of reflecting teams as 'celebrations of redefinition' which highlight and bring forth previously restrained solution knowledges.

The purpose for the establishment of ideas such as leagues, letter-writing campaigns, and co-research projects involves the further circulation of 'local knowledges' around problems to those not in attendance and can considerably widen the scale of operation. These communities of concern might be considered 'virtual communities'.

The voices of the client and their family are privileged in these communities of concern as the means to therapeutic ends. These communities may very well extend their activities from concern to more organised co-research, or in the case of the Anti-Anorexia/Anti-Bulimia League to frank political activism on behalf of its membership and others.

Narrative Ideology and Practice

Leagues, letter-writing campaigns, and co-research are situated in a narrative ideology that acts 'as if' it were true that the problem is the problem rather than the person is the problem (Epston & White 1992; Madigan 1992b; Roth & Epston, in press; White 1995). These practices challenge both therapist and client to revise their relative positioning to, and beliefs about, knowing and not knowing about problems. Briefly, narrative ideas are situated in a therapeutic context that does the following:

1. Privileges the person's lived experience.
2. Encourages a perception that change is always possible and occurring through linking lived experience across the temporal dimension.
3. Encourages multiple perspectives and acts to deconstruct claims of 'expert knowledge'.
4. Encourages the carnival of possible futures through the reconstruction and re-remembering of alterative stories.
5. Invites a reflexive posture and demands that therapists be accountable for their therapeutic stance.
6. Acknowledges that stories are co-produced and endeavours to make the clients the privileged authors of their own experiences.
7. Believes that persons are multistoried.

Leagues

During the early 1980s my co-author (DE) began to circulate his client's knowledges to others who were still trapped within the confines of particular problem lifestyles. He collected his client wisdom in what he called an archive. The archive contained an assortment of audiotapes, letter writings, and artwork that represented a rich supply of solutions to an assortment of long-standing problems such as temper taming, night fears, school refusing, asthma, and, of course, anorexia and bulimia. He came to redefine his clients' knowledge as expert knowledge.

He was able to patch together a network of clients with the purpose of consultation, information, and mutual support. He called these client networks leagues. As the leagues grew, he realised that he had ready access to a wealth of consultants. His clients became his colleagues. The archive is now a vast offertory shared by David around the world.

Leagues are a gathering of persons who have a desire to protest the effects of a particular problem on people's lives. The membership constituency usually involves a majority of clients, mixed with an assortment of therapists, family members, friends, teachers, journalists, and community activists. They are structured in similar ways to many other grassroots political organisations, such as Youth against Violence Committee, or a Doctors for Peace Group. A league's focus is directed toward combating a particular identified problem (e.g., anxiety and depression) and the structures that support the problem.

Leagues allow for the distribution of client knowledge from one client to another. In addition, they often voice strong opposition to those cultural and professional institutions that are problem supporting. A league's mandate acts to undo the knotted dichotomy of difference, distance, and status presently wedged between therapists and clients. Leagues can be seen as another step in stretching the ideas of transparency and reflecting teams into the community.

The Anti-Anorexia/Anti-Bulimia League

The Anti-Anorexia/Anti-Bulimia League encourages a different kind of self-directed healing and encourages persons to retrieve, and reflect upon, what lies hidden in the wings of their imaginations. Members of the league realise that their ideas represent the tip of an untapped therapeutic iceberg. To assist the readers of this chapter, David compiled a series of written questions about the league's history and membership involvement. Vancouver league members, Jennifer and Lisa, volunteered to co-research and present the idea of their Anti-Anorexia/Anti-Bulimia League.

Lisa's Co-research

David: *How did you think professionals regarded the problem of anorexia/bulimia?*

Lisa: *I think that, generally, 'professionals' regarded the problem of anorexia/bulimia as a part of those afflicted.*

David: *Who do you think they thought had the problem?*

Lisa: *It was the person, not the 'eating disorder', that was the problem!*

David: *Where was the problem located?*

Lisa: *Before hearing about the league, I was strongly indoctrinated with the belief that anorexia was a deeply rooted and integral part of me, and that without it I would in fact lose parts of my own self.*

David: *How do you recall first becoming aware of the league in the context of your 'treatment'?*

Lisa: *Oh God! When I first heard about the league I was involved in a transition group through a hospital youth clinic. Let's just say that, at that point, having been given a rather biased opinion of the league by the staff, I was not exactly in favour of its principles.*

David: *Did your impressions change over time?*

Lisa: *Yeah, my impressions have changed and continue to change over time. I think most often my impressions change according to how I feel about myself - when I am feeling strong my impressions of the league's activities in anti-anorexia are very strong and that everything is going to work out. When I am feeling fragile the voice of anorexia says 'it sounds good in theory but in practice it is wrong'. I think people supporting one another is a great idea, and living by the principles of the Anti-Anorexia League is much easier doing it alongside other people than doing it on your own. Being part of the league, and seeing it begin to get together has been a great help to me and has the potential to help a lot of other people.*

David: *Did the league offer you anything different from the other forms of 'treatment' you had undergone in the past or were undergoing?*

Lisa: *Definitely! The league offers a reality that is not offered in therapy. Most often in therapy you are viewed as the problem - that some thing has to be fixed, that there is a wrong in your past, that you have to overcome this or that. The league has a different view of the problem - that it is something that has visited upon you, that you don't need it to live. In the past, and especially at the youth clinic groups, I would be asked to 'check in with my problem', but there was no action taken or offered to relieve anorexia. The league is different; it says, okay, this is the way that it was, and this is what anorexia has taken away from you, and these are the pro-anorexic parts of our society. We don't dwell on the horror stories, we just go from here by taking action against anorexia. I think for me that the only way to get free is by taking action against the problem of anorexia and those things that support its life. I think action is the only way to combat eating disorders and the league does this in a variety of ways.*

David: *Did you sense that this was somehow different than a conventional, run-of-the-mill support group?*

Lisa: *The difference between the league and your run-of-the-mill support groups and 12-step programs is that in these other groups there tends to be a lot of comparison and story telling, and it is like these worst of the worst stories keep people there - and keep people feeling hopeless and horrible. The person who lost the most weight is the one to be the most pitied and most envied! The support groups often just fed into anorexia by supporting ideas of specialness and perfection. However, the Anti-Anorexia/Anti-Bulimia League is supportive of the non-anorexic, non-bulimic steps the person has taken. This is really important and very different. The League's way of thinking needs more attention by other 'professionals' and support groups. Also, the League moves within the realm of political activism and does something about it, not only in ourselves but in the realm of the society - changing society. When your anti-anorexia media campaign really gets off the ground I think there will be potential for an anti-anorexic/anti-bulimic revolution - I really do!*

David: *When did you feel that you started to have a 'voice' in matters of your life and death?*

Lisa: *Recently I have come in contact with my own voice and not the voice of anorexia. For so long, I believed that anorexia's voice was just who I was, and anorexia just told me what to do - other people believed this as well and helped anorexia along. Now I am able to stop and say no to the anorexia. I feel that I have the power and the real desire to say no - this voice is not who I am, I want to have a life and I am going to!*

David: *When did you feel you were being attended to and taken seriously?*

Lisa: *I think only when a person begins to take anti-anorexic steps will they begin to be taken seriously. I mean a person in a support group can tell you that they are doing fine, but you can see they are not. It is only when they begin to fight back can they be taken seriously, because all of us who have suffered through anorexia and bulimia are experts at saying one anti-anorexic thing and doing another anorexic thing. When you really begin to take back your voice everything changes.*

David: *In your experience of human associations is there anything about the league that is unique in your experience?*

Lisa: *I think what is exciting about the league in Vancouver, and that which makes it different to a team or club or a family, is that there are so many aspects of support to the league. There is the community-building aspect of it, there is the goal that we are doing something for the community aspect of it, and there is the not blaming the person aspect of it. What I like most about the league through, is that it has the potential to not only help people break free of anorexia and bulimia, but to be able to change the society little bit by little bit. The league helps women claim back their voice to say, 'No, this is not acceptable'. The advertising, the standards we are made to live up to in the media, what the media considers 'normal' is not acceptable by the league. Our society that supports anorexic activity commits violence against women and their bodies and we in the league will not accept this. When people begin noticing our league banners, newsletters, T-shirts and stickers, there will be change and we will make a difference.*

Jennifer's Co-research

David: *How did you think professionals regarded the problem of anorexia/bulimia?*

Jennifer: *I believe professionals have viewed anorexia and bulimia as a disease.*

David: *Where was the problem located?*

Jennifer: *I believe that if a professional has to point his or her finger at a spot where anorexia and bulimia is located in me they would point to my brain ... they would say that the problem is located in the way I think. I, of course, would respond that the problem can not be removed from the context of history, society, and politics.*

David: *How do you recall first becoming aware of the league in the context of your 'treatment'?*

Jennifer: *Gradually, I began to look forward to league meetings where I felt I had a voice and I was listened to. I also began to feel an immense relief from 'guilt' which I had been carrying around with me. I began to recognise bulimia was not only what the medical model suggested (e.g., distorted body image, relentless drive toward thinness). I became aware that bulimia and anorexia had convinced me that I could not fight back.*

David: *Did the league offer you anything different from the other forms of 'treatment' you had undergone in the past or were undergoing?*

Jennifer: *The league differs from the normative support group in that it calls on the so-called patient to be the* expert. *Family members are taught ways to fight anorexia and bulimia from league members themselves. The individual is empowered and encouraged not to be passive, victim or patient. Furthermore through externalising the problem the league calls on* all *members to consider their values and to critically examine the society in which they are embedded.*

David: *What would you say to a person who asked, 'Isn't this just another kind of Alcoholics Anonymous? Another kind of 12-step recovery movement?'*

Jennifer: *An Anti-Anorexia/Anti-Bulimia League is entirely different from a 12-step recovery program. While I want to fully recognise and respect those individuals who have attained a sense of 'well-being' via the 12-step program it doesn't fit for me. To me the 12-step process is about 'letting go' - giving up control and finding peace. Philosophically different, the Anti-Anorexia/Anti-Bulimia League empowers the individual through externalising the problem. Anorexia and bulimia are proposed as a separate entity in themselves which the non-patient, non-victim is fighting back against. The league's perspective also demands responsibility not only from society, community, and the immediate context, but from the individual's own resources. The league acknowledges and respects the power of the individual. It fights back against the problem.*

Leagues utilise an 'anti-language' for explaining their philosophy and ideological position (e.g., the Anti-Depression and Anti-Anxiety leagues). In doing so league members act to externalise previously internalised problem discourse. For example, the Anti-Anorexia/Anti-Bulimia League utilises an anti-language to:

1. Establish a context in which women taken by anorexia/bulimia experience themselves as separate to the problem.
2. View the person's body and relationships to others not as the problem; the problem is the problem (counters the effect of labelling, pathologising, and totalising descriptions.)
3. Enable people to work together to defeat the effects of the problem.
4. Consider the cultural practices of objectification used to objectify anorexia/bulimia instead of objectifying the woman as being anorexic/bulimic.
5. Externalise and objectify the problem, which challenges the individualising

techniques of scientific classification and looks at the broader context for a more complete problem description.

6. Achieve externalisation by introducing questions that encourage the individuals taken by anorexia/bulimia to map the influence of the problem's devastating effects in their lives and relationships.
7. Externalise by deconstructing the pathologising 'thingification' and objectification of women through challenging accepted social norms.
8. Externalise, thereby allowing for the possibility of multiple descriptions and restorying by bringing forth alternative versions of a person's past, present, and future.

Currently the Vancouver Anti-Anorexia/Anti-Bulimia League works in conjunction with the league in New Zealand in establishing numerous anti-anorexic/anti-bulimic networks of activity, through consultations with clients, families, and therapists residing in Australia, the United States, and Canada. Prior to joining the league, members have usually taken part in a variety of anti-anorexic/anti-bulimic therapeutic activities such as individual, group, and multiple family group therapy from a narrative perspective.

The purpose of the league is to traverse the questionable ideological and fiscal gaps that lie within the traditional treatment terrain of mental health. The league promotes the idea of independence and self-sufficiency. Its playing field is twofold: (1) preventive education through a call for professional and community responsibility and (2) an alternative and unconventional support system for those women caught between hospitals and community psychiatry.

Through regular meetings, league members, families, lovers, and friends often take a direct-action approach to the problems of anorexia and bulimia. For example, through the development of a media watch committee it can act to publicly denounce 'pro-anorexic/bulimic' activities against women's bodies through letters written to a wide variety of magazines, newspapers, and company presidents. This enables the league to possibly return the gaze through anti-anorexic/anti-bulimic surveillance directed toward professional, educational, and consumer systems.

The school action committee has developed an anti-anorexic/anti-bulimic program for primary and secondary school students; however, they are finding out that diets and concerns with body specification are now the talk of toddlers as young as four.

League T-shirts have the words 'you are more than a body' emblazoned across the back of them with the league name and logo printed on the front. They were a hot selling item throughout this last year.

Radical in its philosophy, the Vancouver Anti-Anorexia/Anti-Bulimia League's mandate is to hold accountable those professional and consumer systems that knowingly render women with 'eating disorders' dependent and marginalised. Dependency and marginalisation can occur through practices of pathological classification, long-term hospitalisation; medication; funding shortages; and messages of hopelessness, dysfunction, and blame.

The league's battle is to win the war being waged on women's bodies on both the professional and the consumer front. Through the process of reclaiming their lives from anorexia and bulimia, league members refuse to accept the popular misconception that they alone are responsible for their so called eating disorders. League members are beginning to make a crucial shift in their identities - from group therapy patients to community activists and consultants. In helping at the level of community they are assisting other women and families and, in turn, are helping themselves.

Given the choice of utilising a league member or another therapist for an anti-anorexic reflecting team, I (SM) would prefer, whenever possible, to access a league member. Clients are always struck by the members' compassionate and direct reflections. It is now common practice for us to pay ex-clients and league members to act as consultants to therapists in training and as reflecting team members.

Below is an excerpt from a videotape that was made by a league member for the explicit purpose of circulating her ideas in the training of therapists on what they might need to know when working with the problem of anorexia and bulimia.

SM: *What do therapists need to know when working with persons taken by anorexia and bulimia?*

Lorraine: *There are points in the healing process when the words and actions of a support person/therapist can be very helpful and instrumental in the fight against anorexia and bulimia. Anorexia/bulimia relies on anti-logical tactics to keep a person in its grips. I'll give you a more concrete example: A person has just enjoyed a three-day camping trip with friends and for the duration of the trip she felt relatively free from the abusive and controlling voice of anorexia, but upon returning, she is launched into a drastic campaign against her health and towards anorexia's plots and plans for her destruction. At this point, she is feeling like a failure, like the freedom of the past three days is erased and as if she could never turn this destructive path around. The most critical thing for a supporter/therapist to do, at this point, is to hear the panic as a reaction to the vicious messages that anorexia/bulimia is relaying and identify them as such. Once anorexia is heard out and the panic is shared and validated - because it is scary and lonely when one is feeling swallowed by anorexia- then the conversation can turn to how it was that she made a three-day escape and how she might do it again. The most dangerous and unhelpful thing that can occur is that the panic is ignored and unheard because this can fuel anorexia to prove just how ferocious it can be, thus driving a person further into its grips.*

SM: *When might a therapist be considered pro-anorexic?*

Lorraine: *There are many times, but I will give you just two examples that therapists and hospitals might consider. Something that can be very unhelpful in a relationship between client and therapist is the perpetuation and maintenance of a power differential. Traditionally, there has been the assumption and acceptance of a power differential between therapist and client, but if the intent of a therapist is to be helpful and supportive then it is to both parties' benefit if the fight against anorexia is waged on equal ground. Because doctors and patients have often been segregated by the gap in power, perspective, and background, it is challenging to enter into this unfamiliar territory of equality - even more frightening still to recognise that perhaps the real expert is he/she who has lived the experience rather than he/she who has spectated. Anorexia/bulimia acts as a power over a person, and if the therapist takes on this power-over position even the best intentions to help may act in collusion with anorexia instead of against it.*

I am wary of the current practice of weight and body-fat focus that is occurring through weekly weigh-ins and skinfolds in many recovery programs. In my experience, this type of surveillance acts as a double-edged sword, and the negative effects seem to far outweigh the positive ones. If anything, the focus on weight and skinfolds acts as a medium through which the ideas of perfection, comparison, and not measuring up are reinforced and fuelled.

SM: *When might a therapist be considered anti-anorexic?*

Lorraine: *Something that is helpful is to focus on moments of freedom from anorexia/bulimia and to celebrate health and wellness. A very dangerous message to be relaying to people suffering the effects of anorexia/bulimia is the idea that he/she is not sick enough for help - this too can drive anorexia to prove itself. It is important to recognise anorexia and bulimia as operating on a continuum that begins with body surveillance and weight preoccupation.*

Because anorexia/bulimia relies on convincing its victims that they are powerless, that the future is hopeless, that they are unworthy of a compassionate relationship with themselves and others, a great amount of work needs to be done to recognise and to counter these lies that anorexia and bulimia tell, and to create new versions of possibility. At the times when anorexia/bulimia is challenged by an anti-anorexic/anti-bulimic action or thought, there is a strong tendency for anorexia/bulimia to wage an assault on the person in order to try and convince them against attempting any future moments of freedom and enjoyment. This is a sort of anti-logic that occurs on the path to freedom, and it is something that I feel helping professionals and other support persons need to be aware of so that they can help in the fight.

Focusing on issues of power, voice, individuality, and uniqueness have been very helpful for me in my battle against anorexia/bulimia and I believe that these issues are common to the struggle of many persons living in our Western culture.

The element of the sociocultural manufacturing and perpetuation of anorexia/bulimia is a piece that is often ignored in therapy and research on anorexia/bulimia. Taking the focus off the person/self as the problem and returning the gaze back to the place where the problem originates has been incredibly empowering and relieving for me. Once the blame is relieved, there is so much energy available to use in the construction of a new storyline for one's life. Anorexia/bulimia predicts a mundane story with an ending in death and disappointment. I, as the author of my story, have the freedom to create one of endless possibilities, full of interesting characters and exciting conclusions. A therapist can assist in the authoring of either of these stories with a client -clearly the latter is desirable, yet it presents a large challenge, both to the client and the therapist. The client must take back his/her power and the therapist must relinquish some of their power. In my experience it has been the most helpful thing that a therapist/helping professional/supporter can do.

SM: *Would you like to say a few words about the League?*

Lorraine: *Definitely! The League is a wonderful thing because it takes these ideas and puts them into practice. Because this has never been done before, it has been a constantly evolving concept and group. Presently, the focus of the group is to bring together people suffering the effects of anorexia/bulimia, their families, friends and all other supporters and to implement the power of collectivity against anorexia and bulimia. The focus of our work is on addressing the perpetuating elements in our culture by offering conversation, education, and action.*

Another aim of the league is to experience the benefits of health, power and voice and to combat the glamorisation of anorexia/bulimia. A medium like the League's publication, 'The Undead,' which is free from the constraints of advertising regulations, et cetera, offers a chance for voices that are often unheard to be heard and will work to promote these ideas and spread them further.

It is any wonder that upon viewing the league's 'What every therapist needs to know about anorexia and bulimia, but were afraid to ask' videos, the room thunders with applause, interest, and tears? I (SM) asked psychiatrist Dr. Elliot Goldner, director of St. Paul's Hospital eating disorder program in Vancouver, to offer his reflections after reading excerpts of the league's ongoing co-research project. Dr Goldner writes:

The writings of Lisa, Jennifer, and Lorraine underscore a potent fact - people struggling against anorexia and bulimia possess a wisdom and expertise that must not be marginalised. Their research is pulled from the pores of experience and has not been limited to eight hours a day, academic blinders, and political or financial motivations. To ignore their insight would be folly. Yet, psychiatry and therapy practices have too often disregarded such careful and painstaking research, and have preferred promises of quick fixes, and electrifying solutions from technology and scientism.

When I listen, instead, to the words of Lisa, Jennifer, and Lorraine, these are some of the things I hear:

1. *Collaboration is helpful in fighting anorexia and bulimia; leagues such as the Anti-Anorexia/Anti-Bulimia League can offer such collaboration.*

2. *Anti-anorexic/bulimic actions help to combat eating disorders for individuals and societies; in contrast, non-action (which characterises some 'therapy' or 'support efforts') is not helpful.*
3 *Empowerment of those persons fighting anorexia and bulimia is helpful in combating eating disorders; such empowerment is supported by respect and by separation of the person and the problem.*
4. *Anorexia and bulimia can hold a person with the vice grip of an abusive partner; secrecy and shame can form the glue that adheres these problems.*
5. *Others (including those in 'helping professions') may worsen the problem; this often occurs when people confer certain knowledges about a person and constrain that person's identity and selfhood.*

When presenting the league ideas in a public forum, we are continually reminded of their social impact on therapeutic possibilities. It is from within the wisdom of these co-research projects that therapists can be moved (shoved) toward a reflexive accountability. We would argue that the weight of therapeutic accountability should privilege and be mediated through the knowledges of the once marginalised; not through a professionalised discourse.

Letter-Writing Campaigns

Letter-writing campaigns assist in the re-remembering of unique aspects of a client's life, now restrained by problem saturation. The campaigns are likened to a eulogy or an obituary made on behalf of the client while the client is still living. Members of the family and friends are asked to assist in a re-remembering process through written accounts that outline their memories of their relationship with the client separate from the problem's relationship with the client. The letters, by documenting alternative versions, counteract the infirming effects of the problem story. These accounts hold a tremendous potential for the restorying of persons' lives.

Nigel's Story

The psychiatry department of a local teaching hospital asked if I (SM) would 'see' Nigel, a sixty-year-old man. Nigel was described as 'very suicidal and depressed', and as a consequence had undergone over 40 electro-convulsive therapy 'treatments' over the previous year. I was informed that Nigel was at great risk of taking his own life, was unresponsive to 'talk' therapy, and they had done everything they could for him.

Nigel and his wife Rose had eight visits with me over the course of four months (on three of those meetings we were joined by a reflecting team). I learned from Nigel that he was having great difficulty remembering much of his life. The problem which he referred to as 'depression', had taken over his daily life from waking to retiring at night. Rose was of the opinion that the effects of the ECT had eroded Nigel's capacity for believing that he had accomplished anything in his lifetime. However, she was quick to inform me that Nigel was well respected by his five children and his community, which was located 300 miles north of Vancouver.

My thinking here was to reinvolve Nigel with the relationship context of his community from which 'depression' and 'suicidal thoughts' had separated him. It was out of this concern that Nigel, Rose, and I reached an agreement that 'depression was a strong foe' and that we needed to recruit an 'anti-depression team'. We collaborated on writing a letter to possible recruits, which Rose said she would be only too happy to distribute.

Dear friends of Nigel and Rose,

My name is Stephen Madigan and I am a Family Therapist working alongside Nigel and Rose. Nigel, as you may be aware, has unfortunately been taken over by depression, so much so that the depression has tried to convince Nigel to take his own life on several occasions. The depression tells Nigel that he is 'a worthless person', that he 'never accomplished anything of value', and that 'no-one ever liked him'. The depression is trying hard to make Nigel blind and deaf to all of his qualities, and wants him to turn away from all of the people who love and care about him. We are writing to ask you to draft a letter in support of Nigel and against the depression's version of him. Thank you for your help in this matter.

Yours in anti-depression, Nigel, Rose, and Stephen.

Within two weeks, Nigel was inundated with mail. One of the hospital staff on Nigel's ward said she thought he might have to get his own special mail delivery person. More than 100 letters and cards poured in. At first, Nigel modestly tucked the anti-depression notes away in his hospital night table, but before long, he felt able to put them on display all around his room. He then began to give 'anti-depression' consultations to interested staff and patients on the ward, by reading them his letters and lecturing on ideas of anti-depression.

Nigel is now free of depression and has on occasion offered consultation to therapists training with us in narrative ideas on 'how I went free of depression'.

Oscar's Story

A colleague referred seventy-year-old Oscar and his wife, Maxine, to me (SM). Oscar informed me that he had been struck down by a truck a year before. He was not supposed to live but he did; he was not supposed to come out of his three-month-long coma, but he did; it was predicted that he would never walk again, but he did, and so on. It didn't take me long to realise I was sitting before quite a remarkable man. However, it seemed that Oscar had paid dearly for his comeback, for now he had lost all confidence in himself and would panic if Maxine was not in attendance 'twenty-four hours a day'. Maxine had spent the year before organising the complicated task of Oscar's medical care and was at this time looking forward to getting back to her own business pursuits. Unfortunately, her interests were being pushed aside and taken over by the anxiety.

The anxiety that had been the legacy of Oscar's accident had him believing that 'I am only half a man', and further more 'Maxine will leave me for another man ... she is planning to put me in an old-age home'. And there was an odd twist in that it had him also believe 'I did not deserve a good life' and furthermore 'I should kill myself'. The anxiety was making him forget the life that he had lived prior to the accident and, like Nigel, he was becoming more and more isolated and depressed.

Oscar and Maxine had moved from England to Canada 10 years earlier. We all agreed that the anxiety was gaining on Oscar and that the situation was desperate. With this in mind we agree to design an international anti-anxiety letter-writing campaign. Below is the letter we co-authored in five minutes near the end of the third session. As Oscar was concerned that his friends might consider the letter 'a crazy idea', he insisted that I include my credentials to give it credence.

Dear Friends of Oscar,

My name is Stephen Madigan and I have a PhD in family therapy. Your friends Oscar and Maxine have asked me to write to you so that we might solicit

your support. As you are probably aware Oscar suffered a terrible accident 14 months ago, and has instituted a remarkable comeback. What you may not know is that the after-effects of the accident have left Oscar a captive of anxiety, and that it is currently bossing him around. We think you can help Oscar win back his life from this terrible anxiety. You may not believe this but one of the messages anxiety is giving to Oscar is that 'he is a good for nothing', that 'he is a useless human being', and that 'sooner rather than later all of his friends will come to know Oscar the way anxiety knows him'. Through anxiety's influence, Oscar is beginning to give up on himself, and we ask your support in bringing Oscar back from anxiety's grip. We hope that your letters of support are not too much to ask, and we want you to know that they will be greatly appreciated. Oscar would like you all to know that he will respond to all of your replies.
Warm regards, Stephen Madigan, PhD, Oscar's anti-anxiety consultant.

During the weeks that followed, Oscar would bring the campaign letters to my (SM) office, requesting that I read them out loud to him. I happily did so and my recitations were accompanied by Oscar's crying, laughing, and telling me of his 'good fortune'. You see, Oscar had affected the lives of many, many people and, not surprisingly, they welcomed the opportunity to reciprocate by writing to him. His anti-anxiety support team wrote from around the globe - Europe, the United Kingdom, and North America.

Oscar recently wrote to me (SM) from his long-awaited anti-anxiety trip to France with Maxine, which would mark 'my arrival at health'. He told me that he was sitting alone, drinking espresso, while Maxine had gone shopping for the day. He wrote, 'I am thanking my lucky stars that I am no longer a prisoner of anxiety'. His only problem now was keeping up with all of his return correspondence, but this was a problem for which he was willing to take full responsibility.

Without the recruitment of their community of concern, Nigel and Oscar might never have rebounded to re-remember all their personal qualities and the contributions they had made during their lifetimes, which their problems were 'insisting' they overlook and dis-remember.

Letter-writing campaigns are viewed as attempts to counter this dis-information and to inform both the client/family and their community of 'stories' of the person that are at odds with the problem-saturated story. Campaigns are viewed not only as ceremonies of redefinition (White 1995) but as protest and counter-struggles that undermine a problem-context-dominant story.

In the circumstances involving Nigel's life, there was a dominant professional story to overthrow, which inadvertently supported the 'life' of depression. Upon returning to his home community, the psychiatrist responsible for all of the ECT treatments contacted Nigel to resume treatment. Shortly thereafter, Nigel called to tell me (SM) 'that I have just given my psychiatrist his walking papers'. A short letter followed announcing he was depression-free.

Notes

1. First published 1995 in Friedman, S. (ed), *The Reflecting Team in Action: Collaborative practice in family therapy*, pp.257-276. Co-authored by Stephen Madigan & David Epston. New York: Guilford Publications. Republished here with permission.
2. For further reading in relation to narrative approaches to so-called anorexia/bulimia see: Zimmerman & Dickerson (1994); Madigan & Goldner (1998); and *Anti-anorexia/Anti-bulimia: Archives of Resistance* which Rick Maisel, David Epston and others are currently preparing for W.W.Norton (New York) - we are hoping it will be released by mid-1999.

References

Andersen, T. 1987: 'The reflecting team: Dialogue and meta-dialogue in clinical work.' *Family Process*, 26(4):415-428.

Bakhtin, M.M. 1986: *Speech Genres and Other Late Essays* (V. McGee, Trans). Austin: University of Texas Press.

Elliott, H. 1994: 'Decentring the subject.' Paper presented at the 2nd Annual Narrative Ideas and Therapeutic Practice Conference, Vancouver, BC, Canada.

Epston, D. & White, M. 1992: 'Consulting your consultants: The documentation of alternative knowledges.' In Epston, D. & White, M., *Experience, Contradiction, Narrative & Imagination*. Adelaide: Dulwich Centre Publications. (Previously published in the 1990 No.2 *Dulwich Centre Newsletter*.)

Foucault, M. 1979: *Discipline and Punish: The birth of the prison*. Middlesex, England: Peregrine Books.

Foucault, M. 1980: *Power/knowledge: Selected interviews and other writings*. New York: Pantheon Books.

Foucault, M. 1982: 'The subject and power.' In Dreyfus, H. & Rabinow, P. (eds), *Michel Foucault: Beyond*. Chicago: University of Chicago Press.

Foucault, M. 1984: *The History of Sexuality*. New York: Pantheon Books.

Law, I. & Madigan, S. 1994: 'Power and politics in practice.' *Dulwich Centre Newsletter*, Winter, pp.3-7.

Lax, W. 1991: 'The reflecting team and initial consultation.' In Andersen, T. (ed), *The*

Reflecting Team: Dialogues and dialogues about the dialogues, pp.127-142. New York: Norton.

Madigan, S. 1991a: 'Voices of demystification: Questions as performative texts in therapeutic discourse and practice; a post-structural analysis.' Unpublished dissertation.

Madigan, S. 1991b: 'Discursive restraints in therapist practice.' *Dulwich Centre Newsletter,* Autumn (special issue).

Madigan, S. 1992a: 'Questions about questions: Situating the therapist's curiosity in front of the family.' In Gilligan, S. & Reese, P. (eds), *Therapeutic Conversations.* New York: Norton.

Madigan, S. 1992b: 'The application of Michel Foucault's philosophy in the problem externalizing discourse of Michael White.' *Journal of Family Therapy,* 14(3):265-279.

Madigan, S. 1996: 'Undermining the problem in the privatization of problems in persons: Considering the socio-political and cultural context in the externalizing of internalized problem conversations.' *Journal of Systemic Therapies.*

Madigan, S. & Goldner, E. 1998: 'A narrative approach to anorexia: Discourse, reflexivity and questions.' In Hoyt, M. (ed), *Handbook of Constructive Therapies.* San Francisco: Jossey-Bass.

Myerhoff, B. 1982: 'Life history among the elderly; performance, visibility and remembering.' In Ruby, J. (ed), *A Crack in the Mirror: Reflexive perspectives in anthropology.* Philadelphia: University of Pennsylvania Press.

Roth, S. & Epston, D. (in press): 'Developing externalizing conversations: An introductory exercise.' *Journal of Systemic Therapies.*

Sampson, E. 1989: 'The deconstruction of the self.' In Shotter, J. & Gergen, K. (eds), *Texts of Identity,* pp.3-11. Newbury Park, CA: Sage.

Shotter, J. & Gergen, K. 1989: *Texts of Identity.* Newbury Park, CA: Sage.

Shotter, J. 1990: 'The social construction of remembering and forgetting.' In Middleton, D. & Edwards, D. (eds), *Collective Remembering.* London: Sage.

Waldegrave, C. 1990: 'Just therapy.' *Dulwich Centre Newsletter*, 1:6-46.

White, M. 1995: *Re-authoring Lives: Interviews and essays.* Adelaide: Dulwich Centre Publications.

White, M. & Epston, D. 1990: *Narrative Means to Therapeutic Ends.* New York: Norton. (Also published as *Literate Means to Therapeutic Ends*, 1989, Adelaide: Dulwich Centre Publications.)

Yeatman, A. 1994: *Postmodern Revisionings of the Political.* New York: Routledge.

Young, J. 1989: 'A critical look at the one-way screen.' *Dulwich Centre Newsletter,* Summer, pp.5-11.

Zimmerman, J.L. & Dickerson, V.C. 1994: 'Tales of the body thief: Externalizing and deconstructing eating problems.' In Hoyt, M. (ed), *Constructive Therapies,* pp.295-318. New York: Guilford.

12

A Narrative Approach to so-called Anorexia/Bulimia[1]

co-authored by
David Epston [2], *Fran Morris* [3], *Rick Maisel* [4]

This paper is written in the memory of Ellen West:

> *I don't understand myself at all. It is terrible not to understand yourself.* I confront myself as a strange person. *I am afraid of myself; I am afraid of the feeling to which I am defencelessly delivered over every minute. This is the horrible part of my life: it is filled with dread. Existence is only torture ... Life has become a prison camp ... I long to be violated ... and indeed I do violence to myself every hour.* (Binswanger 1958 - emphasis added by Binswanger).

I (DE) have been using a narrative perspective in my work for the past eight years. This framework derives from a collaboration with Michael White. The practices I will be presenting in this paper have emerged over time through our working, talking, and teaching together (Epston 1989; Epston et al. 1992; Epston & White 1992; White 1989; White & Epston 1990). Since 1986, I have become passionately committed to better understand and assist those persons oppressed by so-called anorexia/bulimia. What prompted me, amongst other concerns, was my dawning realisation of the ways by which the objectifying practices of weighing, assessing, and measuring of women associated with the discourses of psychology and psychiatry could very well co-produce what is referred to as anorexia/bulimia in those very persons oppressed by anorexia/bulimia (Tavris 1992).

In October, 1986, Svetlana Ripon wrote me a letter which incited my concern. Her letter became one of the first inquiries on which the Anti-Anorexia/Bulimia League collaborated. It led to a day-long workshop entitled 'The Co-Production of Anorexia/Bulimia versus The Co-Production of Anti-Anorexia/Bulimia'.[5] The presenters were seven members of the Anti-Anorexia/Bulimia League, aged 16-51. I was one of them. I continue to serve in the capacity of archivist/anthologist of The League. This League is not a support group in the conventional sense of the word. It invented itself as an underground resistance movement. Tomm (1992) referred to The League as 'a community of counter-practice'.

Steps in the Process of Getting Free of Anorexia/Bulimia

The first step in getting free from anorexia/bulimia typically begins when a person becomes more fully aware of the physical, emotional, spiritual, and relationship costs of an allegiance to an anorexic/bulimic lifestyle. This 'disenchantment' has often been foreshadowed by a feeling of losing control over, or being controlled further by, anorexia/bulimia. These persons have come to realise that the proverbial tail is now wagging the dog and that anorexia/bulimia has usurped their lives and occupied their minds. People often report that their lives have become almost unendurable. At this juncture, people feel required to choose between self-execution (through starvation to death or by other means) or a commitment to the repudiation of, and the opposition to, anorexia/bulimia. Several anti-anorexic/bulimic practices support their efforts to break the spell of anorexia/bulimia.

Breaking the Spell of Anorexia/Bulimia

1. Engage person(s) in an externalising conversation about anorexia/ bulimia.

By speaking about anorexia/bulimia as something separate from and external to persons, linguistic space is opened for persons to engage in their own assessment and evaluation of anorexia's 'Rules of the concentration camp', its 'voice'[6] and the practices of self and relationship it requires, e.g., exile and isolation, self-surveillance, self-hatred, self-punishment/torture/ execution, etc. Externalising anorexia/bulimia also undermines guilt and self-blame and replaces them with 'anorexia-blame'. It challenges totalising descriptions of the person as anorexic/bulimic. It provides a landscape in which to identify current or historical acts of resistance to the dictates of anorexia/bulimia and, thereby, recognise the real possibility of furthering that opposition in the present and future (Allen 1993; Epston 1993; Madigan 1992; Tomm 1989; White 1984; White & Epston 1990).

Julie, aged thirty, commented in a recent meeting (7/15/93):

> *If I hadn't objectified anorexia (bulimia), I'd feel scared and I'd soon be bingeing. I'd have no choice. The most I could ever have done in my life is what they told me at the hospital. It was to phone someone up for them to rescue me. But I'd say to them at the hospital: 'I don't want to phone anyone; I want to eat and be sick'. They would say: 'You just have to try harder!' I'd say in reply, 'If I could phone someone up, I wouldn't be in the situation I'm in'. They were conflating my identity with the voice of anorexia and giving it (the voice of anorexia) a platform in therapy to speak itself. If speech is like an act and I was isolated, I would go into those hospital offices and speak 'anorexia' for an hour and would not have put myself forward in speech anywhere else that week. That happened for years ...*
>
> *Now when I recognise the voice, saying things like 'You've left it so late in life to get your act together ... you might as well give up because you are so old now ... there's just no point ... you are never going to find anyone to love ...' instead of just feeling victimised by it, believing that IT is me, I think: 'That's anorexia!' If I can get through this five minutes of it trying to tear me down, I will be all right, even though the voice of anorexia is compelling and horrible. I have this unshakeable faith that it is really not that powerful. It is anorexia thinking ... that's all.*

2. Provide ready access to the archives of the Anti-Anorexia/Bulimia League

Initially, persons in the thrall of anorexia/bulimia will have difficulty recognising the destructive and lethal practices of self and relationship that anorexia/bulimia demands of them, even after prolonged or repeated hospitalisations and tube feedings. These persons are offered ready access to the archives of The League. They are invited to hear and/or read anorexic/bulimic accounts and how such persons 'unmasked' anorexia's purposes/intentions, betrayals and lies. The significance of the archival material cannot be over-stated. These 'readings' replace the well-known pathologising practices of assessment interviews.

Excerpted from an interview with Rhonda, aged nineteen (5/8/90):

D: *You were just reflecting on Sarah's comments about how when I asked her some sort of diagnostic, assessment-type questions, she immediately said: 'I'm shrinking inside'. You have some comments about that?*

R: *Absolutely typical feeling. I've been to eight other therapists before and the questions they ask, they put you ... I feel like I fly back in the chair, into the corner and just sort of sit there and tense up. It's horrible!*

Unlike conventional pathologising stories regarding persons' lives, these conversations, stories, that are in the archive are plotted around 'liberation', 'resistance', and 'oppression'. These stories, which can be conveyed through writing, or stored on audiotape or videotape, begin to provide an alternative vocabulary which is a prerequisite for any sense of oppression and any notion of resistance. These stories make available some hope for an anti-anorexic/bulimic future. As Julie has said, 'In a way, the first time I, self consciously, took the side of outrage, or perhaps self-consciously did anything at all, was when I listened to the tapes and in some way anorexia was exposed'

3. Offer metaphorical descriptions of the 'regime' of anorexia/bulimia

Metaphorical descriptions, (e.g., 'the concentration camp of anorexia/ bulimia', 'living death', 'being on death row', etc.) can help persons 'unmask' or see through the ways anorexia/bulimia operates on people's lives, inviting associations which can enliven and enrich these descriptions. Persons can be invited to assess the extent to which such descriptions match or capture their experience of anorexia/bulimia in their lives. Persons are encouraged to invent metaphorical descriptions of their own. A high value is placed on the production of anti-anorexic/bulimic discursive practices and any novelties are hastily added to the anti-anorexic lexicon. In an anti-anorexic/bulimic therapy, persons are not a product of language but instead produce what W. Halliday refers to as an 'anti-language', the primary purpose of which is to subvert medical and lay discourses on anorexia with a new vocabulary, and new language forms (Halliday, 1978). Language is politicised. The stripped down language of objectivity which holds these persons prisoner in an anorexia 'talk', a talk that minimises, restrains, restricts, undermines, and diminishes, is replaced by the 'play' of a lush, extravagant and polysemic language. The 'play' involves the unpacking of the implications of the metaphors on their experience of anorexia/bulimia in their lives in particular, and women's lives in general.

4. Encourage the personification of anorexia/bulimia

Personifying anorexia/bulimia allows for the attribution of intentions (for example, 'Does anorexia intend to have you sign your own death warrant?'), beliefs (for example, 'Does anorexia believe you are worthless?'), or practices (for example, 'Has he turned you against yourself by talking you into self-blame and self-torture?').

The following questions were directed to Bridget, aged fifteen, in the company of her older cousin and her partner, in order to personify anorexia/bulimia. Just prior to the meeting, Bridget and her caretakers had been warned by her medical adviser that she could very likely perish at any moment.

D: *I think you have to understand its motives, its purposes. Why do you think it would do this, would hurt people and make them think they were happy to die with an anorexic smile on their face? What lethal practices does it use to confound you, to confuse you? Now you're on death row, but somehow anorexia's keeping it from you, and the more it keeps it from you, the more likely it will kill you.*

B: *Well, I feel physically fine.*

D: *How does it do that? How do you think it confuses you? How do you think it tells you you're feeling fine when you're on the point of death? ... Most people, when they are near death know they're being murdered or dying, right? How's anorexia doing this to you? ... Why does it say to you that you are feeling good? Why does it do this? Why does it want to murder you? Why doesn't it want you to protest? Why doesn't it want you to put up any resistance? Why does it want you to go to your death like a sheep?*

Turning Against Anorexia/Bulimia

5. Identify the cognitive, affective, interpersonal and behavioural components of anorexia/bulimia

Once the person can break the spell of anorexia/bulimia, it becomes possible to identify and defy the requirements of anorexia/bulimia. Compliance with the demands of anorexia/bulimia often include the requirements:

a. to work the body to exhaustion, typically between 15-18 hours per day,
b. to engage in mindless, compulsive rituals often involving cleaning, folding, menu preparation, etc.,
c. to attend exclusively to the needs and feelings of others without a thought for oneself,
d. to reject loving relationships, including those with family members in favour of isolation/exile or relationships which promote their servitude and degradation,
e. to reject pleasure and the satisfaction of any desire,
f. to measure every action against the 'curse of the idea of perfection' and continually fail, and
g. to subject themselves to severe self-blame and self-punishments, to vilifications such as 'ugly', 'worthless', 'useless', 'trash', etc., or to mortifications and mutilations of the body.

As the person defies the tyrannical dictates of the anorexic/bulimic 'deathstyle', she begins to call into question the anorexic/bulimic threats that had previously compelled her to acquiesce. Defiance and repudiation can take place in any of those areas of a person's life over which it has been established that anorexia/bulimia had extended its influence. The following are examples:

When I first saw you, I only knew it as saying to me the moment I put food in

> *my mouth that I was bad and deserved to be punished.* (Julie)
>
> *Anorexia has left me to a certain extent with eyes - in that I can see her and her 'ridiculousness' - but she has her anorexic hand gripped so tightly around my heart and won't let go ... Anorexia demands allegiance through a ceaseless taxing of your flesh, energy, and self-love. She is a cruel, merciless, vindictive bitch.* (Rebecca)

During this stage, people often report connecting with feelings, appetites, and desires that anorexia/bulimia had anaesthetised. They report moving in the direction of self-acceptance and away from self-denial and self-punishment.

Once the thinking and doing of anorexia/bulimia have been identified, these can be contrasted with their anti-anorexic/bulimic counterparts. The person is faced with the dilemma of living through two alternative stories: an anorexic/bulimic story with its associated sub-plots (self-hatred, unworthiness, perfectionism), lines of action (living for others, self-recrimination, self-denial, self-starvation, physical torture, mindless rituals) and outcome (death), or an anti-anorexic/bulimic story with its associated subplots (worthiness, self-appreciation, being a pleasure to oneself and allowing oneself pleasures), lines of action (self-nurturance, assertion, mutual relationships) and outcome (freedom, creativity, happiness, and compassion). These distinctions emerge from the play of what Tomm (1991) refers to as 'bifurcative questions'. Here are some examples, excerpted from a therapeutic letter I (DE) wrote.

> *You informed me you refused to go along with anorexia's 'command', even though it attempted to blame you for everything. How was it possible at this particular point for you to be so disobedient and defiant of anorexia? How were you able to trust in your thoughts, ideas, opinions, etc.? Do you think this was something of a milestone in your struggle with anorexia? Does it tell you that you are making some headway? Can you see a future for yourself up ahead and is that future a 'concentration camp' or your freedom? If you were to attend to your own pleasures, appetites, desires, thoughts, ideas, etc., how do you think you might develop differently? What would an anti-anorexic personal development look like to you? Feel like for you? Be like for you?*

6. Deconstruct anorexia/bulimia

The commands and dictates that lie behind anorexia/bulimia can be 'unpacked' and brought forward for inquiry and contest. The outcome of this can be referred to as 'seeing the light', 'unmasking anorexia', 'exposing anorexia', 'undoing anorexia's ruse', etc. The taken-for-granted realities and practices of anorexia/bulimia can be further subverted by situating them in cultural, historical and gender contexts. Persons can be invited to reflect on how they became recruited into anorexic/bulimic realities and practices. Through this deconstructive process, anorexic 'truths' become far less compelling, and persons are far more able to entertain anti-anorexic/bulimic realities and alternative modes of relating to self and others. The following is excerpted from a letter to Rosemarie, aged twenty-three (3/5/92):

> *When I inquired if you had UNMASKED anorexia, you told a remarkable unmasking story. But before you did, you made me realise that unmasking anorexia 'is crucial ... it's the crux of the matter.' Permit me to re-tell your story: 'I had had a fight with my parents. The fight heralded several pro-anorexic days. Because straight after a fight, I can't eat. It's like a button being pushed. I was tremendously upset and decided to hide down by the pool in the back yard. I then saw this ugliness that scared me witless but at the same time, I was able to face it. I really identified it as an evil spirit. I felt its grip ... its bite. We were locked in combat for between a quarter and a half hour. It started with panic and guilt over what I had eaten over the day. Physically, I was feeling sick. I felt a gut dread ... an unfocused dread. But then for the first time, I was able to see anorexia as an influence I had placed my trust in. I saw for the first time its true face. I had never seen anything so hideous. It's a monster ... black with indistinct features. It was more an emotional concept - MY TORTURE! It did manifest itself as a force of being ... an evil power. I got the feeling I could oppose it. I struggled with it in hand to hand combat. I prayed to strengthen my resolve. I won that fight but it wasn't a fight that was all mine.'*

7. Attend to anti-anorexic/bulimic thoughts, feelings, and actions with both curiosity and enthusiasm

When persons have anti-anorexic/bulimic thoughts, feelings and actions they can be understood as 'unique outcomes' (White & Epston 1990, pp.55-63). Persons can be helped to perceive the significance of these 'unique outcomes' by inquiries relating to (1) how they were able to achieve them, (2) the implications of these events in their fight against anorexia/bulimia, (3) what this says about them as persons (e.g., their intentions, values, beliefs, personal qualities, etc.), and (4) how an alternative future could become possible through these developments. At the same time, anti-anorexic/bulimic knowledges, actions, slogans are documented and added to the archive of The League or circulated through The League for commentaries.

Reclaiming a Life and Making an Appearance in it

8. Attend to person's identification and expression of previously obscured thoughts and feelings deemed by them to be descriptive of their subjectivity (personhood)

Anorexia/bulimia encourages people to become invisible to self and others, physically and emotionally. When people turn against and refuse to engage in anorexic/bulimic practices, previously forbidden emotions such as anger, dependency, and vulnerability return. Persons must cope with anorexia-influenced fears that these feelings and desires will prove to be overwhelming or burdensome for others or will provoke rejection or attack. This has to do with the person substantiating herself *as a person* rather than as an insubstantial bodily object. Associated with this is the recognition of and entitlement to feelings, appetites, desires, opinions and thoughts. This will obviously impact upon not only what they consider they deserve, but even what they require in a relationship. Often existing relationships are subjected to very severe challenges and many of these are either ended, deferred, or revised. These relationships are now eligible for redescription as abusive, one-sided ('all take and no give'), degrading, master-pet, etc. Distinctions can be drawn around an anorexic and an anti-anorexic relationship: What would each entail and how would each party to either experience it? Hope for liberation is deepened and people start reclaiming their future visions and dreams, although there is often considerable grief for what has been lost. So-called relapses are now viewed as the inevitable cost of fighting for one's life. These times can be utilised as opportunities for reviewing strategies and renewing anti-anorexic/bulimic offensives. They are no longer cause for despair. The therapist might even respond to such events with relish rather than disappointment or concern.

D: *Do you think there is such a concept as 'anti-anorexic/bulimic daughter-father' relationships?*

J: *I think there is such a thing as an anti-anorexic father-daughter relationship. I think such a father would instil, somehow or other, a sense of self-worth in his daughter and treat her as a valid individual with legitimate thoughts and feelings of her own ... With my father, I often feel I am not really there or that he is unable to recognise and acknowledge what is important in my life ... I agree with Lee (a member of The League) saying that anti-anorexic father-daughter relationships would be equal ones. My father was always domineering over my mother. He was never wrong in a disagreement nor would he even accept that there could be another point of view. I definitely believe that if I felt a sense of impact or effectiveness and felt I really existed, anorexia's grip on me would be greatly weakened or perhaps never have got hold of me in the first place.* (Jane, aged twenty-two)

The person's increasing capacity to identify and tolerate strong feelings (both positive and negative) in the present can be compared to anorexia/bulimia's refusal to allow this in the anorexic/bulimic 'past', however recent. The therapist should attend to persons' developing capacity to believe in their feelings, desires, thoughts, opinions, etc., or to 'know one's heart and mind', 'connect heart and body' as significant moments in opposing anorexia/bulimia (e.g., 'Do you think if you make more room for you in your life, there will be less room for anorexia in it?'). Space should be made in the therapy for the elaboration of these 'self-discoveries' (e.g., 'What are you learning about the nature of your pleasures that anorexia previously had forbidden you to experience?' 'When you told anorexia to 'shut up' and instead you listened to your own voice, what did you say to yourself about the delight and satisfaction you provided for yourself eating that peach?'). This fosters a sense of progression and renewed hope.

9. Searching for the foundations of current anti-anorexic/bulimic capacities in the person's recent and distant past

By establishing a 'history' of the qualities, attributes, and 'know-how' which underlie the current anti-anorexic/bulimic achievements, these aspects of the person can be integrated into an alternative story of strength, power, blameless innocence in protest of evil, etc., and liberation from that evil. This alternative narrative or story recognises and validates these qualities, attributes, and knowledges, reinforcing the likelihood of their endurance and performance.

10. Externalise anorexia-encouraged fears of interpersonal rejection or attack in response to self-expression and assertion

Positive responses from others (including the therapist) to persons' self-expression and assertion (e.g., responses that contradict the dominant story about relationships) can provide a basis for challenging impoverishing views of relationship. Persons can be invited to evaluate relationships from an anti-anorexic/bulimic perspective (e.g., 'What do you imagine your sister would say if we asked her if she found you more companionable when there was less of you in anorexic times, or now that there is more of you as a person?' 'Now that you have decided to take a stand for your rights, do you feel that people are still treating you like a dog - as you described it - or more like a person? Which is your preference, now that you have had a taste of both relationship styles?').

Post-Liberation

By this time the person has a secure, self-embracing anti-anorexic life-style and has clearly separated herself from anorexia/bulimia, although the anorexic/bulimic voice can still be heard. There is no requirement whatsoever for a *perfect* anti-anorexia/bulimia; if anything, imperfection becomes almost an article of anti-anorexic/bulimic faith. Kati (aged thirty-two), for example, when asked to develop an anti-bulimic measure of anti-bulimia came up with the following: 'You vomit whenever you feel like it without feeling guilty' and laughed. Great emphasis is placed on caring for oneself physically and emotionally, learning about one's desires, appetites, etc., and coming to respect and believe in one's own thoughts and opinions. Concern for the ways and means that persons start expressing themselves and their abilities is high. The therapist is unrestrained in the pleasure s/he takes in the pleasure the person is taking in herself and the world around her. Out of context, many of these first events would seem trivial, for instance, 'the first pleasure bath', or 'the first cup of coffee in which you didn't feel required to serve everyone else first and yourself last', but they are surely not. Self-appreciation now replaces self-hatred/torture, etc., and much of that can be attributed to the defeat of anorexia/bulimia.

11. Invite the person to elaborate their story of struggle against and liberation from anorexia/bulimia and circulate this story to a wider audience

The elaboration and writing up (or any other means of documentation) can be accomplished through interviews in which the person is invited to serve as an anti-anorexic/bulimic consultant to other persons resisting anorexia/bulimia in their lives. Family members, friends, and other significant persons can be provided with the same accounts of this new narrative for their reference. This often heals many of the breaches of relationships that anorexia/bulimia fostered through either the person's feelings of unworthiness as a friend/relative, etc., or the frustration and irritation others felt watching helplessly as the person perished in front of their eyes.

12. Ritually celebrate the person's 'liberation' from anorexia/bulimia

A celebration can be used ritually to mark a person's arrival at a new status in life, and to further authenticate their new social identity. Much use is made of the 'consulting your consultants' protocol described in Epston & White (1992). Another ritual is the 'handing over' ceremony in which an anti-anorexic veteran is invited to join us and present the incumbent with The Anti-Anorexic/Bulimic League T-shirt. The recipient is asked to remember all those women executed by anorexia, all those languishing in the private 'concentration camps' throughout the Western world, and is requested to walk forward into her own 'freedom' and if it suits her, to speak out against anorexia/bulimia and all those beliefs and social practices that support it. The mood is lightened when the League's logo is revealed to them on the front of the T-shirt: A circle inside of which is the word DIET with a slash bisecting the 'T'.

From the Archive of the Anti-Anorexia/Bulimia League Correspondence *between* Fran Morris & David Epston

The following is a partial record of an anti-anorexic/bulimic therapy in the form of letters, authored by DE and authorised by FM. Fran referred herself, having had DE recommended by her sister. At the time of our first meeting, she was considering self-execution, given how she had experienced and was experiencing her life as unendurable punishment and torture. The letters record meetings that were held on 4/29/92, 5/22/92, 6/8/92, 7/13/92 and 8/13/92. *(Note from Kathy Weingarten, editor of the Special Volume [see Notes 1 and 2 at the end of this paper]: Unfortunately, because of space limitations, it has not been possible to publish the entire correspondence. David Epston has generously consented to allow a portion of the correspondence to be published although we both feel that this does violence to the integrity of the work that he and Fran did together. However, I felt it was important to make the work available to readers of this book.)*

With explicit consent, written notes are zealously taken throughout each meeting. I favour verbatim recording so that the person's voice can stand on its own in the letters (White & Epston 1990). Letters are written up immediately after a session and sent to clients along with copies of any audiotapes made of the sessions. Fran Morris, when interviewed about her judgement as to the part the letters played in her liberation, deemed the letters to have been 90% responsible.

It is the co-authors' decision to allow these documents to stand on their own and for themselves without being framed by professional discourses which analyse them.

4/29/92

Dear Fran,

You reassured me that 'I want to fight for my right as a human being and woman to be!' You said you were seeing 'liberation' from the 'concentration camp' of anorexia/bulimia where you were put, without trial, in 1969. Even if you had murdered two or three people, you would have done your time by now and be walking the streets as a free person. Why is it that your human rights have been abrogated? Why have you been imprisoned? Are these questions you are willing to entertain? Is your freedom something you believe you are entitled to? More importantly, why is the 'concentration camp' of anorexia invisible to its inmates and to the wider community? Do you wish to join The League in its mission to make 'visible' the 'camp' along with that 'power' that set it up in the first place? But first things first!

The League is interested and concerned about the latter because you have survived anorexia longer than anyone we know. For that reason, we accord you a special respect and sympathy. Anorexia has not been able to kill you off and despite it, you have been able to make something of a life for yourself. Svetlana referred to it as 'a small death': others a 'living death', but you seemed very much alive. It got me wondering how you have been able to keep something of yourself from its grip. And by no means has it turned you mindless or 'zombie-like' as Jacky described it.

From an anti-anorexia point of view, I gave considerable significance to your comments: 'Also it's only recently that I've even begun to feel what things I do want to do; and what my needs are. I didn't know I had needs until three years ago. Or I knew I had needs but I didn't know what those needs were, let alone know how to ask for them to be met. I was a doormat!'

Now this was particularly relevant, given your description of your training as the dutiful, eldest daughter with an even more dutiful mother, burdened by six children and a workaholic/alcoholic doctor-husband. And you had all been deracinated from your home country. You told me you had no choice but to take up the 'good girl' role by your mother's 'right hand'. At times, you felt the mother to your mother at the same time as being trained to serve men and ask nothing of them. You summed it up: 'Don't bother Daddy!' and 'Be a doormat!' As you said, you set to work in your life being 'all out for everyone else'. And you followed in your mother's footsteps here as 'she did everything for everybody else'.

Is it any wonder, you and everyone else overlooked you? Did you sense your mother's despair and longing, something she wasn't allowed to express, (even to herself)? She was to do her duty as a doctor's wife. How do you think your father conceived his duties to his wife? Was she expected to soldier on as if she didn't have any needs or desires or appetites of her own? Did your father expect himself to deprive himself of his desires and appetites or did he satisfy them in his own ways? It seems inevitable, given your circumstances, that you might conclude: 'I didn't want my mother to have all this problem ... I wanted to ease her load'. Did you feel required to take her burdens onto your own young girl's shoulders? Is that where you got your education in 'subservience', 'self-denial', and 'selflessness?' Feed the men and starve yourself!

How do you imagine anorexia was stalking you as you were growing up? Looking back, do you think you were living in its shadow, before it really darkened your life? Am I right in thinking that you have four sisters and anorexia has only claimed the lives of two of you? Or better put, half of your sisterhood? How did your other two sisters escape? Would you be even willing to wonder how they made their escape? Do you think this therapy might engage them in its inquiry? What would be the most pertinent questions to help them remember the information that might guide you out of this hell on earth? And if your sisterhood becomes avowedly anti-anorexic, what contribution could that make to bringing your other sister out of the 'concentration camp' that she, according to you, remains blind to?

Fran, did your anti-anorexia commence when you refused your recruitment into the 'perfect wife and mother' role and started making demands on your husband of fifteen years? Fran, there must have been some preparation for this action. It just could not come out of the blue.

What were the foundations for your anti-anorexia? What paved the way for it? Could you go back and trace the history of this resistance? How would that history be different from the history of anorexia in your life? Which history would you prefer to associate yourself with? And might you consider on behalf of yourself and others in The League who will come after you to write it up, all the better to appreciate it and see if it predicts any more initiatives on your part? If you look back and see where you have come from, it often guides you in your next steps. That is my experience and that of many others in The League ...

Fran, I know I don't know you well but I have met other women on 'death row'. I believe that you are further along the way than you can appreciate because you have had no one to share that experience with, no 'map' to tell you where you are and how far you have come. If I am any judge you are more than half way. By saying this, I in no way want you to think I am diminishing your suffering, oppression, and torture. It is just my considered opinion, having watched many liberations over the past seven years, that you are doing well! However, there is an anorexic ruse that could betray your progress. Let me inform you what it is. Anorexia's last ruse is to accuse you that you are not doing anti-anorexia perfectly or 'good enough' It might then tell you: 'So you might as well give up and return to my loving but lethal embrace'. It might also attempt to convince you that you are not perfect enough for anti-anorexia, or that anti-anorexia is too good for you. There are probably some others it will try on you, so BEWARE!

I very much look forward to reviewing the above with you at our next meeting. I enjoyed making your anti-anorexic acquaintance.
Yours anti-anorexically, David.

5/22/92

I rang Fran several times before our next meeting on the 5/22/92 to reassure myself of her well-being. She informed me that she was 'hanging on!' At our next session we were joined by a 'reflecting team' (Andersen 1987), hastily recruited from all those attending an Advanced Intensive Training Program/Seminar. The impact of their reflections, according to Fran, was so profound that she demanded a written version of their comments.

6/8/92

Dear Fran,

What an anti-anorexic day today was! There was so much you had to tell me and I don't feel the following really will do justice to the joy you radiated. You informed me that there was an 'embryonic feeling of being free ... now I feel I want to not binge and throw up and I want a normal course of living'. You said that this was related to what you described as 'a shift inside of me' and that shift was following from your decision that you had a right 'to be on the planet', 'get real and honest', and that 'anorexia just had to get out of my life'. You had seen through anorexia too, alleging it to be 'a form of deception'.

Then we got to wondering how you had construed as a little girl that you were to be held responsible for your mother's weight gain following your birth. And how by holding yourself responsible as the guilty party, guilt coached anorexia in your life! This must have been a burdensome thought, knowing how weighed down by life your mother already was. Your mother's weight gain had to do with her pregnancy with you which added 28 pounds to her weight. You came to believe, in a young girl's way, that 'I destroyed her self image by making her fat'. No wonder, 'I hated seeing her tired ... I took on so much ... I wanted to give her some relief'. But, in fact, guilt started to operate in your life and 'I felt guilty I couldn't do more'. You thought you might have, quite unconsciously, even exceeded your mother in terms of giving. At times, you even took up the role of 'acting mother' and acknowledged that 'it was difficult to give up the reins'.

If your mother realised that guilt supported anorexia and that you felt guilt for having made her fat, do you think she would require you to do penance or do you think she would say such guilt was unnecessary and unwarranted? Do you think your mother would subscribe to anorexia's torture, punishment, and near execution of you for this selfsame 'guilt?' What do you think the connection between this guilt and perfection is?

Still, as you put it, 'I reached a point where I can't take it anymore'. And, in fact, you came to the conclusion, moreover, that 'I didn't want to do it any more ... I'm bored with it'. You informed me that 'it (anorexia) makes everything into a ritual and an obsession that has to be done 150% perfectly'. Previously, you had 'acquiesced' to anorexia but today you came up with an anti-anorexic slogan: 'ACQUIESCENCE IS TO ALLOW ANOREXIA TO ANNIHILATE YOU'. When I inquired as to how you had been so defiant to and subversive of anorexia, you came up with some striking examples of your anti-anorexia. You had been deliberately doing different behaviours, like not going for a swim, not allowing anorexia to coerce you into exercise, and, in fact, are starting to believe that your 'life is free'.

You are now, according to you, 75% free of anorexia and all that that entails. You are feeling a 'new energy ... my own soul energy' and no longer in the grip of the 'black spectre'. You were of the opinion that 'anorexia has held my self away from me' and had the effect of divorcing you from your very own self. You have opposed this divorce by reuniting mind, body, soul as a woman-person.

You informed me that 'I am staying a lot more in the present moment and just enjoying being with no strings attached, no guilt, just freedom'. Fran, did you cut the strings on guilt? How did guilt keep you from your life up until the point at which you severed your connection with it? Did your mother saying you weren't to blame have anything to do with this? Did turning 40 and knowing that you had martyred half of your life have anything to do with it? Do you think you were entitled to the second half? You now are finding that 'my energy is coming from inside out' rather than being tyrannised by anorexia. Does this suggest to you that there is more of you on the inside and that you are no longer so vulnerable to the surveillance and tyranny of anorexia?

Fran, beware of anorexia's last ditch stand. If other accounts from those who have liberated themselves are anything to go on, prepare yourself for some desperate moves to undo your anti-anorexia by telling you that you aren't good enough at it, it's too good for you, or you are unworthy of anti-anorexia, and the only course you have open to you is anorexia's 'fatal embrace'.

As spokesperson for the Anti-Anorexia League, I invite you to your freedom and you are most welcome to join us. When you do, it will have a special significance for us because you have suffered longer than any of us. For that fact alone, you are especially welcome.

I look forward to reviewing your anti-anorexia at 3.00 p.m., the 16th of July.

Yours anti-anorexically, David.

7/13/92

Dear Fran,

In my absence, anorexia seemed to have departed your body, admittedly, in a very strange way. I am wondering if this didn't have a lot to do with your making the connection between 'guilt' and 'perfection'. 'Because I felt so guilty, I had to make it up by doing everything 150% perfectly'. You thought that this realisation has assisted you in your unmasking of anorexia, even though as you put it, 'I'm still in the middle of it'. Fran, you may be in the middle but you are no longer muddled. In fact, you say that some clarity 'has come about through a very strong glimmer of light' into the darkness of a life lived according to the requirements of anorexia. You concluded that you 'can now separate anorexia from me'. When I asked what you imagine would have become of you if you hadn't done so, you replied: 'If not, I wouldn't have been here' and anorexia would have claimed another woman-victim. You realised too that you had grown up 'full of worry and fear of not being good enough'. Still separating yourself from anorexia 'was more of a feeling rather than being able to put it into words'. But you thought that 'getting to have a close connection with a Divine source' was another. You considered a 'political focus' was a third possibility. You summarised: 'I have chosen to carry a legacy of what women have been left with and are doing about it'. You realised that you now have a mission of your own: 'to free myself as well as others'.

When I inquired as to some of the sources of these developments, you thought that the question: 'HOW COULD I HAVE CAUSED IT ALL?' was crucial to your calling guilt into question rather than trying to satisfy its requirements of you to lay down your life to it. In fact, you thought of late you were 'pretty free of guilt' even though its legacy is still with you in the practices that it has encouraged you to do all your life: for example, 'apologising all the time to the point of apologising for my existence', 'minimising and putting myself down' and 'people-pleasing'.

You provided me with some evidence of that in the incident with your employer and how you were able to assert yourself so as to be able to attend this appointment. You had to admit this was certainly a 'break-through'. You realised too that 'I am enjoying being with myself and not bingeing ... I can sew, write, be there for others'. You were even able to watch a movie. How's that for ANTI-ANOREXIA!

In addition to separating yourself from anorexia, you have taken this 'unmasking process' a step further by 'seeing what was anorexic behaviour and what was me'. When I asked if you could provide me with some instance of anorexic behaviour, you came up with 'exercising to the point of dropping' and contrasted 'choosing to exercise for fun or choosing not to' as an anti-anorexic form of exercise. Denying your needs was anorexic while the acknowledgment of your needs and not feeling guilty for doing so was anti-anorexic.

We then put our heads together and came up with some questions you might like to revise or amend and send to your sisters.

1. *"Why didn't you live your life according to guilt the way I have? I felt so guilty about our mother's lot in life and thought I had to carry and be responsible for everyone's burdens. I think I did this in part because our parents weren't there in terms of emotions because they themselves didn't acknowledge the legitimacy of their own needs. Our mother was a door-mat and our father was a workaholic/ alcoholic.*
2. *Were you at any time in your growing up or adult years beset by guilt? If so, how did you prove your innocence to yourself? Were you in any way like me driven by perfection?*
3. *Do you think over-eating is connected to the same set of circumstances as under-eating (anorexia/bulimia)?*
4. *Was your independence and aloofness your means of escaping a life of self-punishment and self-torture? Please advise me.*
5. *You get a kick out of life and always seem to land on your feet. How have you taken advantage of life more than being taken advantage of by others? Please advise me.*
6. *What was your experience of life in our family just before I got taken over by anorexia (1970-1)? Would you be surprised if I told you that for me, then, anorexia was a sort of reprieve from my experience living in our family.*

Please help me with this, my beloved sisters."

Yours anti-anorexically, David.

8/13/92

Dear Fran,

Well, what can one say but 'Congratulations!' for walking away, a free woman-person, from the 'concentration camp' of anorexia in which you served 23 years of a very precious life. As you put it so well, 'Some of the anorexia is in the past ... not all'. And when I inquired how you had made this possible, you suggested a number of ways. Firstly, you are no longer 'working hard at letting it go' but instead have adopted an anti-anorexic policy of relaxation and peace. You did mention that this has led you to permit yourself more substance in the form of seven pounds and that that has not scared you or panicked you. Do you think you deserve to have more substance as a person? You are even allowing yourself 'to go to bed earlier' instead of anorexia burning you out. You now have 'time for people ... I am not so isolated'. When I wondered what your new friends might see in you, you found it too new to answer that. However, I am still wondering. You are no longer going along with anorexia's demands to 'be too fussy ... I don't burn myself out ..'. And you went on to describe yourself anti-anorexically: 'I am now care-free', after 23 long years of being care-worn. You have even become so anti-anorexic that 'I am not getting so worried about organising things ... I am more spontaneous'. And to top things off: 'I am putting people ahead of perfection ... they can accept me as I am ... I feel a self-acceptance ... they can like me, warts and all'.

'So where now?' I asked. 'Now that you are looking, have there been some opportunities that you are seizing upon, some doors that you now can see are open to you?' And sure enough there were. You informed me that 'I now can do a yoga teachers' training course ... 2 years ago, I didn't'. Do you think if you were still an inmate in the 'concentration camp' of anorexia that you would be embarking upon what you refer to as 'a good medium' for me? Fran, do you think the torturing is over?

You acknowledged that 'anorexia comes up now and then ... but I am now able to go with MY gut feeling not anorexia's gut feeling'. And then you told me that 'I am no longer counting calories'. Nothing could be more convincing than that.

I wondered how much time anorexia used to take up in your day and you mockingly replied: '48 hours'. 'How much of your life have you rehabilitated' I inquired. You said, '98%'. Even here, Fran, you refused to go along with perfection by giving anorexia its due. 'What was it like to have your life back after 23 years of imprisonment?' You said with some delight: 'It was hard at first ... now I am feeling like normal ... I have a lot more freedom'. And this has meant that you are now able to express your creativity. In fact, you thought you had retired from over-responsibility.

You have also started revising your relationships with your parents. You remembered something which you considered was 'a real plus'. You were able 'to be relaxed around eating at home'. From an anti-anorexic point of view, Fran, what do you make of this? What does this tell you about the person you are becoming? What does this suggest to you about a new kind of relationship with your mother and father?

You then generously agreed to review your anti-anorexia with us. Here are some of your considerations as to what might constitute an anti-anorexic therapy:

1. *Knowing there is someone else who had similar experiences so I didn't feel strange.*
2. *Seeing the progression when my mind sorted out who I am and what anorexia is.*
3. *You accepting me as a person and not someone who is sick or diseased.*
4. *Finding out I could be free.*
5. *The political slant opened up new doors and made me aware of how much I and other women have been manipulated into being overpowered by men. It made me see too how I was part of a big machine and I wasn't guilty for it all. I had got caught up in a web of power.*
6. *You created a therapy for me/us ... you weren't working to a set pattern. I wasn't being type-cast.*
7. *The letters were food for thought ... things I could go back to.*

And when I sought your advice as to how one might experience oneself as more care-free, your counsel was as follows: 'Accept yourself as you are. Accept yourself as a human being without a label. I would trust you in whatever you do. And I would advise you not to try too hard to get free. There is no right or wrong, only is-ness.'

You thought too that going free of guilt was 'a crucial part' of your anti-anorexia. You described guilt as 'a metal helmet sitting on my head' and then you came to know that: 'I wasn't responsible for it all'. And that had quite an effect on you: 'Guilt dropped. A heaviness went. I felt myself taking responsibility for what I needed to take responsibility for. I can now stand back, be detached, and not get embroiled.'

You also thought that going 'public' was an important part of your anti-anorexia and we worked out that anorexia is 'shame' and that anti-anorexia is 'pride', anorexia is 'secret' and anti-anorexia is 'public'. I forgot to tell you that our Anti-Anorexia/Bulimia T-shirts are on the way. Do you want

me to order one for you? Better yet, what if I present one to you on your 'freedom day', a day I will look forward to whenever it comes. I believe you will know it when it arrives. In the meantime, I will be digging out some recipes to bake an anti-anorexic 'freedom' cake to mark the occasion.
Freedom is yours! David.

Follow up

Fran and I met on two occasions early in 1993 (2/3, 2/15).[7] Since we had last met, Fran had made a 'voyage of discovery', travelling to places she had never been before in New Zealand. When she returned, she informed her parents that 'you haven't lost me but I've found myself'. She had decided that 'it's okay to be here on this planet ... I let go a heap of the past ... I feel like I'm flying ... before I was locked in fear'. She informed me she was 'tending herself like a young plant ... I want to feel that deep rooted sense'. She then amazed me by informing me she had decided to sell her house and travel to the US to do yoga training and 'reclaim' her life. When I inquired as to her recent developments in her relationship to anorexia/bulimia she had a great deal to say. I will let Fran's words conclude this paper.

I was very close to death in the early stages but I didn't even realise it. I have thought of ending my life seriously two or three times to the point where I was going to get a doctor's prescription and end it all. That's when I came to you. You saved my life, old bean! You were one of the first people who took me as me and didn't treat me as sick. You offered the essence of unconditional acceptance ... no weight requirements, I didn't have to stop vomiting ... no rules ... no blackmail. You were not perpetuating the prison. You helped me to see I could get out of my own prison.

I am now saying 'hello' to anorexia and asking it what it has got to say to me. Why are you separating me from being who I really am? Sometimes now, it doesn't answer back. It's frightened of losing its power. But it hadn't realised we could work together. I want to learn from it. I am integrating those parts of me that have been separated. It's happening. I've always had the feeling of being split. I've often felt 'I'm not me ... I'm separate ... I'm different ... divided into various aspects of my personality.' However, this led me to either kill myself or get on and live. I don't deserve this crap anymore. I really want to be and be here and to accept that it is okay for me to be human.

Yes, I am getting better, I came to a realisation that my feelings were just feelings, not me. I am not my feelings ... I am not my thoughts.

I am still dealing with the fear that if you eat, you'll never stop. The body has its own wisdom and I have to believe in it. Anorexia had cancelled that out. I will get balance. I no longer give it power by obsessing about it.

I would advise other women that there is hope. It can seem like you try everything and nothing works. But all the time you are doing the spade work and there comes a point when all that pays off. Then there is a shift ... I couldn't tell when it would come. Anorexia started for me when I was 17 and I'm now 40. But I allowed for change. I kept on telling myself I could change. I kept learning who I am and I am still learning and will do so until the day I die. All my compulsions (swimming, walking, cycling) are just gone, It just happened. An almighty shift in focus. An abrupt change of focus. There is a newness about me. I am having a new relationship with myself.

Author's Note (DE)

Acknowledgement is given to the Anti-Anorexia/Bulimia League of New Zealand: This work in general owes a great deal to fifteen years of Michael White's work in this area (White 1983; 1986) and the colleagueship, lively discussions over lunch, and encouragement of my partners at the Family Therapy Centre in Auckland, Johnella Bird and Joan Campbell.

Notes

1. First published 1995 in the *Journal of Feminist Family Therapy*, and republished in *Cultural Resistance*, edited by Kathy Weingarten, Guilford.
2. David Epston is Co-Director of The Family Therapy Centre, 1 Garnet Road, Westmere, Auckland, New Zealand. He would like to acknowledge Kathy Weingarten for the considerable editing that was required and the integrity to the spirit of the work with which she undertook it.
3. Fran Morris, c/- Solar Hill, 61 Western Avenue, Brattleboro, VT 05301, USA.
4. Rick Maisel, PhD, is in private practice at the Redwood Centre, 2428 Dwight Way,

Berkeley, CA 94704, USA; and is an adjunct faculty member at the California School of Professional Psychology, Alameda, CA; and at John F Kennedy University, Orinda, CA. He was responsible for the first draft of the non-correspondence part of this paper, drawing in part on the doctoral dissertation of Christie Platt, PhD (1992).

5. This day-long workshop was presented at the New Zealand Family Therapy Conference, 1991, Auckland. Since then, I have read two papers strongly advancing a parallel point of view (Gremillion 1992; Swartz 1987).
6. The 'Voice' of anorexia/bulimia is often gendered and 'it' is typically given male status. According to feedback, this has provided one of the most provocative and helpful questions: 'Why is the 'voice' of anorexia/bulimia most often gendered male?'
7. Judith Myers-Avis (Professor of Family Therapy, University of Guelph, Guelph, Ontario, Canada) spent a week at The Family Therapy Centre as a Dulwich Centre Scholar in February, 1993. She allowed the League to reflect on itself by interviewing many of its current membership and me. We are grateful for her contribution and her encouragement.

References

Allen, L. 1993: 'Politics of therapy - An interview with Michael White.' *Human Systems: Journal of Systemic Consultation and Management,* 4:19:32.

Andersen, T. 1987: 'The reflecting team: Dialogue and meta-dialogue in clinical work.' *Family Process*, 26(4):415-428.

Bakhtin, M.M. 1994: *Problems of Dostoevsky's Poetics.* Minneapolis, Minnesota: University of Minnesota Press.

Binswanger, L. 1958: 'The case of Ellen West.' In May, R., Angel, D. & Ellenberger, H.F. (eds), *Existence.* New York: Basic Books.

Epston, D. 1989: *Collected Papers.* Adelaide: Dulwich Centre Publications.

Epston, D. 1993: 'Internalizing discourses versus externalizing discourses.' In Gilligan, S. & Price, R. (eds), *Therapeutic Conversations,* pp.161-177. New York: Norton.

Epston, D. & White, M. 1992: *Experience, Contradiction, Narrative and Imagination: Selected papers of David Epston and Michael White, 1989-1991.* Adelaide: Dulwich Centre Publications.

Epston, D., White, M., & Murray, K. 1992: 'A proposal for a re-authoring therapy: Rose's revisioning of her life and a commentary.' In McNamee, S. & Gergen, K. (eds), *Therapy as Social Construction.* London: Sage Publications. (Republished in this book.)

Gremillion, H. 1992: 'Psychiatry as social ordering: Anorexia nervosa, a paradigm.' *Social Science & Medicine*, 35(1):57-71.

Halliday, M.A.K. 1978: 'Antilanguages.' In Halliday, M.A.K., *Language as Social Semiotic: The social interpretation of language and meaning*. London: Arnold.

Madigan, S. 1992b: 'The application of Michel Foucault's philosophy in the problem externalizing discourse of Michael White.' *Journal of Family Therapy,* 14(3):265-279.

Platt, C. 1992: 'Formerly chronic bulimics' perspectives on the process of recovery (Doctoral dissertation, California School of Professional Psychology-Berkeley, Alameda, 1992).' *Dissertation Abstracts International*, 53:3162.

Robertson, M. 1992: *Starving In The Silences: An exploration of anorexia nervosa.* North Sydney: Allen & Unwin.

Swartz, L. 1987: 'Illness negotiation: The case of eating disorders.' *Social Science & Medicine,* 24(7):613-618.

Tavris, C. 1991: *The Mismeasure of Woman*. New York: Simon & Schuster.

Tomm, K. 1989: 'Externalizing the problem and internalizing personal agency.' *Journal of Strategic and Systemic Therapies*, 8(1):54-59.

Tomm, K. 1991: Personal communication.

Tomm, K. 1992: Personal communication.

White, M. 1983: 'Anorexia nervosa: A transgenerational system perspective.' *Family Process,* 22:255-273.

White, M. 1984: 'Pseudo-encopresis: From avalanche to victory, from vicious to virtuous cycles.' *Family Systems Medicine,* 2(2):150-160.

White, M. 1986: 'Anorexia nervosa: A cybernetic perspective.' In Harkaway, J.E. (ed), *Eating Disorders*. Maryland: Aspen Publishers.

White, M. 1989: *Selected Papers.* Adelaide: Dulwich Centre Publications.

White, M. & Epston, D. 1990: *Narrative Means to Therapeutic Ends*. New York: Norton. (Also published as *Literate Means to Therapeutic Ends*, 1989, Adelaide: Dulwich Centre Publications.)

13

David Consults Ben[1]

In this paper, which I hope is a good example of what are now known as 'co-researching' practices, I think Ben does a fine job of speaking with authority on a problem conventionally referred to as obsessive-compulsive disorder in children. After all, were you aware that such a problem always comes up from behind? Would you have guessed the benefits of throwing Mr O one? Or that those who have taken their lives back from such a problem do so by courageously looking IT in the eye and, by doing so, expose it as fearful rather than terrorising?

The following is a typical consulting-your-consultants interview, although it is my (DE) second meeting with 'Ben' and his parents, 'Maggie' and 'Jim'. The first interview was an emergency consultation at a psychiatric hospital in the United States. The consultation was attended by Ben, his parents, the attending doctor, and all eight hospital staff who were involved with Ben while he was an inpatient. This meeting, scheduled at the request of Ben, occurred approximately two months later and took place at a family institute near his home. The reader should be aware that in the interval Ben remained in the care of the hospital staff.

This consulting your consultants is located (see Figure 1) in what is being referred to here as a genealogy of this 'knowledge'. It demonstrates the extent to which persons such as Ben, myself (DE), and his parents have recourse to this knowledge and contribute to it. For example, the videotape of this meeting was returned to both Tim and Al for their opinions as to Ben's candidacy for the award of the Diploma of 'Impurfection', and then eight months later was forwarded to Ron and his family prior to our first meeting together. This 'knowledge' is mediated through the therapist-archivist and passes backwards and forwards between members of the League. A league is what I refer to as a 'community of concern', which may best be conceptualised as more virtual than real. Such communities form around shared concerns and the 'knowledges' that emerge from them. The league discussed here has named itself the Anti-Habit League. The 'problem' itself provides persons and their families with the right to membership in the League and the associated privileges. However, before availing ourselves of these privileges through the therapist-archivist, the conditions of consent and what Fran Morris (Epston, Morris & Maisel 1995) has referred to as respectful confidentiality is discussed at length. With the informed consent of the members, letters (Epston 1994; White & Epston 1990), videotapes, audiotapes, stories, and so on, become the shared property of the League itself. The therapist-archivist can be granted discretion to excerpt letters, exchange videos, and so forth, although each member may wish to have specific conditions attached to this use (e.g., to be known by their first name only, or to be contacted ahead of time and to have their permission sought on each occasion of a 'loan'). I have found people to be very generous indeed, and much of what I have referred to as therapist discretion has to do with protecting members. My main concern would be the possibility of new members in distress putting undue demands on their sources. For this reason, all contacts are mediated through the therapist-archivist. At times of great risk or despair, I have arranged for face-to-face consultations. One example (see Figure 1) involved Bryce and Jerry. Bryce (aged nineteen), a first year university student, had tried to comply with the demand of the 'curse of the idea of perfection' for his failure to achieve perfection in everything he did, especially combing his hair which could occupy up to four hours of his day. He 'consulted' to Jerry (aged seventeen), who had recently graduated from high school but failed to have a straight A+ average (thanks to one A-). Jerry had tried to take his life, and his parents, justifiably, were desperately concerned about his welfare. We met prior to this consultation in order to co-operate around constructing appropriate questions for Bryce. We also agreed that I would intervene on Bryce's behalf should any further discussion seem to be intrusive. On this occasion, Bryce waived all my concerns in this regard. This was the only time Anti-Habit League members had ever met on purpose, although such meetings would certainly be worth considering. It is my practice in face-to-face consultations to split my fee 50/50 with my consultants. The consulting persons have to agree to this arrangement. If such 'knowledges' are to be valued, they must be paid for.

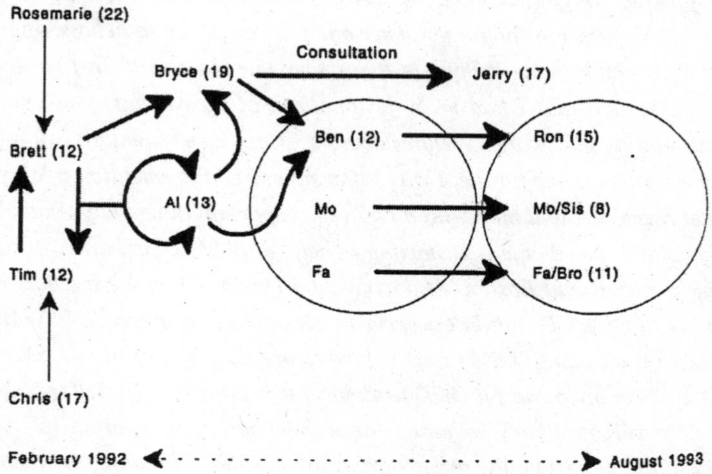

Figure 1

In Figure 1, the 'genealogy' of this league is charted through time (February 1992 to August 1993) and from person to person and family to family. The heavy arrow indicates the exchange of archival material (e.g., letters, videotapes, audiotapes, stories, drawings, and slogans), whereas the fine lines indicate the therapist either excerpting and reading from letters or other reminiscences from the therapy (e.g., 'The problem Bryce was experiencing was calling him names like … Did your problem do anything similar or did it come up with some new insults?'). By detailed inquiry, cross-referencing of 'knowledges', and so on, it does not take long to be knowledgeable yourself, nor does it take much contact with a problem through the people you meet before you get to know it reasonably well.

Ben's thoughts and recollections (December 1994)

In October of 1992 I was diagnosed with OCD (obsessive-compulsive disorder). *I had been having symptoms for as long as I can remember but they were getting a lot worse. Depression also made things hard. Some of my symptoms were touching or doing things a certain number of times, counting, and repeating certain phrases. In general I felt I needed to do things until it felt 'perfect'. I also had negative obsessions about my sister and felt compelled to behave aggressively toward her, which made it hard to live under the same roof. In February 1993 things got so bad that I had to be hospitalised at a psychiatric hospital. At the hospital things got worse. While doctors were experimenting with possible medicine combinations for me, I was suffering more, and spending a lot of time in the quiet room. Around mid-March two very important things happened. The first one was that the medicine was starting to help, and the second one was that I had a meeting with David Epston. At this meeting David taught me a whole new way of dealing at my OCD. I didn't deserve to get pushed around by OCD. Although I had known it all along, I didn't know how to use it to my advantage. David really helped me turn my powerful OCD around so that it barely affected me. Of course, there were still problems here and there, but they were a lot easier to handle. Thanks to the medicine, the great staff at the hospital, including the doctors, and the support of my family and friends, especially David, my life went from terrible to terrific. I am so thankful for David's help.*

Interview with Ben, Maggie and Jim

David: *We are making a tape to record this historic event, Ben, Maggie, and Jim. Also, I think Al and Tim* [veterans of the problem and now consultants in their capacities as president and vice-president of the Anti-Habit League of New Zealand] *would be interested in hearing from you. They knew a little bit about you. But these people don't know very much about the fact that we met about ... how long ago was it Ben?* (Note: Dialogue continues on p.290.)

I had met Tim, aged twelve, and his mother, Donna, over a ten-month period (December 1992 to October 1993) on eight occasions. When I first met Tim he had been involved with compulsive hand-washing relating to concerns about dirt, animals, dust, and 'dirt' on TV. He would go berserk if anyone watched people kissing on TV and would not desist until they covered their faces with cushions like himself. He had had an eight-year-long headache and vomited most days on the way to school. He described himself as 'suspicious'. He felt himself to be forbidden to have friends because they were having fun, and he was not permitted to have more than 'a minimum of friends'. He was preoccupied with his schoolwork and, in the first session, described himself as 'on the verge of a nervous breakdown'.

This 'story' was written after the second meeting and presented to me at the third:

> *Once my mind was plagued by guilt. I was forced by my mind to conduct a series of rituals, such as hand washing. My life was like a bowl of dust blowing away in the wind. I had hardly any activities or clubs to go to. My life usually centred around my schoolwork. I didn't have many friends and, if I did, I would usually argue or get nasty to them as they were happy. My life was going down the drain. Then one day, a day in which freeness would finally invade the 'infected' areas of my mind, my mother decided, after seeing me go through a time of pain and guilt, to take me to see David Epston. After only one visit the shell of guilt that had covered me crumbled and light and freedom came back to me again. I started making new friends and tying the old tethers back together that at one time had been left to rot and slowly decay. So, after a long time of horror, I live in peace again.*

I had met Al, aged thirteen, along with his mother and his father, over a five-month period (July 1992 to December 1992) on four occasions. The problems commenced five years previously after the family moved from the capital city to a small rural town. Al was severely teased and had a series of overwhelming and distressing nightmares. This was followed by a succession and accumulation of what we referred to as 'habits'. He was currently obsessed by germs and the fear that he was suffering from a terminal illness such as AIDS. His schoolwork was deteriorating and he was refusing contact with others and, when he was in contact with others, was obliged to enter into touching back whenever touched so as to return the 'germs'.

This story was written after the third meeting and presented at the fourth:

It all started when I was eight. I moved from a large city and a happy life to a small town where I was plagued and terrorised by fears and habits. They first began with a dream and, although I cannot and do not wish to remember it, it upset me a lot at the time, so much, in fact, that it opened the way for fears and the habits to enter my life. My main fear has always been disease and with it came many others. The first of my habits was a constant need to clear my throat and always needing to wash my hands. These habits have continued to terrorise me up until recently and, although I have done my best against them, I still needed help to get rid of them. I believe if you know what habits are, you can get rid of them; otherwise they're invincible. Fear could have ruined my life, and it nearly did. I'm happy to be rid of it and I don't want it back!

As a result of my nightmares, fears started to take over my life. After the move to the small town, I felt insecure and that opened the way for fear. My fears included fear of the dark, fear of disease and unnecessary worry. I seemed to catch worries off other people and accidentally used my imagination to scare myself. In the small town I found it hard to make friends and was upset very easily. When I was nearly nine, my family moved back to Auckland. I was happier there but my habits still didn't leave. Once there I felt more secure so I began trying to make my habits go away. It didn't work perfectly but it did help. As one habit went away, another came in its place. Some of the habits I've had were clearing my throat, blinking at things, washing my hands, not eating all my food, missing the top and bottom steps when I went upstairs, and touching everything I walked past.

My worst habit was that I felt other people were giving me germs so if they touched me I had to touch them back.

The last habit is what made my mum look for help as she realised the habits weren't going to go away by themselves. After asking around, Mum found out about David Epston so she got an appointment with him. When I first went I didn't know what to expect. We arrived early and were all nervous when we went in. But he told me there were other people with the same problems and, best of all, it could be disposed of.

Since then, I've visited him on three times. All my habits have gone and no new ones come. Well, to tell the truth, most have gone and the others are still disappearing into the background. With less to worry about, my schoolwork and attitude have improved. I'm glad I'm not afraid any more.

The therapist sets the scene by decreeing it to be an 'historic event' rather than a mundane therapy event and specifying the potential audiences. In this instance, there are three potential audiences: Tim, Al, and the Anti-Habit League, those therapists attending this training at the Family Institute of Cambridge, and what Lobovits, Maisel & Freeman (1995) refer to as the introduced audience - those young persons, their family members, and possibly their therapists struggling with similar problems who may find a measure of relief and hope, ideas, or incitement to their own creativity in consulting such an 'archive' of an 'alternative knowledge'. 'These people' here are the audience of thirty-five professional therapists (dialogue continued from page 188):

Ben: *About two months ago.*

Maggie: *St Patrick's Day - March 17th.*

David: *You wrote me a fax in Sweden. Is that okay if I read it out loud?*

Ben: *Go ahead.*

David: *First of all, I was glad to hear about Mike. How is he doing?*

(Mike was a young man suffering from severe cerebral palsy who required caretakers to support his efforts to walk and whose speech was quite aphasic. Until I met Ben on the first occasion, I had been informed that Ben had adopted the almost indecipherable speech of Mike. This made communicating with Ben extremely difficult. Almost within several interchanges on meeting Ben, Ben consented to my question: 'Did Ben just say "hi!" or was that Mike speaking?' Ben replied: 'Ben!' 'I enjoy speaking to Ben. Do you mind continuing as Ben and I will be David?' And, sure enough, we did carry on for the next hour and a half as Ben and David. When I saw Ben on the second occasion, I enquired about Mike. I had heard from Ben's parents that Ben's relationship with Mike had changed after my first meeting with Ben. Although Ben had previously shown discomfort about his compulsive mimicking of Mike and had made some atoning gestures after our meeting, Ben began to reach out in a very heartfelt way to this boy who was the only child on the unit with physical disabilities and significant developmental delay.)

Ben: *He is doing great! Well, when we both were in hospital in the same unit, some of the kids would make fun of him. And when I started feeling better I was very supportive of him. And I did stuff with him. I came to learn what a great person he was in that he expressed love to me as to how thankful he was.*

David: *Was that a big surprise to you?*

Ben: *Yeah, it was ... but that just proves more that he is a great person. I am glad he is doing well.*

David: *Are you in touch with him?*

Ben: *No, but my doctor said he would try to get his address or phone number.*

David: *Do you think if it wasn't for you, Mike wouldn't be living so happily with his new foster family?*

Ben: *I haven't thought about that.*

David: *If you did think about it, what would you think?*

Ben: *I think I had some impact on him. I met his foster mum.*

David: *Did you? Did you give her any advice?*

Ben: *I just told her he was a great kid. And she is very nice and caring. I think he would still be happy but not as happy.*

David: *You know there are a lot of people in this world who, for whatever reasons, aren't able to show love. How did you bring that out in him?*

Ben: *By giving him love so that he would have the sense that he was loved. You know, set free the love that was trapped inside his heart!*

David: *Was it touching for you to see his love get free of the trap that it had been in?*

Ben: *Very ...*

David: *Did it happen overnight or gradually?*

Ben: *It happened gradually over the course of time.*

(This series of inquiries, aside from my interest in learning of Mike's wellbeing, also intends to implicate Ben in his own agency - that he could make an appreciable contribution to Mike's freeing his 'trapped' love and his wellbeing, in spite of his physical disabilities and the humiliations associated with them. I wish I had been more explicit here and asked: 'Did you learn this practice of "giving love" so the other person could sense he or she was loved from your brother-sister relationship with [his sister] Julia? Or was it just a fresh hospital learning? Where did you learn this practice of giving love?')

David: *Was that the highlight of your time in hospital?*

(Undoubtedly there were 'lowlights' and dark times during Ben's hospital admission, but my preference here is to ask about the 'highlights'.)

Ben: *That was one of them.*

David: *What were your other highlights?*

Ben: *The meeting that I had with you.*

David: *Why was that? Because you beat me in ping pong?*

Ben: *No, that wasn't it even though I liked that. It was sort of I felt someone really knew what I was going through, almost as if you were feeling the same pain I was feeling and could reach out and show me how to deal with it in the best way I could.*

David: *Did you have some sense that I wasn't entirely happy with the way Mr. O had intruded upon your life?*[2]

(For me, one of the most appealing advantages of an externalising conversation is that it allows you out of the position of the 'objective observer' or 'fake neutrality'. I have no problem whatsoever avowing my position against such a problem, given my experience-near 'clinical knowledge'. This was derived from relative influence questioning, that is, those questions that ask in an ethnographic rather than merely a psychological manner: 'What effect is this problem having on your life and the life of those in your life?' I might add that that is an exceedingly complicated question and can best be broached by any number of questions. By allying all the concerned parties against the problem, my distaste for the problem does not have to be concealed by any such requirement of 'being on everyone's side at the same time'. I am on everyone's side against the influence of the problem. And, you know, a problem such as so-called obsessive-compulsive disorder can be very compelling of professionals to find the perfect answer. Here the intention of this question is to review Ben's recollection of my avowed position against the problem. In the first meeting I might have asked, if he was in doubt: 'What do you think I think about the way this problem has intruded into your mind, heart, and soul? How do you think I feel about witnessing this happening to a nice, ordinary kid like you?')

Ben: *Well, you can't really help the problem because it sort of creeps up behind your back. But I think what you thought was 'there's a problem so let's do all we can about it'.*

(For me, this comment is of profound interest and one that I have been researching ever since, and that is the spatialisation of the problem. Once again, this is an experience-near 'knowledge' and is hard-won by ethnographically precise questioning 'unpacking' such metaphors over Ben's experience of this problem. And, in my research so far, some of it retrospective, this problem seems to be located behind the person and the solution seems to arise when the person relocates the problem in front of them. This would suggest to me such processual questions: 'Where is the problem now? Behind you, beside you, above you, below you, or in front of you, or somewhere else?' If a person replied: 'Beside me', I would further my investigation with: 'Look, last time we met you indicated to me that it was behind you. Did you put the problem beside you in some way or other? Or did you command it to get out from behind you and stand alongside you? Or what? Can it pull you down from behind if it is beside you? Can you keep your eye on it better? etc.')

David: *I'm not asking you to be critical or anything, but how were the other people helping you with the problem that was different? Did they have a different idea about problems?*

(Such questions assist us as professionals to reflect on our practices regularly by having the people we see evaluate our helping efforts as we all know the way to hell is paved with good intentions but unexpected consequences.)

Ben: *It wasn't so much what they were doing wrong but the amount of stuff they did right. Like, my parents were very supportive but they didn't know as much about these things as you did. They did all they could, but people like you who understand and can help, you know ...*

David: *But don't you think you are giving me overmuch credit here because I only met you for an hour or so and, until I got your fax, I didn't know which way it was going for you? Are you sure you are not giving away too much here?*

(It is important here to contest Ben's willingness to give me all the credit, for fear that by doing so he would be very likely to discount and disqualify all his efforts, 'knowledges', and genius, and that of his family, therapists, friends, and so on. This work concerns itself with generating 'communities of concern' rather than therapist veneration. On the other hand, I am not arguing for false modesty or the assumption that therapists can't play an important role, but I construe that role as akin to opening a door, a door Ben had to walk through and then find his way from there.)

Ben: *No.* [shaking head and grinning]

David: *Well, that is very nice of you, especially saying that in front of all these people.*

Ben: *But just remember you owe me ten bucks afterwards.* [laughter all around]

David: *We were talking amongst ourselves, Ben, about this young boy. What he said was that he thought he had a small problem but then found out it was a giant problem and that was what got his determination going. You know, when I met you, your Mum said in the fax that you thought that you were the size of a crumb and your problem was the size of the Empire State Building.*

(In the fax, Ben had metaphorically described his relationship with the problem [crumb vs Empire State Building] at a point in time: 'When I was going into hospital'. This admits of the possibility of his revision of that relationship in the following series of questions.)

Ben: *Yeah, I felt like when I was going into the hospital I was just a teeny little breadcrumb. This guy, Mr O, was as big as the Empire State Building but, as I grew over time, he shrunk. And now I am proud to say that I am taller than him.*

David: *How tall are you? About 5'?*

Ben: *About 4'11" and he is about ... the size of my parakeet's brain.* [loud laughter all around]

David: *Well, you have turned the tables! Just to give it some respect, how did it sneak up on you and how would you warn others ...?*

Ben: *I didn't expect it.*

David: *Looking back now from where you are, what were its ways and means of sneaking up on a young person and taking over their lives like it did you? Do you have any warnings to other young people?*

(These 'warning' questions can only be asked of 'veterans' of the problem and are asked on behalf of 'others'.)

Ben: *Well, I guess the only thing I could say is that if something bad happens, just think about it. And make sure this problem doesn't get overblown because you can go through a lot.*

David: *How would you warn another person that this problem was sneaking up on them and getting bigger than they were? Are there any signs or clues to forewarn another person?*

Ben: *A lot of stress was building up ...*

David: *What do you mean by that?*

(It is important to have some consensual meaning for such a popular psychological term, for it is vital for me to understand what Ben understands by this rather than what I might mean.)

Ben: *The normal stuff to do with school ... I almost felt it was bigger because I didn't know about it.*

David: *Hold on ... are you suggesting that it's knowing about the problem that made you see through it? Did you not know about it?*

('Because I didn't know about it' catches my attention here and I will enthusiastically interrupt him in order to pursue the putative significance of his comment. At times, you have to be quick.)

Ben: *Well, I knew I was compelled to do things but didn't know why. My parents said: 'Well, you have a mild case of obsessive-compulsive disorder', but it got a lot worse and, as I shrunk, Mr O got a lot bigger.*

David: *I guess the question that all of us are wondering is: 'How did you shrink it? Did you shrink it, blow yourself up, or do both at the same time?'*

(Instead of asking, 'How did it shrink you?' I go back to the above [4'll" vs the size of a parakeet's brain] and convert Ben's metaphor into a question implicating yet again his agency in relationship to the problem. This is a much richer question than say a straightforward solution-oriented question such as, 'How did you do that?')

Ben: *Well, there are a couple of things. One is that the medicine kicked in. Two is the support of everybody and* that *makes me feel stronger.*

David: *What kind of support makes you feel stronger and what kind of support could weaken you? Is there a difference?*

(Once again, I invite Ben to unpack the meaning of a rather taken-for-granted word in both professional and lay discourses - 'support' - by asking about the potential effects on him of different kinds of support.)

Ben: *Well, the support that makes me feel stronger is people letting me know I am a good person even though it seems like I'm not, and let me know they are on my side. And, in a way, this isn't you doing it, there is something inside of you that at that time you had no control over.*

David: *Did you think for a while that Mr O was you? He owned your mind?*

Ben: *Yeah, because he did own my thoughts.*

(My guess is that Ben at times must have felt unsupported by others and himself for attempting to physically harm his sister. The externalising conversation has offered him the linguistic resources to think this anew, and he certainly has asked us to 'condemn the sin' rather than him. However, this must not be understood to be an abrogation of any responsibility but rather the encouragement of responsible action on his part, supported by his 'community of concern',)

David: *When you were a crumb, what percent ownership did he have of your thoughts?*

Ben: *Basically everything. I had a little basic commonsense. I still knew how to walk.* [laughter all around]

David: *Well, look, this is quite a shock to me because when I met you I thought there was a fair bit of you there. Do you remember on that day - March 17th? You were certainly ahead of Mr O on that day?*

(This is an attempt to resurrect an historical 'unique outcome'. My recollection of the hospital meeting with Ben convinced me at the time that he was a young man of considerable wit, charm, and grit. On that occasion his mind was certainly his own if I was to be asked to judge.)

Ben: *'Cos of all the support. I was sitting in a room. Twelve people and I knew all of them were on my side and all of them cared about me. That gave me a lot of growing power. And in turn at that meeting I was a little taller than Mr O.*

David: *I thought so. Do you think Mr O has any ways and means of separating people off from support? Turning you against people or turning people against you?*

(This is an ethnographic question seeking for information as to the 'practices' of the problem.)

Ben: *Well, I think that to the normal person, if someone does something bad when really it is Mr O ... okay, they think this guy has done something bad. The best way to look at it is to think of getting* him *help and wiping Mr O out of the picture.*

(Ben's account is an apt description of his 'positioning' in this externalising conversation - support for the person and opposition to the problem.)

David: *Okay, in your fax you offered some thanks to Tim and Al. These people won't know that Tim and Al are people who freed themselves from Mr O in New Zealand. They sent you some letters, didn't they?*

(I cannot recall what archives from the Anti-Habit League I sent Ben and his family, but the two 'stories' on page 189 & 190 written by Tim and Al are regularly circulated, and for me 'speak' to this work far better than anything I know.)

Ben: *You included some stuff about them in your letters.*

David: *And you said: 'Thank you, Tim and Al. Mr O is a bad loser. Your strategy worked!'*

Ben: *It* did *work.*

David: *What strategy of theirs did you put into use here in America?*

(Can you imagine my curiosity here? I had no idea whatsoever what it was from the archival material that Ben selected out, put into his practice, labelled a strategy and, more important, found effective, but I certainly wished to pursue this in some detail. I immediately discerned that 'giving him one' was of vital importance. I wish I had reviewed this in reference to the externalisation of this 'curse of the idea of perfection' with such enquiries as: 'Is this your means of sabotaging perfection? Would you consider this as getting back at it, a small dose of revenge? How did perfection react when you refused to do its bidding? Were you making fun of perfection? Does perfection expect to be taken seriously?' etc.)

Ben: *Because if I am getting really strong and I keep on beating Mr O and then he is down for the count. And I am just standing there in the ring saying, 'I am number one!' he will come up from behind and grab my leg or something because he is a very poor loser so I learned to get lots of stuff on him but give him one so he doesn't feel like he has to start creeping up on me again. That's even worse when you know the problem is there because he takes you by surprise.*

David: *Did you become more vigilant, more watchful of Mr O? You didn't turn your back on him?*

Ben: *Yeah I did. In the beginning, when I started to recover ...*

David: *Did you have to stand face-to-face?*

(Here I am using the practice I have come to associate with the co-construction of 'local knowledges' cross-referencing one person's experience with another and inviting the latter to comment on it [see Madigan & Epston 1995]. This requires therapists to keep an available inventory of this at the forefront of their thinking/practice. If you expect a person, young or otherwise, to articulate a 'local knowledge' without considerable 'scaffolding', you will be waiting for a very rare bird. The therapist's contribution at this stage is considerable. This is certainly not a time to rest.)

Ben: [after considerable reflection] *Yeah.*

David: *That's funny because what Tim said was that he had to put him in front of him and keep him there for quite a while. He said: 'Then Mr O threw in the towel in the first round ...'*

Ben: *That's very, very, very true.*

(Ben's response is typical and is often associated with vigorous head-nodding, grins of recognition, and so on. These are to be watched out for.)

David: *It didn't take very long. And then what he said was: 'He would come back after a while but it wasn't much of a fight. It was more like a spat. And one flick of my finger and I could make it go away'. Do you feel you are in Tim's shoes in terms of a return engagement?*

(This is the 'matching up' question, in an attempt to augment and thicken Tim's 'knowledge'. I very much like Kenneth and Mary Gergen's (1991) metaphor of 'lamination' to describe this process rather than 'reduction'. This knowledge clearly builds in a very different manner than theory-generated positivist knowledge.)

Ben: *Yeah, Yeah, I do, but I also know not to get too overconfident because he will just take me from behind.*

David: *So how do you keep yourself alert and attentive?*

Ben: *I don't know because I guess it has almost become an instinct ...*

David: *Second nature.*

Ben: *Because I feel like as long as this is inside of my head that Mr O* is *a bad loser, I know that I can throw him one every so often. If I just keep on thinking I can beat Mr O, 'I'm the best', he's just going to grab your leg and take you down.*

('Give him one' gets further elaborated into 'throw him one'. This is a very unique way Ben has of actively resisting the 'curse of the idea of perfection'. It is a very commendable conceit, one I intend to explore and elaborate in my future work opposing such a problem. I might have asked, 'If Mr O is a bad loser, as you say, does that mean you have to be a good loser to go against him? Would you describe your policy here as one of "winning by losing on purpose"? How is this different from Mr O's policy?')

David: *You tell me that you have been working hard to earn your degree in Impurfection ...*

Ben: *Imperfection spelled with a U ...* [laughter all around]

David: *Do you think you are ready to make your application for the New Zealand Diploma in Impurfection? Is it time yet or do you think you need more training in Impurfection?*

(The steps of [1] preparation for application, [2] the application process itself, and [3] the award/non-award of the application in this ritual process are taken very seriously, although I suspect some people reading this transcript may consider this a joke. This practice is clearly an application of the rite-of-passage analogy.)

Ben: *There is only one more thing I have to do. I have to say this. I am 'reedy'!* [mimicking my New Zealand accent; laughter all around]

David: *You're reedy! Can I just check? I know it could be over-confidence talking here.* [to parents] *Do you think he is ready to submit his application for the New Zealand Diploma in Impurfection?*

Jim: *Yes.*

David: *What about you Maggie?*

Maggie: *Mm hmm!*

David: *This will have to go to Al and Tim because they are the president and vice president at the moment. Shall we write an application to them? And your Mum and Dad could be your references?*

Ben: *Sure. Tim and Al were in a way my teachers and they had been through it and they knew what to do and what not to do and they passed that knowledge on to me. And I am grateful to them for that.*

David: *Can I write that to them?*

Ben: *Sure.*

David: [writing] *'Tim and Al, I feel like you have been my teachers.' What else did you say? I thought it was interesting what you said.*

Ben: *I said that because they had gone through what I was going through that they could tell me what to do and what not to do and pass that knowledge on to me. David, did you misspell a word in there?*

David: *Yeah, look at that ... see the d and the j. Well I put them together.* [laughter all around] *These people don't know that one of the tests of impurfection is to make spelling mistakes on purpose. Now I think Tim and Al might be interested to hear what it was you found useful from them. Was there anything you would like to say thanks to them for? Any ideas or practices ...*

(This tape is also being made for Al and Tim and I expected to forward copies to them. I can only guess what it was like for Al and Tim to review this tape. At this stage I have a great fondness for 'saying thanks' questions. Furman & Ahola [1992] have developed a parallel practice.)

Ben: *They didn't have to tell me all this. They didn't have to give up some of their time to help* me. *But the fact that they did, I almost feel like they are really on my side and up in the front lines with me.*

David: *They will be pretty pleased to hear that, I think. What evidence do you have to support your application for the Diploma in Impurfection?*

Ben: *Because I know and am aware of the* curse *of perfection.*

David: *These people here might not know exactly what that is though they might guess. Can you fill people in on that?*

Ben: [shaking his head ruefully] *The curse of perfection. It's almost as if you try to be too perfect, something is bound to go wrong.*

(In Ben providing his 'evidence' and my assisting him to elaborate on it as to its significance qua problem, Ben's parents and I had many surprises in store for us, as is usually the case.)

David: *What else would you like to tell Tim and Al so they can be reassured that you are ready? Are there any good examples that you would like to say to them?*

Ben: *Well, a little story. Before I went into the hospital, I had a compulsion to make my last basketball shot. I needed to end on a perfect note. And about a week ago I was at a doctor's appointment. And we were shooting around and I missed a shot. He asked: 'Can you leave without making the last shot? And I said: 'Yes, I can!'*

David: *And you did it? Was that hard?*

Ben: [smiling proudly] *No.*

David: *Now in the old days when you were unaware of perfection and the effect it was having on your life, would you have been compelled to do that?*

(These are important 'bifurcative questions' [Karl Tomm, personal communication, 1991] that invite a person to compare his/her relationship with the problem at two points in time in order to draw distinctions [e.g., 'a week ago' vs 'in the old days']. Note also the careful use of verb tenses to add considerable 'pastness' to the past.)

Ben: *I would have had to make my last shot. If I missed a layup I would have to hit a layup.*

Jim: *What would happen if someone stopped you from doing that?*

Ben: At *that time, it was sort of inconceivable. I felt I couldn't stop this urge I had. And, if someone did, I almost felt shattered.*

David: *Was Mr O lying to you about some things like it did to Tim and Al?*

(This is an example of the personifications typical of work with 'extreme' or 'deadly' problems such as obsessive-compulsive disorder, anorexia/bulimia, life-threatening asthma, or psychotic experience [see White 1995]. Here the 'problem' is enriched by personifying it, permitting it to have a 'voice', tactics, strategies, personal characteristics, and indeed pathologies of its own [e.g., 'What kind of problem do you think your problem has got? What would your diagnosis be for a problem with such "a nature"?'[3]])

Ben: *What do you mean by that?*

David: *It told him that if he didn't do this he wouldn't have any happiness for the rest of his life. Or he was trash. Or he would fall apart.*

Ben: *Yeah ... yeah.*

David: *Did the New Zealand Mr O speak in any way similar to the American one?*

Ben: *Very much so.*

David: *Not any cultural differences?*

(This is more than a jest. Such a question deprivatises the problem and globalises it as 'worldwide ... multinational'. Still, it is only a step down to 'culture' [e.g., 'Do you ever wonder if Mr O is as prevalent in Polynesia or the Third World as it is in western capitalist countries?'].)

Ben: *Nope ... no accents ... It was like a feeling if I didn't do this, that I was nothing.*

David: *Did it call you names if you didn't?*

Ben: *No, more like the thoughts I had. Then I realised that if I was going to be controlled by a bad force then I was a nothing.*

David: *Well, I am glad you became your own person rather than a person for Mr O. Tim and Al are insiders so they will know what you are talking about ... what else would convince them that you are ready for this Diploma because you could help other people now?*

(At this stage in the process, considerable reference is made to the 'introduced audience', which also assists in marking Ben's new standing as 'veteran' [e.g., 'You could help other people now'.].)

Ben: *That I have strategies and one of these strategies is to think, say I have an urge to make my last shot, I try to reverse it and say: 'I should have an urge to miss the last shot'.*

David: *Oh, really! Is this counter-compulsions or something? An urge to oppose the urge?*

(I think I would be hard put to find a better idea/strategy than this one in any professional text I have read over the years. This, to my way of thinking, is an act of genius and clearly Ben has a fine mind. But I want to reassure you that such ideas/practices 'pop up' on a regular basis talking to young persons in this manner and with this expectation. As is the case here, the young person rarely considers informing his/her parents, even though I suspect Maggie and Jim would have been delighted to know about it.)

Ben: *That was the most successful one. It doesn't work every time.*

David: *Oh, that's good. You don't want to be perfect.*

Ben: [crossing his hands in front of his face] *No, I wouldn't want that.* [laughter all around]

David: *Where did that idea come from ... was that your idea, your Mum's or Dad's or a hospital idea ... where did it come from?*

Ben: *It just came from myself.*

David: *Do you consider that a good idea? Would you recommend that to other young people?*

(These are questions to discern the 'genealogy' of this practice and the ideas that resourced it. Other questions are asked to have him evaluate it, both for his own use and for export to others. This kind of inquiry is at the heart of this work.)

Ben: *I think that if it works for me it's not necessarily going to work for someone else.*

David: *Give me an example ... let me think of Al. Al was driven when he was coming down the stairs to miss the last step ...*

(Cross-referencing his 'knowledge' back in time allows him to stand back from it and describe its deployment. By doing so, this practice will be more available for his use, should he require it.)

Ben: [postulates] I had that! *I didn't have that very long. I had it some times.*

David: *What else ... oh, he felt he had to touch people.*

Ben: *I sometimes felt I had to do that.*

David: *These are international. This is a multinational, Mr O.*

(Once again, many therapists might have been tempted to follow a pathology track here. Rather, once again, I return to the frame of reference of 'culture'.)

Ben: *Worldwide.*

David: *So say Al had that. Mr O was compelling him to miss the last step, what would you recommend he do if he followed that particular strategy?*

(This question invites Ben to refine and elaborate this strategy and at the same time to publicise it.)

Ben: *He would miss the last two steps.*

David: *Is that right! Is that like doing Mischief? Being a bit noncompliant to Mr O?*

Ben: *In that case, yeah, I guess.*

(These questions invite Ben once again to refer this strategy back into a revised relationship with Mr O - one in which he is certainly no longer Mr O's puppet. Instead, 'mischief' and 'noncompliance' might appeal to a young man of Ben's age and feistiness.)

David: *Have you got any other ideas like that?* [to parents] *Did you know about these ones?*

Maggie: *No.*

David: *That's a good idea, don't you think? Why do you keep those secret? Did you not think they were worthy of mention?*

Ben: *No, not that ... they have just never really been brung up.*

David: *Look, I met Chris. He was about seventeen and he felt compelled to shower and wash himself for hours on end. And the first way he opposed it was to go and have his usual shower but he would leave a little bit behind his knee undone to get back at the compulsion.*

Ben: *And work your way from there.*

David: *Funny ... the fact that he could do that it just vanished overnight. Did you find that by any chance that once you stood up to it, it pretty well backed down?*

Ben: *I was really afraid to. I mean ...*

David: *How did it convince you to be afraid?*

Ben: *Well, it's almost like a big bully coming up to you, who is just really big. He is really afraid ...*

(Here is another opportunity to 'unpack' a metaphor and, in addition, to add it to my stock of counsellor knowledge around such a problem [e.g., 'Do you find that this problem is a bit like a bully?']. It increases the interviewed person's responsiveness by adding 'a bit like' rather than forcing the answer into a yes/no. This is critical when inviting persons to review their relationships according to metaphorical relationships [e.g., a bully in relationship to his/her 'target' person]. For example, 'Why do you say that? Have you had some experiences of being bullied yourself? Or have you read about bullies? Or seen them on TV or in movies?' etc.)

David: *You were afraid?*

Ben: *He's afraid ... you are both afraid of each other. But I think he won't be afraid because he is this big guy. So I give him my lunch* but *if I say one day: 'No, I am not going to give you my lunch', he'll say 'Okay, I'm sorry'.* [laughter all around)

(Once again, this is a revelation to me and something I intend to pursue in my co-researching efforts around such problems [e.g., 'I know this is going to sound weird and I wouldn't have even thought to ask you about it if it wasn't for what Ben told me. He said: "We are afraid of each other". What do you guess he was getting at there?'].)

David: *This is uncanny. Tim said the problem was like a big bully too. He said: 'I realised it was hard on the outside but had a soft centre'.*

(Here is another example of cross-referencing and 'laminating' accounts/ vocabularies/metaphors.)

Ben: *Exactly!*

David: *It's wearing a mask. There is a scared thing behind the mask.*

(I regret I didn't pursue this line of inquiry: 'Ben, where do you think you would be today - crumblike or a young man with growing power - if you hadn't come to think of it that way? Did that way of thinking pave the way, in a manner of speaking, for the road to recovery you have been walking the last month or so?')

Ben: *You just don't think of it that way at all.*

David: *Can you be frank? For a while there did Mr O terrorise you?*

Ben: *Yeah ... for a while there he was asking me to do his home-work, carry his back-pack ...*

David: *Did you feel enslaved?*

Ben: *Yeah.*

David: *When did you feel you got your freedom?*

(The 'enslavement' metaphor 'naturally' allows for the next question: 'When did you feel you got your freedom?' Again, such an agentic question is far preferable to less agentic questions such as: 'When did you go free? Who let you go free? Was your time up?' Such metaphors have much more room in them than psychiatric/psychological metaphors such as diagnoses. I have always found that diagnostic descriptions limit a person's capability of expressing their experience, both the suffering and the freedom.)

Ben: *It wasn't overnight. It was very gradual. I'd say ... when I was in the hospital, I was an inpatient for a little over a month and a half ... I was an outpatient for another month. And think after the first four weeks of my inpatient time, that's when things started turning around.*

David: *I know there was a struggle but when you went ahead of it was that a very clear experience for you? Did you know it when it happened or is it only on looking back that you experience it that way?*

Ben: *Yeah, I guess I say I knew it but ...*

David: *Did you tell anyone? Your Mum or your Dad?*

Ben: *I let them know I was feeling better.*

David: [to parents] *Would either of you have guessed exactly when that was? Can you date it?*

(This is an attempt to locate this event in time so it can be marked ceremonially and remembered in years to come. I think you will agree that there is cause for celebration here, even if the problem is still hanging around in the background.)

Jim: *February first he became completely overwhelmed. He was in the hospital February 22nd.*

Maggie: *David saw him March 17th. And I would say we were seeing very slight signs then but the month of April was just incredible. Every day he was so much ...*

Ben: *And late March.*

Jim: *It was over about a six-week period.*

David: *If you were to celebrate freedom day, could you assign it to a date?*

Ben: *No ...*

David: *What about even arbitrarily? Even somewhere in the middle so you could acknowledge it. I could send you a card next year.*

Jim: *Ben's first day out of the hospital being able to be in a social situation with the family was Margaret's birthday - April 28th. It was the first time the four of us were able to be together since December.*

David: *Was that a special day for you? What do you think Julia thought about it ... Was she pleased?*

Ben: *It was almost like my birthday as well. I don't know exactly how Julia felt but I think she would be* extremely happy *to have the sense that a family of four could go out to dinner and have a nice conversation and sleep under the same roof.*

(This interview goes on for another half hour with me closely interviewing Maggie and Jim as to their reasons for supporting Ben's application for membership. They added an immense amount of information to support Ben's 'knowledge' being such loving and concerned parents, as well as close observers. I regret that I do not have the space to include most, if not all, of their commentaries.)

After reviewing the videotape of Ben along with his family, Al and Tim independently provided me with their decisions:

Dear David:

Thanks for your letter and video about Ben. I watched the tape and could understand his problems, though they were far worse than mine. He must have worked really hard to overcome them. I think he has earned the New Zealand Diploma of Impurfection with Distinction. And in my capacity as Vice President of the New Zealand Society, I would recommend the award go to Ben, though I was a little surprised at my selection to the Vice President position but still honoured.

My habits are now well under control but occasionally they try to come back. This is getting less and less though. Since we last saw you, I have been fairly busy. In the May holidays I went on a week-long bike tour and was able to ride much faster without my habits dragging me back. In the August holidays I went to stay on my uncle's farm again and really enjoyed my time there. I wasn't even afraid of the MUD!!! I have also joined a church youth group, partly because of the church side of the bike tour and also because I wanted to make new friends. We have now finished the aviary and, as well as having four adult budgies and two adult quail, we now have an addition in the form of a newly hatched baby quail.

Next time you write to Ben, could you congratulate him from me on having beaten Mr O. By the way, my Mum has the same birthday as his Mum. Thanks for your help in sorting out my life. Please keep in touch.
Yours (without habits), Al.

Dear David,

I was greatly impressed by Ben's battle with Mr O. When I read your letter how he was before he was hospitalised and then seeing him on the video, I noticed his great change. He has really changed. I do believe he has worked hard enough to receive the New Zealand Diploma in Impurfection. At the moment, life is going good for me. I'm in the top class in the 3rd Form and have recently turned 14. The only bad thing has been the death of my grandmother some time ago and I am just about over it. And, as for perfection, my borders have been closed to him. Mr 'O' as you called it has not visited me ever since.

Best wishes, Tim.

The letters, along with a diploma, were forwarded to Ben.

Eight months later I was meeting with the Smith family along with a 'team' whose members were attending a week-long intensive training. The Smith family was invited to join this training week by their therapist, who was attending it. We met them on three consecutive days for a period of two hours. On the second to last day I met with Ron, aged fifteen, while the men attending met with Ron's father, Jim, and his young brother, Barry, aged twelve, and the women met with Ron's mother, Denise, and his younger sister, Carrie, aged ten. The following is the letter faxed to Ben, Maggie, and Jim, which first outlines the desperation of the Smith's situation and then directs questions to Ben, Maggie, and Jim.

Dear Maggie, Jim and Ben,

I and a Team have been meeting with Denise and Jim Smith and their children, Ron, aged 15, Barry, aged 12, and Carrie, aged 10. They have driven up from a small New Zealand town, 400 miles south of Auckland. It seems that, for the past four years, Ron has become more and more a slave to what he refers to as IT (this is his unique version of what you have called Mr O). And, by the way, Ron is a very unique person. He is required by IT to be perfectly clean which means he is living quite a lot of his life in the bathroom. He is becoming concerned that IT is driving him mad. Denise and Jim worry pretty much that this is the case. In fact, I suspect up until recently they have been more aware of the ambush Ron was innocently walking into than he was. His brother and sister are upset that they are losing their older brother to IT. At the moment, the only way they can relate to him is by being part-time slaves to IT and doing such things as opening doors and turning the TV on for Ron because IT 'tells' him crazy stuff like he will be contaminated if he opens his own doors or turns his own TV on. Would you believe that IT has even trained him into turning on the TV with his feet and toes?

Maggie, Jim, and Ben, I suspect none of the above will be at all new to you. As you said, Ben, Mr O (IT) is 'worldwide' and 'doesn't even have an accent'. They watched your videotape before they came up to Auckland and, not surprisingly, everyone was quite impressed with your family's opposition to Mr O (IT). And if you had the time and energy we would all be grateful for a consultation with you. I am sorry I didn't have the time to fax you and ask for your permission in the first instance but things have reached a crisis for the Smiths. If this is inconvenient, we all, naturally, will understand; however, if you could assist us, we would be more than grateful.

Questions for Ben from Ron:

1. *Do you think it is best in the beginning to give the problem a bit of your life while you get most of it back? Is it a bit like taming a wild animal where you throw a bit of meat to it every so often and it gradually becomes tamer?*
2. *Right now, what percentage do you have of your mind and what percentage does Mr O have of your mind? This problem has been bugging me for four years but really started to get bad at the end of 1992. I have been thinking of a 90% (me) - 10% (IT) split? Is that a good way to begin from your point of view?*
3. *How did you get around your attitude to other people who weren't supposedly 'perfect' as Mr O instructed you to be?*
4. *I think it is like a perfection syndrome because it wants you to be perfect. It is like trying to make everything perfect. How did you start opposing it? Did you begin with little or big things? I am confused as to how to make my start.*

Questions for Maggie from Denise and Carrie:

1. *Maggie, how did you cope before Ben started winning his life back from Mr O?*
2. *Did you cope better when you gave in to Ben's compulsions or stood against them?*
3. *Did it go better for your family if you gave in to keep the peace or stood firm despite Ben's distress or rage?*

Questions for Jim from Ron and Barry:

1. *Did the problem with Mr O only have a bad effect on Ben? Or other people in the family as well? If so, what were the effects on other people?*
2. *How was your family able to help Ben increase the amount of time he was in control of the problem rather than the problem being in control of him?*
3. *How was the family able to help Ben oppose the problem head-on rather than retreating from its influence?*
4. *Did you find that the problem had a 'logic of its own'? Did you have any success trying to talk Ben out of Mr O's 'logic'?*
5. *When Ben took control over Mr O, did this lead to Ben engaging in activities that he used to engage in before Mr O took him over?*
6. *What tricks did Mr O use to try to convince Ben he had no control? Did he have any tricks to try to talk Ben out of your capacity to help him oppose Mr O?*

Thanks very much, in anticipation. Sorry for the brevity of this. It is a race against time.

Yours sincerely, David, Ron, Denise, Jim, Carrie, and Barry.

This is an excerpt of the response. I have deleted Jim's and Maggie's responses because of the limitations of space.

Dear Smiths,

I am very sorry to hear of your situation. I am sure that this must be a tough time for everyone in the family. Denise and Jim, seeing your son pushed around by IT must be heartbreaking. As parents of a son being pushed around by IT you must want to have your son completely take control of IT. From experience, I know that IT is like a tyrant with a goal to control people's lives.

With David Epston and others giving help to you, you are in very good hands. With David Epston's help, cognitive-behavioural therapy, and medicine, I have been able to smash what I call Mr O and you call IT. It was not easy to defeat Mr O, and sometimes he tries to get revenge, but he is weak and I am strong.

Barry and Carrie, it's tough knowing that your brother is going through tough times. As his siblings, it is good to support him in any way you can and show total disregard for IT. It will make your brother stronger and it will make your lives easier. Under all the blackness lies your brother, a good human being. Try your best to brush away the blackness and find your brother, pure and natural.

Answers to the questions that Ron asked Ben:

1. *Yes, it is in many ways good to give the problem a little bit while you get your life back. It is too hard to carry a big load in one trip. Many trips of small loads will get the job done.*
2. *Right now, I have about 82% control and Mr O has 18%. Mr O has the 18% of my life that I value least - spare time. But when something important has to be done, Mr O runs and hides. It is a very good idea to think of yourself as higher than IT with any numbers. It is terrific that you have such great confidence in yourself, but do not go higher than 90% or you will get overconfident and you will then be vulnerable to IT; 80-90% are the best numbers to start with. It is a good sign that you have such an accurate idea about the situation. This shows that you have control over your basic thinking. You have a very good approach to such an obnoxious enemy.*
3. *When Mr O had the control to instruct me to be perfect, it made perfection such a big thing on my mind that it made me notice other people's imperfections. Then I thought, at least they don't have the inconvenience of being pushed around by Mr O. Once I went into battle with Mr O, who was my big problem, it was easier for me to feel*

sympathetic with other people who were battling big problems.

4. *A good way to get started is to believe that you can defeat IT. Once you have that idea inside you, you're ready to make your start. Little things are good to begin with, but, as time goes by, it is good to slowly change those little things to big things. If you want to climb a ladder with 12 steps it will always be tough to jump 6 of them. Go one at a time and, as you get higher, it is good to slowly but swiftly beat IT to the top.*

Good luck and remember Mr O is scum; I would be happy to hear from you and to hear how things are going.

Your teammate against Mr O, Ben.

Conclusion

In this chapter, we have described a process that we refer to as an archaeology of therapy. In this process, the solution knowledges that have been resurrected and/or generated in the context of the therapy and the history of, or conditions, that made the production of these knowledges possible become known. By using the rite of passage signalled by therapy termination to attend to and document the hard-won know-how that helped free persons from bondage to their problems, they become knowledge-makers, and knowledge-makers become knowledgeable. Both their knowledge-making capabilities and their knowledgeableness are authenticated, not only in the presence of the therapist but also in the presence of other relevant present and future audiences.

The consulting-your-consultants interview with Ben and his parents is an extension of this practice in that such knowledgeableness comes to reside with and be further co-produced by league members. Here this league has named itself the Anti-Habit League of New Zealand, and is merely one of many such leagues (see Madigan & Epston 1995). We have come to consider such a knowledge akin to what Foucault (1973) referred to as a 'local knowledge', often hidden from view or lacking sufficient credibility to be either voiced or heard. And this knowledge might not only serve the interests of its membership, but become 'an effective criticism of the dominant knowledges' (White & Epston 1990, p.26). Many means have been explored to archive such 'knowledges' and circulate them around the leagues. The league acts not only to legitimate these 'knowledges', but also to discern gaps. Such gaps become the stimuli to further co-researched projects on behalf of co-researching participants and the league in general.

The practices outlined in this chapter encourage persons to deploy their knowledges more knowingly, increase their own authority in matters of their concern, and decrease their dependency on expert knowledges. We believe that such personal solution knowledges can be more viable, enduring, and efficient, than imported 'expert' knowledges which too often disable those we seek to help and induce in them a stupefying patienthood. Viewed in this perspective, the artful use of therapeutic questions can help transform the process of therapy termination from one marked only by loss and diminishment to one offering the prospect of genuine gain and fuller authorship of the story of one's life.

Acknowledgements

Portions of this chapter originally appeared in the *Dulwich Centre Newsletter* (1990 No.4) and are republished here with permission.

Notes

1. This is an extract from the paper entitled 'Consulting your consultants: A means to the co-construction of alternative knowledges' that was first published 1995 in Friedman, S. (ed), *The Reflecting Team in Action: Collaborative Therapy*, pp.277-313. Co-authored by David Epston, Michael White & 'Ben'. New York: Guilford Press. Republished here with permission.
2. 'Mr O' was the name that Ben, his family, and the hospital staff arrived at to stand for 'the problem' so that they could engage in an externalising conversation about it.
3. These questions were suggested to me by Rick Maisel at a Santa Rosa workshop in 1992.

References

Douglas, M. 1982: *In the Active Voice.* London: Routledge & Kegan Paul.

Epston, D. 1985: 'An interview with David Epston.' *Family Therapy Association of South Australia Newsletter*, pp.11-14. (Republished 1989 in Epston, D.: *Collected Papers*. Adelaide: Dulwich Centre Publications.)

Epston, D. 1987: 'A reflexion.' *Dulwich Centre Newsletter,* Summer, pp.16-17.

Epston, D. 1994: 'Extending the conversation.' *Family Therapy Networker*, November/ December, pp.31-37,62-63.

Epston, D., Morris, F. & Maisel, R. 1995: 'A narrative approach to so-called anorexia/ bulimia.'' *Journal of Feminist Family Therapy,* 7(1/2):69-95. (Republished in this book.)

Foucault, M. 1973: *The Birth of the Clinic: An archaeology of medical perception.* London: Tavistock.

Furman, B. & Ahola, T. 1992: *Solution Talk: Hosting therapeutic conversations*. New York: Norton.

Geertz, C. 1976: 'From the native's point of view: On the nature of anthropological understanding.' In Basso, K. & Shelby, H. (eds), *Meaning in Anthropology.* Albuquerque: University of New Mexico Press.

Gergen, K.J. & Gergen, M.M. 1991: 'Toward reflexive methodologies.' In Steir, F. (ed), *Reflexivity and Research,* pp.77-95. London: Sage.

Harré, R. 1983: *Personal Being: A theory for individual psychology*. Oxford: Blackwell.

Hewson, D. 1990: 'From laboratory to therapy room.' Unpublished manuscript.

Kobak, F. & Waters, D. 1984: 'Family therapy as a rite of passage: The play's the thing.' *Family Process,* 23(1):89-100.

Lobovits, D.H., Maisel, R.L. & Freeman, J.C. 1995: 'Public practices: An ethic of circulation.' In Friedman, S. (ed), *The Reflecting Team in Action: Collaborative practice in family therapy*, pp.223-256. New York: Guilford Press.

Madigan, S. & Epston, D. 1995: 'From 'spy-chiatric gaze' to communities of concern.' In Friedman, S. (ed), *The Reflecting Team in Action: Collaborative practice in family therapy*, pp.257-276. New York: Guildford Press.

Mauss, M. 1954: *The Gift: Forms and function in archaic societies.* London: Cohen & West.

Turner, B. & Hepworth. M. 1982: *Confession: Studies in deviance in religion.* London: Routledge.

Turner, V. 1967: *The Forest of Symbols: Aspects of Ndembu ritual.* Ithaca, NY: Cornell University Press.

Turner, V. 1986: 'Dewey, Dilthey, and drama.' In Turner, V. & Bruner, E. (eds), *The Anthropology of Experience.* Chicago: University of Illinois Press.

van Gennep, A. 1960: *The Rite of Passage.* Chicago: Chicago University Press. (First published 1908.)

White, M. 1986: 'Awards and their contribution to change.' *Dulwich Centre Newsletter,* May, pp.15-16.

White, M. 1988a: 'The process of questioning: A therapy of literary merit.' *Dulwich Centre Newsletter*, Winter, pp.8-14. (Republished 1989 in White, M.: *Selected Papers.* Adelaide: Dulwich Centre Publications.)

White, M. 1988b: 'Saying hullo again: The incorporation of the lost relationship in the resolution of grief.' *Dulwich Centre Newsletter,* Spring, pp.7-11. (Republished: 1989 in White, M.: *Selected Papers.* Adelaide: Dulwich Centre Publications; and 1998 in White, C. & Denborough, D. (eds), *Introducing Narrative Therapy.* Adelaide: Dulwich Centre Publications.)

White, M. 1989: 'The externalizing of the problem and the re-authoring of lives and relationships.' *Dulwich Centre Newsletter,* Summer, pp.3-21. (Republished: 1989 in White, M.: *Selected Papers.* Adelaide: Dulwich Centre Publications; and 1990 in White, M. & Epston, D., *Narrative Means to Therapeutic Ends.* New York: W.W.Norton.)

White, M. 1995: *Re-authoring Lives: Interviews and essays.* Adelaide: Dulwich Centre Publications.

White, M. & Epston, D. 1985: 'Consulting your consultant's consultants.' In Chable, B.A., Fawns, R.A. & Paterson, T.R. (eds), *Proceedings of the Sixth Australian Family Therapy Conference.* Melbourne, Australia.

White, M. & Epston, D. 1990: *Narrative Means to Therapeutic Ends.* New York: Norton. (Also published 1989 as *Literate Means to Therapeutic Ends.* Adelaide: Dulwich Centre Publications.)

14

Consulting the Problem about the Problematic Relationship:[1]

An exercise for experiencing a relationship with an externalised problem[2]

co-authored by Sallyann Roth & David Epston[3]

This paper arose from an attempt to find a way for people to have an experience of an externalising conversation. It took the dictum: 'The person is not the problem; the problem is the problem', to its logical extreme and provided the problem - whatever it was - with a 'person' of its own. One thing we found that problems have in common is a tendency to be particularly garrulous. Several narrative trainers that I know of have used this exercise, all coming up with variations of their own (Bird, personal communication; White 1998; and, much more expansively, Zimmerman & Dickerson 1996). What turned out to be essential for the success of this 'exercise' was an insistence that those attempting it were to do so in the guise of a journalist rather than as a therapist.

Externalising conversations, introduced by Michael White and David Epston and developed and expanded by them and other practitioners, depict problems as external to people (White 1989, 1991/1992, 1995; Epston & White 1992; White & Epston 1990). In this way of working, problem-externalising questions replace and exclude problem-internalising questions. By problem-internalising questions, we mean questions that address the person and problem as one and the same. For example, typical questions from a perspective that views the problem as within the person might be phrased like this: 'How long have you been depressed?' and 'When you are less depressed, how does your relationship with Sue change?' Or like this: 'Have you been a fearful person for much of your life or is this new?' Such problem-internalising questions effectively join the problem with the person, so that they are represented as indivisibly unified. Seeing oneself as one with a problem implies that one's identity is the problem or includes the problem, and therefore that change requires the alteration of one's very being (White 1989, 1991/1992, 1995; White & Epston 1990).

Problem-externalising conversations address the person as separate from the problem, and hence, in a relationship with it. For example, in a problem-externalising conversation, we might ask, 'What has Demoralization talked you into about yourself?' and, 'What has Demoralization talked you into about your partner?'[4] Or, we might ask, 'As you tell it, Fears have really been pushing you around for the last year or so. Have there been times when you've pushed them back? Even a bit?' Or 'Have there been times when you have insisted that Fears stop taking charge of the little things and confine themselves to the big ones?' A key realignment of the person and The Problem thus occurs through problem-externalising questions: Seeing oneself as in a relationship with a problem (through its objectification or personification), rather than as having a problem or being a problem, immediately opens possibilities for renegotiating that relationship. Moreover, the prescriptions of many cultures induct us into thinking of emotional or behavioural problems as inside ourselves, into blaming ourselves, feeling guilty or ashamed for having these problems, and into experiencing ourselves as helpless to act against our problems without acting against ourselves. In this way, externalising problems can even be seen as a kind of revolutionary, counter-culture, or counter-oppressive act.

We do not see externalising as a technical operation or as a method (Combs & Freedman 1994; Freedman & Combs 1996; Neal 1996). It is a language practice that shows, invites, and evokes generative and respectful ways of thinking about and being with people struggling to develop the kinds of relationships they would prefer to have with the problems that discomfort them (Epston 1993; Roth & Epston 1996; Tomm 1989; White 1989, 1991/1992, 1995; White & Epston 1990). We believe that engaging the people who consult us in problem-externalising conversations can encourage their capacity to act for themselves in relation to problems, to act upon whatever relational context most immediately supports their problems, and to notice and actively respond to the many ways that their self-stories have been shaped by cultural prescriptions and proscriptions laid down by communities of people in our present, our recalled past, and even the past that came long before our time.

This chapter and the exercise it includes do not describe or teach every aspect of the actual use of externalisation in narrative therapies. Rather, the exercise gives clinicians who have little or no hands-on experience with this approach a sense of what engaging in an independent relationship with an externalised problem is like, and thus enables them to experience the resulting perceptual shift in thinking about a problem and the person it besets. It is this experience of the power of problem externalisation that the exercise is designed to demonstrate, not the complexities of conducting externalising conversations. The complexities include, for example, ways of assuring that any language introduced by the therapist feels accurate and familiar, as well as new, to those consulting with the therapist. They also include ways of being guided by the person's unique language and descriptions, and ways of assuring that externalising conversations develop as joint enterprises and are not impositions of the therapist's ideas. The complexities include the ways that problem-externalising conversations are introduced and co-produced so that they are not experienced as trivializing of people's pain, or as by-passing of their experience. The practitioner attends to the subtle and important differences between working with externalisations of the problem and externalisations of the internalised problem discourse. Beyond the dimensions we have already mentioned, there is also the particularly effective trajectory of problem-externalising questions developed by Michael White, those questions that track the problem's *effects on* ... [people's] *emotional states, familial and peer relationships, social and work spheres* ... [or the ways] *it has affected their view of themselves and of their relationships,* [and the ways they have been] ...

recruited into these views (White 1991/1992, p.126). We elaborate none of these points in this chapter.

The rich resources for those who want to consult well-explicated material about the clinical use of externalising practices include key writings by White and Epston (Epston 1993; Epston & White 1992; White 1989, 1991/1992, 1993, 1995; White & Epston 1990) as well as recent articles and books by other practitioners that discuss these practices through description and example (Adams-Westcott, Dafforn, & Sterne 1993; Adams-Westcott & Isenbart 1996; Combs & Freedman 1994; Dickerson & Zimmerman 1993, 1996; Freeman & Lobovits 1993; Freedman & Combs 1996; Jenkins 1990; Kamsler 1998; Linnell & Cora 1993; Madigan 1996; O'Neill & Stockell 1991; Roth & Epston 1996; The Families 1995; Zimmerman & Dickerson 1996).

Some Common Misunderstandings about Externalising Practices[5]

A common misunderstanding of work that relies on externalising conversations is the belief that it aims to eliminate, conquer, or kill off problems. It does not,[6] although it can seem to have a divide-and-conquer aspect. Rather, it aims to create linguistic and relational contexts in which people experiencing themselves as burdened, crushed, or taken over by problems can imagine and activate alternative and preferred relationships with these problems.

Can problems be kept in their place? Can they be resisted? Can they be flirted with but not married? Can a problem be an old friend, one a person may have grown past? Can a problem be left behind or put on the shelf? Can a problem learn not to speak unless it's called upon? Can a problem be given enough space to stay healthy and stick around for any good it might do, but not be given so much room that it takes over more territory than the person wants to give it? For example, one would never choose to be taken over by Perfection to the point of becoming immobile, anorectic, or obsessive in behaviour. However, one may wish to retain a good enough relationship with Perfection to hand in papers that are not filled with misspellings or to get to work on time. It's not the person who is the problem; it's not even fully The Problem that is the problem. It is, to go the whole way, the relationship of the person with The Problem that is the problem!

Why not try to kill off The Problem? Why do we favor going the whole way, viewing the relationship of the person and The Problem as the problem? First, The Problem may not be only a problem. It may, in some fashion, be a bit of a friend. Second, even if it is of no help at all, a long-time associate cannot be retired or sidelined without paying respect to it. And, if a person frees himself or herself of a problem and it returns and tries to reassert itself at some later time, the person is less likely to be humiliated or deeply demoralized if The Problem can be seen as having been set aside, grown past, risen above, and the like, rather than as not having been effectively conquered or killed off.

Another common misunderstanding is the belief that only one problem is externalised in this work, but that is not the case. What is externalised may shift during a single meeting, and shift again and again over the course of several meetings. And often what gets externalised is not the problem the person names at the outset. We may experiment with externalising anything that a person experiences as a deleterious and intrinsic part of himself or herself. The possibilities are numerous[7]: They include affect states (e.g., Despair, Hopelessness, Excitement), an internalised problem discourse (e.g., Self-Blame, Self-Negation), a behaviour (e.g., Weepiness, Inertia, Mischief), the armor of self-protection that often follows abuse by another (e.g., Silence, Secrecy, Isolation, Numbness), and oppressive social arrangements that have been internalised (e.g., Male Superiority, Racial Disqualification, Standards of Physical Beauty).

Crucial to the effectiveness of a problem-externalising conversation, whatever its content, is the degree to which people experience it as experience-near and refreshing. Does the conversation leave people feeling that their unique experience in living is being fully, complexly, faithfully, and poignantly described? Do they feel that the conversation is bringing forth descriptions and observations, feelings and perspectives that seem very close to their experience as they live it? Does the conversation illuminate the obscure and overshadowed; does it go just a step beyond what has previously registered in their consciousness? Do people feel that they are sharing an experience - not a theory - of what is, what has been, and what might be? Are their lived experiences being storied rather than deduced and explicated?

We do not want to support inadvertently the limited and limiting view that externalisation is merely a technique, by presenting the exercise that follows in isolation from the larger body of theory that supports the use of externalising practices in the context of narrative work. For this reason, we will say just a bit about narrative work and the way that these practices fit with it.

Narrative Therapies and Problem-Accommodating Storylines

Narrative work is based on the belief that the stories we hold about our lives are mined from our relationships and experiences, both past and present, and that these stories shape our present experience and future possibilities. They shape what we see ourselves as being able to do and as well as the ways that we interpret what we and others do. Here we refer to the full panoply of individual, couple, family, institution, culture, and gender stories. When we are in a problem place (troubling predicament), the story lines we draw on and draw forward, those that shape and are shaped by our present meanings and actions are, not surprisingly, generally those that accommodate the problem place and that accommodate us to the problem place. These problem-accommodating stories limit or even block our access to the full vein of resources available to us. The narrative work we discuss here aims to open access to a greater range of story-line choices for people at those times when the stories they currently live are limited and dominated by meanings that restrict their current lives and foreclose future possibilities (White 1989, 1991/1992, 1995; White & Epston 1990).

Emerging Narratives of Contrary Experience

We try to develop clinical and training contexts that cultivate attention to those less noticed - even previously unnoticed - experiences that can be instrumental in countering the dominant, limiting story while promoting stories and actions the person prefers (Epston & White 1992; White 1989, 1991/1992; White & Epston 1990). We focus on aspects of people's experience that are contrary to their problem-accommodating and discouraging way of seeing and describing themselves - and on the generation from that contrary experience of at least one encouraging additional story that has coherence across time. That is, we work with emerging narratives of contrary experience.

The work of drawing forth narratives of contrary experience is often initiated by attention to what White and Epston have called 'unique outcomes' (White 1989; White & Epston 1990): times when the problem could have prevailed but did not, or when it could have influenced the person more than it actually did. These events are likely to become cornerstones in constructing novel and contradictive narratives - that is, full, historically situated, forward-projected narratives of experience (and identity) that are contrary to the usual story (White 1993).

Crucial to the emergence of enriched narratives and the new thinking and behaviour that they generate is the creation of a context that encourages these narratives of contrary experience. Such a context is more important than the person's recall of individual events or specific acts by the therapist. We foster such a context largely, but not solely (Roth & Chasin 1994), through the use of externalising questions. An externalising conversation is rich in powerful linguistic descriptions that are so at odds with many conventional ways of thinking, talking, acting, wishing, needing, wanting, and evaluating in relation to problems that they often catalyze a swift and fluid transit into new meanings, new observations, and fresh storying. In other words, these descriptions are alternative constructions of reality that enrich the future possibilities available to the person.

A Word about the Training Exercise

Next, we present a training exercise we have found to be a lively and potent introduction to the transformative power of engaging in problem-externalising conversations. We have designed other, related exercises, one emphasizing the use of metaphoric language practices in problem-externalising conversations (Roth & Epston 1996), another addressing some interviewing structures that encourage the description of people's relationships with problems in experience-near detail and some specific language practices that potentiate the work (Roth & Epston ms).

We invite readers to approach problem-externalising conversation in this exercise by acting *as if* the statements 'The problem is neither the person nor inside the person', and 'The problem is the person's relationship with The

Problem', were literally true. The aim of the exercise is to provide learners with an experience of a relationship with The Problem so immediate and unusual that it is likely to shift and expand the meanings, questions, and positions available to them as listeners, as inquirers, and as side-by-side allies when they hear clients speak about the challenges in their lives.

Finally, a suggestion: Reading this exercise will not provide the same experience that doing it will. We strongly recommend that learners find some colleagues and do it with them, even if learners have some familiarity with this kind of work.

WHOSE LIFE IS IT ANYWAY?

A Training Exercise for Therapists to Explore the Relationship of a Person and a Problem from the Problem's Perspective

1. *Setting up the exercise*

   (a) Form small groups of four to six people. Each group selects a single, nameable problem familiar to most, such as fear, self-hatred, insecurity, distrust, self-harm, self-negation, nightmares, unwanted habits, intimidation, etc. (3-5 minutes)

   (b) In each group, one person takes the role of The Problem as it might be experienced by a particular person and/or the person's family. We know that problems often tailor themselves to specific people and contexts even though they have a great deal in common with other problems of their general type. (1 minute)

   (c) The person who takes the role of The Problem tells something about the context in which it is operating, one of the stories that situates its activities. For example, 'I am Jack's- Fear-of-the-Unknown and I have confined him to his house, and even to his bed, for much of his 35 years on this earth. He's epileptic, so he needs me to keep him safe. The doctors say the medication is enough to keep him safe, but I know better. I've also kept him from making a really stupid move, from marrying Judy. He's been talking about getting a job, but I'm working on convincing him that that's really out of the question. Sometimes he thinks that his world is so small he should kill himself, but I tell him if he moves into the larger world it will kill him for sure.' (2-5 minutes)

2. *Introduction to interviewing the problem*

Group members who are not enroled as The Problem take the roles of investigative reporters and inquire with great curiosity and interest into its modus operandi. In this sample case, they would interview Jack's-Fear-of-the-Unknown about how it established, how it maintains, and how it tries to extend its influential relationship with Jack, his family, his friends, his potential work mates, and others important in Jack's life. Every question to The Problem should be addressed to it as 'Jack's Fear-of-the-Unknown' or 'Bill's-Perfection', or 'Amy's Temper', or the like.

3. *Suggestions for interviewing the problem about its influence on persons*

Instructions for The Problem:

Remain fully enroled as The Problem throughout the exercise, and don't slip into being the person, even for a minute. If reporters address you as the person and not as The Problem, tell them you don't know who they are talking to, and remind them of who you are. If the reporter asks anything that you feel is an attempt to be therapeutic, say suspiciously, 'You're not a therapist, are you? I thought you were a reporter! If you're a therapist, I'm gone!'

Instructions for reporters:

Ask The Problem questions that invite a highly detailed description of its intentions and practices. Your goal is to develop enough material in this interview to write a ground-breaking exposé that will reveal to all just how The Problem operates, and to what purpose. To do this, you need to find out what The Problem does that it considers accomplishments of influence. In other words, what does it do that serves its purposes, and by what means does it go about making sure it can do it? Inquire as fully as you know how to; do not be shy. Problems are often arrogant as well as boastful, and when asked directly, they will talk about things you would imagine they would keep to themselves. You may be surprised at how easy it can be for you to get them to spill the beans. Go for high degrees of specificity!

A special warning to reporters: It can be hard to move away from the traditional therapist role. You might find yourself tempted to be helpful to The Problem, to 'cure' it, to get it to see the error of its ways, to reform it or to rehabilitate it. Only by refusing this temptation will you get The Problem to clarify the following:

i) Its purposes.
ii) Its hopes and dreams for the person's life.
iii) The myriad techniques it uses to get its way.
iv) The voice, tone, and content that it finds most persuasive.
v) Who stands beside it, that is, what people and what forces are in league with it.

Use your questions to bring out The Problem's description of its relationship with the person it is tormenting. If you get really curious about The Problem's means of going about achieving its goals and follow its lead, questions are likely to come easily to you. To follow The Problem's lead in forming your own questions, listen to The Problem with great precision and openness. There are no one-size-fits-all questions for such interviews. Just to warm you up to the task, however, here are some sample questions. Use them to stimulate your own imagination about what kind of interview this can be.

The sample questions below contain more information than the reader was given. We assume that each question develops from the responses to the prior questions; subsequent questions are in a sense, responses to responses. For this reason, the sample questions 'flesh out' as we hope your questions will.

4. *Conducting the actual interview: Part One. The problem's ways and means of achieving influence*

Instructions for Reporters:

Conduct the first parts of the interview with The Problem. Remember, the aim of the first part of the interview is to elicit from The Problem its ways and means of achieving influence over the person. (15 minutes)

Sample questions, part one

- Jack's-Fear-of-the-Unknown, did you enter his life as a friend? If so, do you think you are still a friend? Or have you gotten turned around in some way? Are you the legacy of his epilepsy, from the days when he was required to stay close to home and plan ahead for each and every eventuality? The days before he found the right medication?

- Is it your intention to keep him young? As he puts it, 'I feel like a three-year-old child, not a thirty-five-year-old man'.
- Are you exploiting his controlled medical condition for reasons of your own? What are they? How come you warn him about danger just about every time he gets close to someone? Have you warned him away from each and every one of his friends? How have you convinced him to follow your instructions?
- Jack's-Fear-of-the-Unknown, does his reluctance to leave his own neighborhood have anything to do with your insisting that he can only be safe and sound in bed? If so, how does your insistence on this fit with your future plans for Jack? What are your plans for Jack, anyway?
- What did you tell him that got him to break off with Judy? How did you persuade him to listen to you instead of to his heart's desires? By what means did you chip away at his confidence?
- Did Pessimism come on to the scene at your invitation? Did you invite Pessimism to join you because you thought you were getting your way and wanted Pessimism to let loose the final blows? Or did you invite Pessimism in because you thought your influence might be slipping?
- How did you win him over to your opinions about what to do with his life? How did you win him away from the opinions of others who know and respect him? And away from his own opinions and feelings about what gives him satisfaction?
- Are you always whispering, 'Watch out!' 'Be careful!', and so on? Or do you have other things you say to him to convince him to slow down or to stop altogether in following his own dreams? What are they?
- Do you sometimes issue threats like 'If you drive over the bridge to town something will go wrong'? If you do issue threats, which ones have been effective for your purposes? By what means have you gotten Jack to listen to you when you have been threatening him?

- How do you decide when to use threats and when to use whispers? Do you threaten and whisper to his family members, too? To Judy? Which of them, if any, have you been able to enlist to support you in your efforts to keep Jack jailed in his own home?
- What did you convince him about himself that has made him so susceptible to your whispers and threats?
- Is it your wish to keep Jack holed up in his house with no company except you, Pessimism, and Jim Beam[8]? Is Jim Beam a buddy of yours? What does Jim Beam do to Jack that might show me that he's your buddy?
- Are you and Pessimism hoping that Jack's collapse in the face of your restrictions will become so complete that he will do what he has been threatening to do, and take his own life? If he did, would he be taking his own life, or would you have stolen it from him?

5. *Conducting the actual interview: Part Two. The problem's failures to achieve influence* (or, from the Problem's perspective, the effect of the Person on the Problem)

Instructions for reporters:

Now conduct the second of the two interviews with The Problem. The aim of this second interview is to elicit from The Problem material about its experiences of failure to influence the person and The Problem's demoralization. In other words, here you want to find out what kinds of encounters The Problem considers as allowing it little or no influence, and what plans it has to reassert its influence. (15 minutes).

Suggestions for interviewing The Problem about its influence (or rather, lack of influence) on persons:

To develop information for part two of your exposé, ask The Problem about:

(a) Times the person has frustrated The Problem's plans, schemes, and dreams,
(b) What the person has done to keep some of his or her territory safe from The Problem's grasp or to defy The Problem,
(c) What plans The Problem has to re-assert itself in the face of such resistance or defiance,

(d) What voice, tone, and language The Problem plans to use to re-assert itself, to regain influence in the person's life.

Sample questions, part two

- Jack's-Fear-of-the-Unknown, has Jack ever been able to resist your smooth-talking, terror-inducing voice? Even a bit? If not in action, has he defied you in his thoughts? Has he ever tricked you into silence for a time? When has he managed to savor his own purposes and dreams, despite your persuasive silver tongue? How do you account for his giving you the slip on that occasion? Did he divert your attention? Or did he just plunge ahead as if you weren't even there?
- What conditions set the scene for his closing his ears and his mind to your plans and dreams for his life and opening his ears, mind, and heart to his own plans and dreams for his life? What was your first clue that he was doing this?
- Do you think that when he decided to come to therapy - even to drive across a bridge to do so - that this was a sign that he might be growing such a strong voice of his own that it might drown out your whispers and threats?
- Jack's-Fear-of-the-Unknown, have you been chagrined not only by Jack's determination to seek therapy but by his driving over the long bridge into town to get it? Has it been unnerving for you that he hasn't had one seizure in five years? Were you taken back by his jogging all the way to the sea last week and not just around the block as you have always instructed? Has he done other things that have startled, shocked, or frightened you? What are they? Do you feel that you might be losing your grip on him?
- Is it growing harder for you to keep Jack under your thumb? Are you finding him difficult to discipline? To discourage? Is it harder for you to get him to comply? What was your response to his ignoring your dire warnings and engaging in such daredevilish activities last week as driving 200 miles south and then 200 miles back on one weekend to see a football game? Does any of this put you in mind to oppose his opposition to you, Jack's-Fear-of-the-Unknown? Have you already opposed his opposition to you? If so, how? Did he see through you when you did this? What were the clues?
- If he keeps on securing himself by his policy of 'becoming more secure by

being insecure' might he become immune to your policy of 'becoming insecure by being secure'?

- Might you become demoralized if Jack continues to assert that he has 'put a dent in Pessimism' by taking his life into his own hands for the first time since he was seven years old? And by his continued feeling that he's ready to 'get a life'?
- How will you ever talk him out of listening to Judy, who told him the first time she met him, 'I think you are a confident person'? How will you try to talk him back into your idea that bed is safe and sound, when he has started referring to it as a 'trap'? Now that Jack has started to see a 'daring' future ahead of him, do you think you can still forbid him to dream with your threats and your whispers?
- What will you try to slip in to replace Pessimism and Jim Beam, now that Jack says he won't let either of them continue to cloud his vision or to interfere with his plans?
- Do you think if he continues to ignore you that you'll end up going off in a snit, or do you think you might stick around in the wings just to keep him on his toes? How will you decide?

6. *Reflecting on what has happened*

All members of the group become themselves and discuss their experience of doing this exercise. *Because The Problem is likely to be quite demoralized, the person enrolled as The Problem must make sure to de-role completely.* (10 minutes)

- What was it like to be The Problem? To be a reporter?
- How was your experience different from, or similar to, the experiences you have had in other professional conversations?
- How do you account for any differences you noticed?
- What surprised you as The Problem or as a reporter?
- How might anything you noticed influence you with your colleagues and clients in the future?

7. *Reflecting on ways our own practices can inadvertently support problems*

The goal of the following question is to stimulate reflection on, and to increase awareness of, the ways that many of our everyday, taken-for-granted ways of speaking and being with people may serve to maintain an internalising problem discourse. (8 minutes)

- How could we, as therapists, have supported, or coached The Problem to be successful in achieving its aims?

Closing

As you, our readers, use this exercise to guide you in a conversation with The Problem, we hope that you will feel the cognitive and emotional differences between this kind of conversation and other professional conversations in which you have engaged. We further hope that the exercise provides an experience of the differences between problem-externalising as a technique and problem-externalising as a principled language practice that generates alternative constructions of reality.

People who have participated in this exercise have told us that it was fun. They were surprised to find their imagination and their sense of play engaged even in regard to very serious matters. Many have told us that doing the exercise precipitated a kaleidoscopic shift in their own thinking. We hope that this was also your experience, and we welcome feedback about your use of this exercise and your ideas about other exercises that this one may stimulate you to develop.

Notes

1. First published 1996 in Hoyt, M. (ed), *Constructive Therapies 2*. New York: Guilford Press. Reprinted here with permission.
2. This exercise derives partly from the standard psychodramatic practice of interviewing 'parts of people' as 'other' than themselves - as particular feelings, ideas, angst, and so on - in order to develop more complex relationships with these 'parts'. It most immediately draws on David Epston's practice of engaging in clinical dialogues initiated by such invitations as 'Do you mind being the problem

and I'll be you?' or, 'Do you mind being you and I'll be The Problem?' The exercise was partly inspired by a paper by Chris Kinman (in press) and was revised following extensive suggestions by Michael White (personal communication). A variation of this exercise focused on language (Roth & Epston 1996) has been published in the Journal of Systemic Therapies.

3. Sallyann Roth, M.S.W., Family Institute of Cambridge, 51 Kondazian Street, Watertown, MA 02472, USA, and David Epston, M.A., C.Q.S.W., Family Therapy Centre, 1-3 Garnet Rd. Westmere, Auckland, New Zealand, are equal contributors to this paper. We thank Carole Samworth, Richard Chasin and Michael White for their generous and generative comments on earlier drafts of this chapter.

4. These kinds of questions were developed by Michael White as a means of 'externalising the internalised problem discourse'.

5. Dickerson & Zimmerman (1996) discuss common misconceptions about narrative therapy at the broader, theoretical level.

6. Freeman & Lobovits (1993) propose the utility of a variety of relational metaphors for externalising conversation. In particular they question the use of metaphors that denote 'power over'.

7. One proviso is not to externalise abuse or other catastrophic events that have actually occurred. Kamsler (1998) and Linnell & Cora (1993) warn of the futility if not danger of externalising 'Abuse' or other such catastrophic events, since the fact of abuse cannot be altered. Rather, one externalises and works with the effects of the abuse on the identity and abilities of the person, as these effects are subject to change.

8. A whiskey brand name.

References

Adams-Westcott, J., Dafforn, T.A. & Sterne, P. 1993: 'Escaping victim life stories and co-constructing personal agency.' In Gilligan, S. & Price, R. (eds), *Therapeutic Conversations,* pp.258-271. New York: Norton.

Combs, G. & Freedman, J. 1994: 'Narrative intentions.' In Hoyt, M.F. (ed), *Constructive Therapies,* pp.67-91. New York: Guilford Press.

Dickerson, V.C. & Zimmerman, J.L. 1993: 'A narrative approach to families with adolescents.' In Friedman, S. (ed), *The New Language of Change: Constructive collaboration in psychotherapy,* pp.256-260. New York: Guilford Press.

Dickerson, V.C. & Zimmerman, J.L. 1996: 'Myths, misconceptions, and a word or two about politics.' *Journal of Systemic Therapies,*

Epston, D. 1989: "Marisa revisits (includes "Rewriting your history").' *Collected Papers,* pp.128-136. Adelaide: Dulwich Centre Publications.

Epston, D. 1992: 'Temper tantrum parties: Saving face, losing face, or going off your face!' In Epston, D. & White, M., *Experience, Contradiction, Narrative & Imagination: Selected papers of David Epston & Michael White, 1989-1991.*

Adelaide: Dulwich Centre Publications.

Epston, D. 1993: 'Internalizing discourses versus externalizing discourses.' In Gilligan, S. & Price, R. (eds), *Therapeutic Conversations,* pp.161-177. New York: Norton.

Epston, D. & White, M. 1992: *Experience, Contradiction, Narrative & Imagination: Selected papers of David Epston and Michael White, 1989-1991.* Adelaide: Dulwich Centre Publications.

Freedman, J. & Combs, G. 1996: *Narrative Therapy: The social construction of preferred realities.* New York: Norton.

Freeman, J. & Lobovits, D. 1993: 'The turtle with wings.' In Friedman, S. (ed*), The New Language of Change: Constructive collaboration in psychotherapy,* pp.188-225. New York: Guilford Press.

Huspek, M. & Radford, G.R. 1997: *Transgressing Discourses: Communication and the voice of other.* Albany: State University of New York Press.

Jenkins, A. 1990: *Invitations to Responsibility: The therapeutic engagement of men who are violent and abusive.* Adelaide: Dulwich Centre Publications.

Kamsler, A. 1998: 'Her-story in the making: Therapy with women who were sexually abused in childhood.' In White, C. & Denborough, D. (eds), *Introducing Narrative Therapy: A collection of practice-based writings.* Adelaide: Dulwich Centre Publications. (First published 1990 in *Ideas for Therapy with Sexual Abuse.* Adelaide: Dulwich Centre Publications.)

Kinman, C. 1994: 'If you were a problem ...: Consulting those who know about the tactics of a problem.' In Kinman, C.J. & Sanders, C., *Unravelling Addiction Mythologies: A postmodern conversation about substance misuse discourse and therapeutic interactions,* pp.32–45. Abbotsford, B.C.: Fraser Valley Education and Therapy Services.

Linnell, S. & Cora, D. 1993: *Discoveries: A group resource guide for women who have been sexually abused in childhood.* Haberfield, Australia: Dympna House.

Madigan, S. 1996: 'Undermining the problem in the privatization of problems in persons: Considering the socio-political and cultural context in the externalizing of internalized problem conversations.' *Journal of Systemic Therapies.*

Madigan, S. & Goldner, E. 1998: 'A narrative approach to anorexia: Discourse, reflexivity and questions.' In Hoyt, M. (ed), *Handbook of Constructive Therapies.* San Francisco: Jossey-Bass.

Neal, J. 1996: 'Narrative training and supervision.' *Journal of Systemic Therapies.*

O'Neill, M. & Stockell, G. 1991: 'Worthy of discussion: Collaborative group therapy.' *Australia & New Zealand Journal of Family Therapy,* 12(4):201–206.

Roth, S. & Chasin, R. 1994: 'Entering one another's worlds of meaning and imagination: Dramatic enactment and narrative couple therapy.' In Hoyt, M.F. (ed), *Constructive Therapies,* pp.67-91. New York: Guilford Press.

Roth, S. & Epston, D. (in press): 'Developing externalizing conversations: An introductory exercise.' *Journal of Systemic Therapies.*

Roth, S. & Epston, D.: (manuscript). 'Language charged with meaning.'

The Families 1995: 'Reclaiming our stories, reclaiming our lives.' *Dulwich Centre Newsletter*, 1.

Tomm, K. 1989: 'Externalizing problems and internalizing personal agency.' *Journal of Strategic & Systemic Therapies*, 8:16-22.

White, M. 1989: 'The externalizing of the problem and the re-authoring of lives and relationships.' *Selected Papers*. Adelaide: Dulwich Centre Publications. (First published in the 1989 Summer issue of the *Dulwich Centre Newsletter*, pp.3-21. (Republished 1990 in White, M. & Epston, D. *Narrative Means to Therapeutic Ends*. New York: W.W.Norton.)

White, M. 1992: 'Deconstruction and therapy.' In Epston, D. & White, M., *Experience, Contradiction, Narrative & Imagination: Selected papers of David Epston & Michael White, 1989-1991*. Adelaide: Dulwich Centre Publications. (First published in the 1991 No.3 issue of the *Dulwich Centre Newsletter*, pp.3-21. Also published 1993 in Gilligan, S. & Price, R. [eds], *Therapeutic Conversations*, pp.22-61. New York: Norton.)

White, M. 1993: 'The histories of the present.' In Gilligan, S. & Price, R. (eds), *Therapeutic Conversations*, pp.121-132. New York: Norton.

White, M. 1995: *Re-authoring Lives: Interviews and essays.* Adelaide: Dulwich Centre Publications.

White, M. 1998: 'Notes on externalising problems.' In White, C. & Denborough, D. (eds), *Introducing Narrative Therapy: A collection of practice-based writings.* Adelaide: Dulwich Centre Publications. (First published 1994 in the paper 'Schools as communities of acknowledgement: A conversation with Michael White.' *Dulwich Centre Newsletter*, Nos.2&3.)

White, M. & Epston, D. 1990: *Narrative Means to Therapeutic Ends*. New York: Norton. (Also published as *Literate Means to Therapeutic Ends*, 1989. Adelaide: Dulwich Centre Publications.)

Zimmerman, J.L. & Dickerson, V.C. 1994: 'Tales of the body thief: Externalizing and deconstructing eating problems.' In Hoyt, M. (ed), *Constructive Therapies*, pp.295-318. New York: Guilford.

Zimmerman, J.L. & Dickerson, V.C. 1996: *If Problems Talked: Narrative therapy in action*. New York: Guilford.